ANALYSING ARCHITECTURE NOTEBOOKS

Architecture is such a rich and subtle field of human creativity that it is impossible to encapsulate it completely in a single book. I tried to describe some of the basics in an earlier book, *Analysing Architecture*, which has now appeared in four editions, increasing in size each time. But even though that book has almost doubled in content, there is more to cover. So, rather than make the original even heavier, I have decided to add further chapters as a series of separate smaller volumes.

These *Analysing Architecture Notebooks* are the new chapters I would have added to *Analysing Architecture* had not excessive size become a concern. The series format also allows me to explore topics at greater length than if I were confined to just a few extra pages in the original book. Nevertheless the shared aim remains the same: to explore and expose the workings of architecture in ways that might help those who face the challenges of doing it.

Simon Unwin is Emeritus Professor of Architecture at the University of Dundee in Scotland. Although retired, he continues to teach at the Welsh School of Architecture in Cardiff University, Wales, where he taught for many years. His books are used in schools of architecture around the world and have been translated into various languages.

Books by Simon Unwin
Analysing Architecture
An Architecture Notebook: Wall
Doorway
Exercises in Architecture – Learning to Think as an Architect
Twenty-Five Buildings Every Architect Should Understand
The Ten Most Influential Buildings in History: Architecture's Archetypes

ebooks (available from the iBooks Store)
Skara Brae
The Entrance Notebook
Villa Le Lac
The Time Notebook

The Analysing Architecture Notebook Series
Metaphor
Curve
Children as Place-Makers

Simon Unwin's website is at *simonunwin.com*
Some of Simon Unwin's personal notebooks, used in researching and preparing this and his other books, are available for free download from his website.

ANALYSING ARCHITECTURE NOTEBOOKS

METAPHOR

an exploration of the metaphorical dimensions and potential of architecture

First published 2019
by Routledge
2 Park Square, Milton Park, Abingdon, Oxon OX14 4RN

and by Routledge
52 Vanderbilt Avenue, New York, NY 10017

Routledge is an imprint of the Taylor & Francis Group, an informa business

© 2019 Simon Unwin

The right of Simon Unwin to be identified as author of this work has been asserted by him in accordance with sections 77 and 78 of the Copyright, Designs and Patents Act 1988.

All rights reserved. No part of this book may be reprinted or reproduced or utilised in any form or by any electronic, mechanical, or other means, now known or hereafter invented, including photocopying and recording, or in any information storage or retrieval system, without permission in writing from the publishers.

Trademark notice: Product or corporate names may be trademarks or registered trademarks, and are used only for identification and explanation without intent to infringe.

Publisher's Note
This book has been prepared from camera-ready copy provided by the author.

British Library Cataloguing-in-Publication Data
A catalogue record for this book is available from the British Library

Library of Congress Cataloging-in-Publication Data
Names: Unwin, Simon, 1952- author.
Title: Metaphor : an exploration of the metaphorical dimensions and potential of architecture / Simon Unwin.
Description: New York : Routledge, 2019. | Series: The analysing architecture notebook series | Includes bibliographical references and index.
Identifiers: LCCN 2018035234| ISBN 9781138045439 (hb : alk. paper) | ISBN 9781138045484 (pb : alk. paper) | ISBN 9781315171906 (ebook)
Subjects: LCSH: Architecture.
Classification: LCC NA2500 .U59 2019 | DDC 720--dc23
LC record available at https://lccn.loc.gov/2018035234

ISBN: 978-1-138-04543-9 (hbk)
ISBN: 978-1-138-04548-4 (pbk)
ISBN: 978-1-315-17190-6 (ebk)

Typeset in Arial and Georgia

by Simon Unwin

for Jack

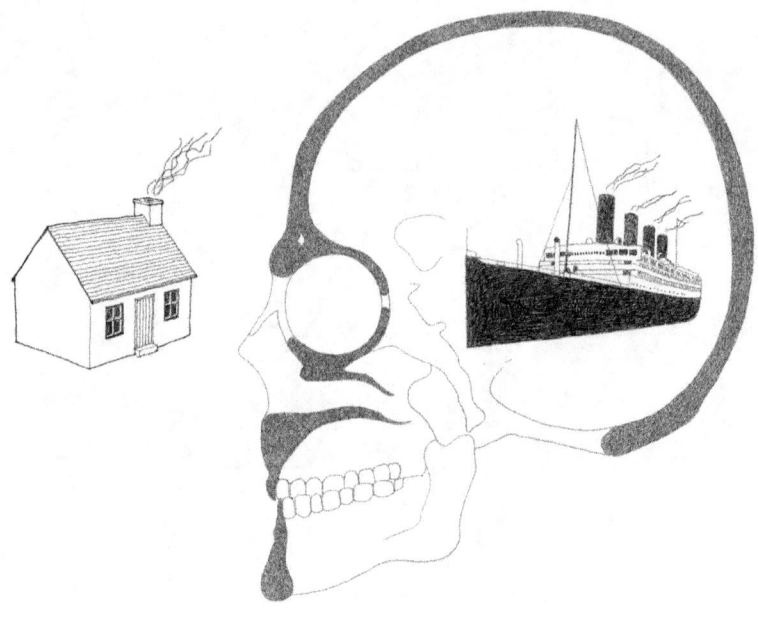

Metaphor is when the mind translates one thing into terms of another. It is a factor in the generation of ideas, in architecture as in other disciplines.

CONTENTS

PREFACE 1
INTRODUCTION 5
SIMILE, CLICHÉ, METAPHOR? 21
BODY METAPHORS 25
GENDER METAPHORS 37
TREE METAPHORS 43
DOORWAY METAPHORS 49
METAPHORS OF PERSONALITY 55
TEMPLE METAPHORS 63
COTTAGE METAPHORS 71
ARCHITECTURE-RELATED WORD METAPHORS 85
THE GENETIC METAPHOR 97
METAPHORS OF SENSE AND NONSENSE 107
MIND METAPHORS 117
LANDSCAPE METAPHORS 131
MACHINE METAPHORS 135
THE MUSIC METAPHOR 145
NARRATIVE METAPHORS 149
ENDNOTE 172
ACKNOWLEDGEMENTS 176
BIBLIOGRAPHY 177
INDEX 180

'But the greatest thing by far is to have command of metaphor. This alone cannot be imparted by another; it is the mark of genius.'
Aristotle, trans. Butcher – *Poetics XXII* (350 BCE), 1902.

'The prophets used much by metaphors
To set forth truth; yea, who so considers Christ,
his apostles too, shall plainly see,
That truths to this day in such mantles be.'
John Bunyan – Preface to *The Pilgrim's Progress from this World to That which is to come: Delivered under the Similitude of a DREAM*, 1678.

'Art is a lie that makes us realize truth, at least the truth that is given us to understand. The artist must know the manner whereby to convince others of the truthfulness of his lies.' *
Picasso, trans. de Zayas – 'Picasso Speaks', in *The Arts*, 1923.

* Metaphor is one of the means used by artists (poets, critics, architects…) to try to 'convince others of the truthfulness of (their) lies'.

PREFACE

This Notebook explores the role of metaphor in architecture. When I began compiling it I asked various friends what their favourite architectural metaphor might be. Many of them looked at me blankly as if the idea of architecture having a metaphorical dimension was strange. It did not take much conversation for them to realise, though it might be a factor they acknowledged only subliminally, that metaphor is a powerful element in architecture. The following pages will illustrate the extent to which metaphor affects our perceptions of architecture, how it is conceived, and how architectural metaphors have been borrowed by other disciplines for their own theoretical explanations.

In the Italian/Spanish language film *Il Postino* (Michael Radford, 1994), the Chilean poet Pablo Neruda (Philippe Noiret), tells Mario Ruoppolo (Massimo Troisi) – the eponymous lovelorn postman – that the essence of poetry is judicious deployment of *metaphore* (metaphor in both languages). We might think of metaphor as a device belonging to the poetry of words but metaphor can also be non-verbal – visual, spatial, experiential... Metaphor is essential to the poetry of architecture too.

Searchers after truth (scientists and logical philosophers) are suspicious of metaphor. Comparisons on which metaphors depend can easily be over-applied turning a useful device for explanation into treacherous deception. Whereas a poet might be happy to describe a man as a tiger, hoping to evoke ideas of primal wildness and a ruthless lack of empathy with victims, a biologist or psychologist would reject such an imprecise comparison. Even non-scientists would recognise their own delusion if they concluded that the poet intended us to think the man had yellow and black stripes and fangs like scimitars.

In architecture the situation is different from in truth-seeking. Though there have been critics that have sought to transfer into architectural discussion the distrust of metaphor felt by logical philosophers and scientists*, metaphors in architecture are generally thought of not as treacherous sources of delusion but as (to use an architectural metaphor) cornerstones of creativity. Some anthropologists think that too. Victor Turner, for example, in *Dramas, Fields and Metaphors* (1967), wrote that 'Metaphor is, in fact, metamorphic, transformative', and quoted Robert A. Nisbet – *Social Change and History...* (1969):

> '*Metaphor is our means of effecting instantaneous fusion of two separated realms of experience into one illuminating, iconic, encapsulating image.*'

Both Turner and Nisbet were talking about the ways in which we use metaphor to help portray an integrated sense of the world to ourselves and to each other. *Sense* is different from *truth*, even though we might sometimes think of them as being the same. Where 'truth' claims to be absolute, 'sense' recognises relativity – i.e. that each of us, in various situations, makes, finds, yearns for or is given – by family, friends, priests, politicians and their spin-doctors, philosophers, journalists, scientists, polemicists, novelists, poets, playwrights, commercial advertisers, bloggers, tweeters... – a sense of how things are, which we might assert/accept, even fight for, as truth, but which is nevertheless never more than a fiction the plausibility of which is conditioned by our situation.

In a creative activity such as architecture, metaphor is less a threat to objective truth and more (to use another architectural metaphor) an arena of conceptual vitality – an arena being a performance area shareable with others. Metaphors illuminate, leaven, stimulate... in architecture as in poetry or any other creative field. We are told by our teachers not to 'mix metaphors' but suggesting that metaphor itself is a 'cornerstone', an 'arena' and a 'field', all on one page, illustrates

---

* notably:
Geoffrey Scott in *The Architecture of Humanism* (1914) where Scott attempted to dismantle what he called 'The Romantic Fallacy', 'The Mechanical Fallacy', 'The Ethical Fallacy', 'The Biological Fallacy'... all in favour of 'Humanist Values';
and
John Summerson in 'The Mischievous Analogy' (1941), reprinted in *Heavenly Mansions* (1963), where Summerson questioned Modern Architecture's claims to be 'organic' and to express 'the spirit of the machine age'.

something of the problematic nature of metaphor whilst also hinting at its creative possibilities.

Architects, as poets, should be aware of the power of metaphor. One aspect of genius in an architect is (as Aristotle suggested for all; see the frontispiece of this Notebook) a capacity for metaphor. We might usefully ask of every (great) work of architecture, whether of the recent or distant past, 'On what metaphor is it built?' For example, and as is illustrated in the following pages, some were built on the idea that buildings should be conceived as 'machines', others as 'organisms' like living creatures – plants, animals, people... The possible variety of apt metaphor in a creative activity is probably infinite. Novel metaphors arise; originality can be linked to them. In this Notebook I have tried to give a broad view of how metaphor has been used in architecture as a stimulus to those who seek direction for their own design.

To its very origins, architecture is infused with metaphor. The metaphors of architecture are protean ghosts haunting a many-roomed labyrinth. They morph and fuse, subtly mutating perceptions; like distorting glass. When you look more closely you realise that the labyrinth of architectural ideology is ruled by those protean ghosts. In relation to architecture, metaphor is not just a matter of what we might call a recognition of intellectual correspondences; it infects all the senses – emotionally and psychologically as well as physically. Any architect who aspires to greatness must learn to exploit and propagate metaphor. Some people may have looked quizzical when I have suggested that architecture might be metaphorical but this Notebook will show how deeply rooted this factor is and how powerful it can be.

Taking advantage of its 'notebook' format, this Notebook is a collection of disparate examples. The general argument is that metaphors live at the conceptual core of architecture; but those metaphors are of many and varied kinds, which change and grow as you try to pin them down. The best I can do is to present this account of my exploration not discursively but by the gradual accretion of fragments of the general tissue of metaphor – varied in character and potential – that may be assembled by the reader into a creature of understanding peculiar to themselves. No fragment of tissue is presented here in more than one or two pages; but to help with the process of assembly I have sorted them roughly into thematic sections. The aspiration is that your own assembled creature will come to life in your architecture...

The air of the language we breathe is infused with metaphor. We identify, characterise, assimilate, make sense of things by metaphor. Metaphor is ubiquitous. It has an extraordinarily powerful influence on our perception and understanding of the world. We describe things to others using metaphor, often subconsciously. Others describe things to us using metaphor, and usually we understand what they mean without undue thought. It is arguable that all religion and much philosophy is based on metaphor. We explain things to ourselves using metaphor. Even scientists, despite themselves, resort to metaphor to help them make sense of the subject of their research; and technologists commonly use metaphors to stimulate new inventions. Often it is metaphor that 'takes control'. Metaphors are, as we are ourselves (according to Prospero), 'such stuff as dreams are made on'. And architecture is nothing if it is not about conjuring up dreams.

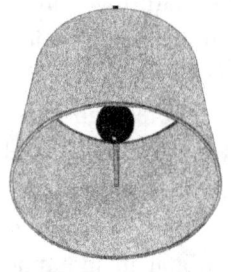

Metaphors can be like magic incantations. They imbue things with mysterious powers. If, lying in bed, I casually look up and notice that the lamp hanging from the ceiling resembles an eye then, to some extent, it becomes transformed into an eye. Depending on my mentality and any paranoid proclivities I might suffer from, that lamp-eye could come to haunt my life. This is no insignificant power and it is rooted in our sense of and fascination with metaphor, in architecture just as much as in other aspects of life and creativity.

Architecture uses the same effects, not just in the images that may be applied to walls but also assisted by the subliminal power of light and axes. In the cathedral above (Cèfalu on the island of Sicily) the gaze of Christ Pantocrator, watching over His flock, is reinforced by the architecture.

INTRODUCTION

Architecture originates in our being in the world. Just by standing on the land we identify a place and project our sense of the world outwards. Such places constitute the beginning of architecture. By walking a line we generate a pathway, straight or meandering, with a beginning and an end. Then we start to change the world physically, to establish spatial structures to frame our being. We develop our architecture through metaphor. In the distant past we looked to those places we recognised and experienced in nature for ideas – the shelter of a cave, the shade of a tree, the original refuge of the womb, our own proud vertical stance and point of view, the communal circle we make with our friends in a forest clearing… – and sought to emulate them in our architecture. We built tombs as metaphorical wombs for the dead and homes as metaphorical wombs for the living. We stood stones on end as sentinels and statues of our chiefs. We made circles as manifestations of and containers for community.

WOMB
metaphor as the seed of constructed architecture

The womb is one of the oldest and understandably most enduring metaphors in architecture.

The womb is the original refuge from the world, from which we emerge through a narrow passageway.

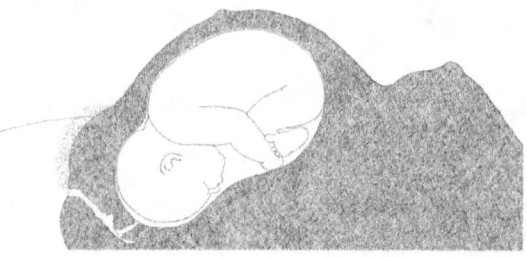

Our relationship with landscape is mediated by our capacity for metaphor. We think of a cave as a womb within the body of a hill.

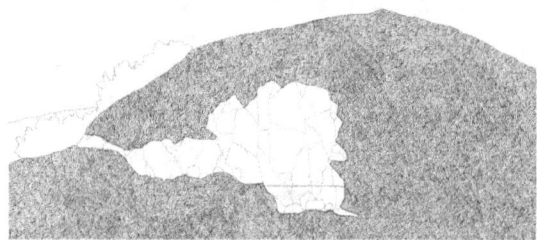

We construct tombs as wombs within mounds, into which the remains of the dead may be returned to 'mother earth'.

Maeshowe, Orkney (c. 2700 BCE)

Such tombs themselves come to be seen as metaphors for (the ultimate refuge of) death itself.

Tomb of Agamemnon (Treasury of Atreus), Mycenae (c. 1250 BCE)

'The house (is) a substitute for the womb – one's first dwelling place, probably still longed for, where one was safe and felt so comfortable.'

Sigmund Freud, trans. McLintock – *Civilisation and its Discontents* (1930), 2002.

Bryn Celli Ddu, Anglesey (c. 2000 BCE)

Burial mounds lie in the landscape pregnant with their dead, their narrow doorways portals leading back to the dark realm outside life.

New Stone Age houses, Skara Brae, Orkney (c. 3000 BCE)

Houses are metaphorical wombs too. Their rooms are refuges from the world, with hearths at their hearts providing the spark and warmth of life.

Religious buildings also allude to the womb metaphor; framing the presence of gods and sanctuary for their 'children'.

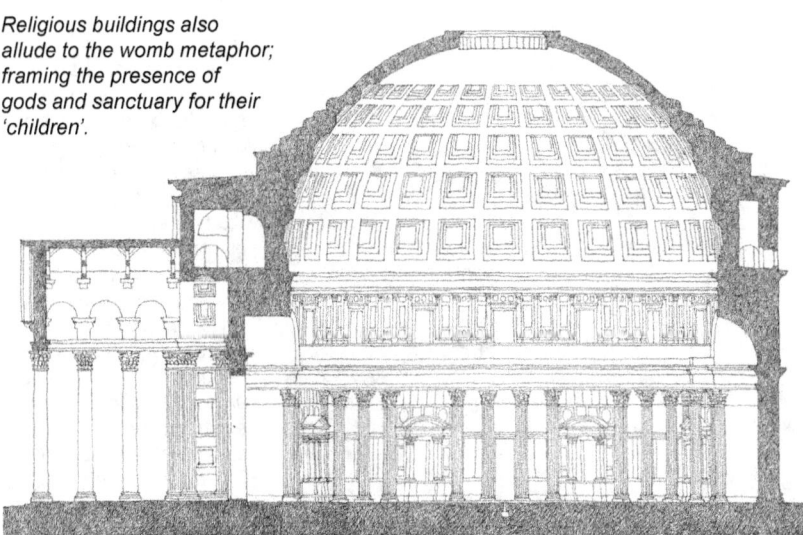

Pantheon, Rome, built by the Emperor Hadrian (c. 127 CE)

METAPHOR

MOUNTAIN AND CAVE
the Egyptian pyramid

The ancient Egyptian stone pyramid is a dramatic sculptural form in the desert. But it is saturated with symbolic meaning based in metaphor too. It is a geometrical mountain containing a small womb-like burial chamber. Its grandeur is a metaphor for the (assumed) greatness of the Pharaoh interred within. Its geometry is a metaphor for discipline and perfection, and its alignment ties it into to the (perceived) order of the universe.

The power of the pyramid is metaphorical. It derives not only from its size but also from: its content – the Pharaoh's burial chamber at its heart; its geometry – perfecting natural irregularity and aligning the tomb with the four cardinal directions (as well as some significant stars); and its position – on the threshold between the life of the river Nile and the realm of death in the desert.

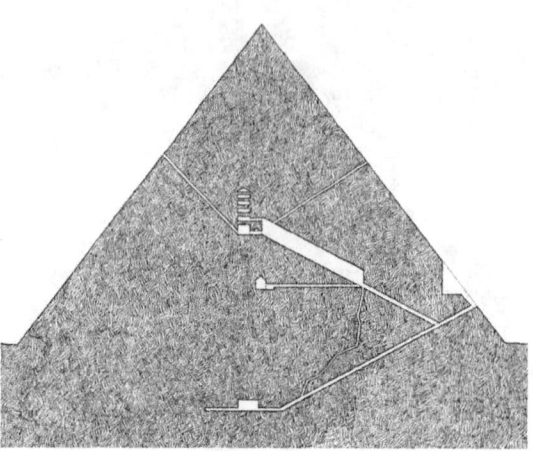

Pyramid of Khufu, Giza (c. 2500 BCE)

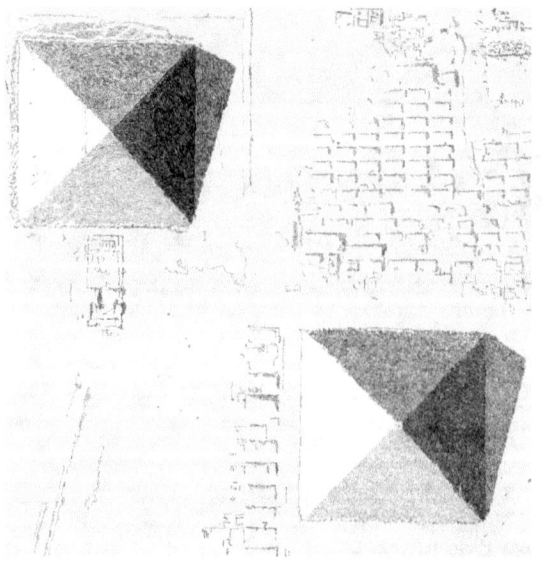

In our imaginations ancient Egyptian pyramids have become symbols of death, of eternity and the endless cycle of day and night, of relationship with the heavens and mystical geometry... They are also powerful memorials – ever-present reminders of people who lived thousands of years ago. In building them, Egyptian architects accessed and exploited some deep stratum of our imagination. The poetry of the pyramid, which depends on metaphor, resonates through time.

PRESENCE
the standing stone

Metaphor is one of the mechanisms by which our imaginations assimilate the world. We give sense to things through comparison. We theorise about things we are trying to understand and describe by alluding to characteristics they share with other things. We create new things by emulating the familiar. The attraction of metaphor is not exclusive to our attempts to make sense of the world through words. Thousands of years ago, architectural construction originated in metaphor. Sometime in the distant past, we began consciously constructing places as lasting metaphors for those ephemeral places we make just by being in the world or adopt in our natural surroundings.

A standing stone is a metaphor for human presence. Not only is there correspondence in their shared verticality. The stone says of the people it stands for that they are here, strong and dominate the surrounding territory.

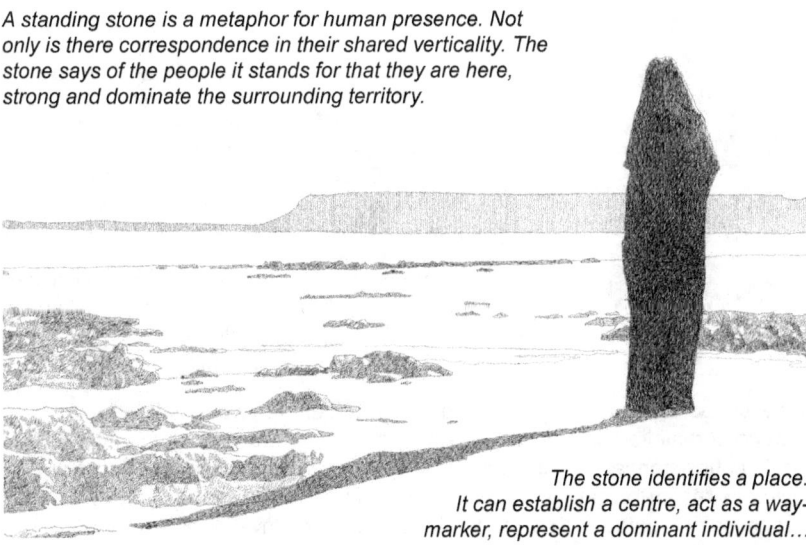

The stone identifies a place. It can establish a centre, act as a waymarker, represent a dominant individual…

COMMUNALITY AND RITUAL
the stone circle

We gravitate to clearings in the forest to settle, and to perform rites and ceremonies. The clearing provides a locus for congregation, for coming together as a community. Entering the clearing we become members of its community, or intruders.

Standing in a circle we demonstrate our cohesion as a group. By forming a circle we establish a place. We are contributors to discussion or spectators at a performance. Those who step inside the circle become a focus of attention, they become performers.

We construct a circle of stones (or tree trunks) as a metaphor for the clearing and the circle of people. The circle is metaphor as active architecture. It identifies a place, assimilating and emulating places we adopt in nature and those we make just by being in the world.

As architects constructing metaphors in physical form we develop and extend our intellectual and imaginative power over the world we inhabit. We assert our potential as poets assimilating what we find, assigning it to our own desires and creating new worlds within the one around us. By the subtle processes of metaphor, correspondences become inventions.

DEATH-RELATED METAPHOR
Woodland Chapel, E.G. Asplund

Metaphorical correspondence may have operated subliminally in prehistoric architects' imaginations; i.e. long ago we may not consciously have thought of a cave as a womb or a stone circle as a circle of friends. Such creative correspondence, as Freud and Jung have indicated, can operate subconsciously. But, when we become aware of the power of metaphor, we can employ it with poetic purpose. I have analysed Asplund's Woodland Chapel in previous books*. Though small, it is replete with apt death-related metaphor. In the sense described by Pablo Neruda in *Il Postino* (see page 1) Asplund's chapel is an architectural poem.

On approach, the roof of the chapel appears to be a pyramid – a form associated with death and memory.

The vertical axis mundi links the chapel with heaven and eternity.

The altar/lectern is in a niche like a hearth – a metaphor for home.

The eight columns inside the chapel are ancestors standing in the form of a stone circle. Raised on two steps, they witness the ceremony as reminders of the cycles of life. They support the chapel's internal dome – an architectural metaphor for the sky.

(Externally, a chimney appears to rise from this 'hearth' – another metaphor for home.)

Walls are made to appear thicker than they are – a subliminally perceived metaphor for security and mysterious separation from the everyday.

The catafalque – on which the coffin containing the dead child rests during the service – is situated between the 'hearth' and the axis mundi, suspended between home and heaven.

The twelve columns of the porch are friends and relatives, amongst which mourners mingle before and after the service. The columns are also the twelve disciples of Christ. They mediate between the everyday world outside and the sacred world of the funeral ceremony inside the chapel. The metaphorical correspondence of columns to significant ancestors and predecessors is old. (See the quotation below.)

The horizontal axis links the chapel with the setting sun.

* see for example: Case Study 9, in *Analysing Architecture*, fourth edition, 2014, pp. 289–91; and *The Ten Most Influential Buildings in History: Architecture's Archetypes*, 2017, pp. 66–7.

'The midst of the edifice ...was suddenly raised aloft by twelve columns representing the number of the Twelve Apostles.'

Abbot Suger, trans. Panofsky – *On the Abbey Church of St.-Denis...* (12thC), 1946.

ARCHITECTURE AND COHESIVE SOCIETY
Abbot Suger and the Church of St.-Denis

Suger was abbot of St.-Denis in Paris in the twelfth century CE. He left a written account of the significant improvements to the abbey church that he commissioned. Architectural historians like to think of him as the client that prompted the invention of 'Gothic' architecture (architecture with pointed windows, and thereby distinguished from the previous style, 'Romanesque'). More relevant to the present Notebook is his understanding of the metaphorical power of architecture in relation to spiritual belief. Referring to his own commissions he wrote:

Rose window, St.-Denis

'Now therefore ye are no more strangers and foreigners, says he, but fellow citizens with the saints and of the household of God; and are built upon the foundation of the apostles and prophets, Jesus Christ Himself being the chief cornerstone which joins one wall to the other; in Whom all the building – whether spiritual or material – groweth unto one holy temple in the Lord. In Whom we, too, are taught to be builded together for an habitation of God through the Holy Spirit by ourselves in a spiritual way, the more loftily and fitly we strive to build in a material way.'

You do not need to be religious to appreciate Suger's argument. He suggests that architecture, in the communal endeavour of its construction, promotes social and moral cohesion. Through building together people are 'builded together' to become (for Suger) 'an habitation of God'. This metaphor may be reversed: a built church is also a metaphor for a cohesive community. Suger represents architecture as an act of worship and infers that the aesthetic satisfaction and pride experienced is evidence of God's approval. (Everyone feels satisfaction when a grand aspiration is completed well.) The intricate and mutually supportive cohesion of stone blocks in the structure of an abbey church is presented as a metaphor for the intricate and mutually supportive cohesion of people in the (religious) community that builds it. Each stone is an individual shaped to fit the architecture of the whole, and the arrangement of intricate windows modifying light* from the sky is a metaphor for revelation. In the above quoted passage, Suger coins a mutual metaphor in which the grand and ambitious church built of stone not only frames its clergy and congregation but also reinforces the aspiration that its community might, in piety and cohesion, emulate its architecture.

The community is, metaphorically, the church; the church (the actual building) is metaphorically the community. This is a mutual metaphor linking people and architecture.

Abbot Suger, trans. Panofsky – *On the Abbey Church of St.-Denis and its Art Treasures* (12thC), 1946.

The Methodist Church in Neath, South Wales (opened in 1914) is called the Penny Brick because the congregation contributed a penny for each brick. The building stands as a metaphor for their cohesion as a religious community.

* Suger was abbot at St.-Denis when extensive improvements were made to the church, giving birth to the Gothic style of architecture. His additions introduced more light into the interior, through large stained glass windows. (See the quotation at the bottom of the opposite page.) This is not a difficult metaphor to appreciate. The Church (institution and building) interprets the Gospels – the 'light of Heaven'.

'Urbs beata... quæ construitur in coelo vivis ex lapidibus...'

'Blessed city... built in heaven out of living stone...'
'Urbs Beata Jerusalem', seventh-century hymn.

A church is the physical embodiment of the efforts of people. It represents huge investment of human resources: imagination, skill, living time, wealth... Its building is an act of worship, of commitment and devotion. Whether seen through the lens of religious belief or not, such an achievement is an unquestionable expression of the coherence and character of those responsible. There is no dead weight in a Gothic church. Every block of stone – members of the church – whether in rose window, buttress, wall or column, plays its part in maintaining the church's form, in defying gravity and keeping those tons of material in their proper place. The whole is a powerful metaphor for the 'building together' (to use Suger's words) of people – the human members – into a living and morally strong society.

'Once the new rear part is joined to the part in front,
The church shines with its middle part brightened.
For bright is that which is brightly coupled with the bright,
And bright is the noble edifice which is pervaded by the new light;
Which stands enlarged in our time,
I, who was Suger, being the leader while it was being accomplished.'

The south transept of the Abbey Church of St.-Denis, built (as was the north transept) in the century after Suger was abbot.

Suger saw that this metaphorical power did not reside only in the finished building. The effort involved in such an ambitious project (which might take many life times) brought people together in a communal endeavour too.

Abbot Suger, trans. Panofsky – *On the Abbey Church of St.-Denis and its Art Treasures* (12thC), 1946.

METAPHOR

GOD AS ARCHITECT
Mimar Sinan

'Boundless thanks to that Architect of the palace of nine vaults, who, without measure or plumb line, without rule or compass, by His hand of creation, made firm its arched canopy! And endless thanks to that Master of the seven-storied workshop, who, with His hand of power, kneaded the clay of Adam and in him displayed His art and novelty.'

Sinan, trans. Crane and Akin – 'The Treatise Charmingly Named Record of Buildings' (1588?), in *Sinan's Autobiographies*, 2006.

Towards the end of his long life, Mimar Sinan, architect of the grandest Ottoman mosques of the sixteenth century, dictated his autobiography to a poet (Sa'i). Through various false starts, Sinan tried to frame his life and achievements in an appropriate form of words. He knew he had to recognise his own insignificance in relation to God (he referred to himself as a 'weak ant') and acknowledge the patronage of the various Sultans he had served, but it is clear that his principal desire was to record (with pride) his own achievements as an architect. It seems that finding an appropriate balance of words was a more delicate challenge for Sinan than constructing a great dome from stone. But he found a way with the help of metaphor.

Sinan's mosques are themselves metaphors expressed in architecture. Places of worship frame prayer and acts of devotion. Architects conceive religious buildings as containers of divinity – i.e. as metaphors, such as 'the house of God', 'the Celestial City', 'Paradise'... Sinan saw his mosques as 'Paradise-like', as 'houses of God', and as emulations of God's own creation – the universe itself.

Architects often turn to precedents to stimulate their imaginations. Sinan was impressed and influenced by Hagia Sophia in Istanbul (below) which became a thousand years old when he was in his forties. For over nine hundred years it had been a Christian church but in 1453, a few decades before Sinan was born, it was

Hagia Sophia, with its gigantic dome, was the inspiration for Sinan's mosque designs. When he was working it was already a thousand years old.

Hagia Sophia

converted into a mosque. With its huge dome like the sky supported on an intricate composition of columns, arches and half domes, it presented the challenge Sinan wanted to meet and to surpass.

The similarity in structural composition with Hagia Sophia is evident in the Süleymaniye Mosque (below; also in Istanbul), one of the grandest of the many grand mosques Sinan designed. Of it he, with the help of his poet scribe, wrote:

> 'And the domes of that noble Friday mosque are ornaments like bubbles of the sea of elegance, and its highest dome is like the revolving heavens. And its gold finial shining upon it is like the brilliant, gleaming sun. And the minarets and dome are like the Chosen Beloved, the canopy of Islam, and of the Four Friends. And the ornamented windows, which are without like or equal, resemble the wings of Gabriel. When they are illumined with the sun's radiance, they are like an embellished rose garden of the springtime.'

Sinan, trans. Crane and Akin – 'Record of Construction' (1588?), in *Sinan's Autobiographies*, 2006.

Sinan saw his own design as a respectful metaphor for God's creation expressed in architectural form, an apt frame for worship.

It was in his fourth attempt at an autobiography that Sinan referred to God as 'Architect' (opposite, top). By the fifth and most complete version he had reverted to referring to Him as 'Creator of the foundation of the seven stories... (and) Builder of the heavenly canopy of nine vaults'. The possibility that architecture might aspire to being a metaphor of the creation was kept, while Sinan seems to have baulked at the suggestion that if God is an Architect, then architects are, by reversing the metaphor, gods. Sinan's humanism (necessary to his achievements) presented a quandary as to which agency – God or the architect – deserved credit for bringing order and beauty to the world.

Like the Hagia Sophia (opposite), Sinan's Süleymaniye Mosque is a metaphorical model of the universe, expressed in architecture.

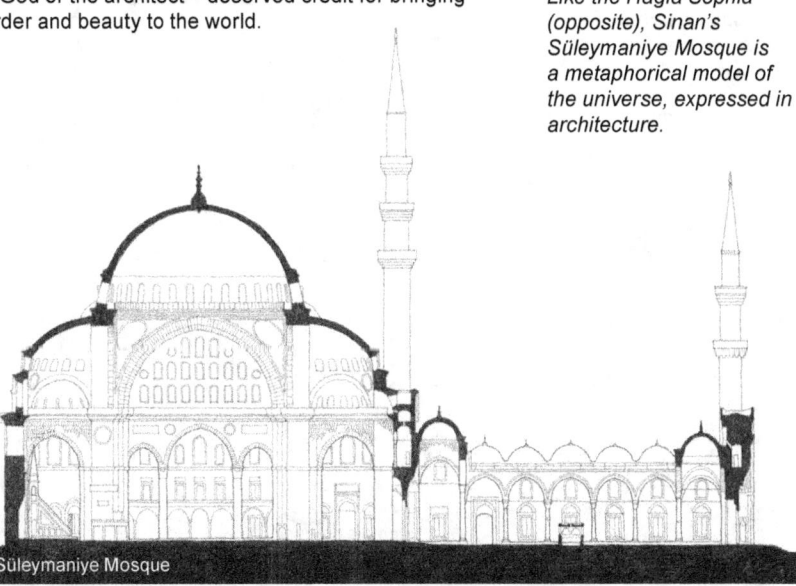

Süleymaniye Mosque

IMAGO MUNDI
building the world/universe, natural and social

'The profound originality of architecture as such resides perhaps in the internal mass. In lending definite form to that absolutely empty space, architecture truly creates its own universe.'

Henri Focillon, trans. Beecher Hogand and Kubler – *The Life of Forms in Art* (1934), 2013.

Sinan believed that in the architecture of his mosques he was emulating that of the universe created by God. This metaphor is by no means confined to his Ottoman culture. It is found in widely disparate cultures.

In her anthropological investigation* of the architecture of the Batammaliba tribe in west Africa, Suzanne Preston Blier noted that the name of the tribe could be translated as 'those who are real architects of the earth'. She found their architecture saturated with metaphor. The tribes use of language made it clear that they thought of their houses as built images of the world: with the lower inhabitable level – occupied by livestock – as the 'underworld'; the terrace level – open to the air and where most everyday family tasks are performed – as the 'earth'; and the conical roofs of the granaries – with their top access – as the realm of the sky.

* Suzanne Preston Blier – *The Anatomy of Architecture*, 1987.

The Batammaliba people think of their houses as models of the world, especially in terms of its levels: underworld; earth; and sky.

See also page 26.

section facing east

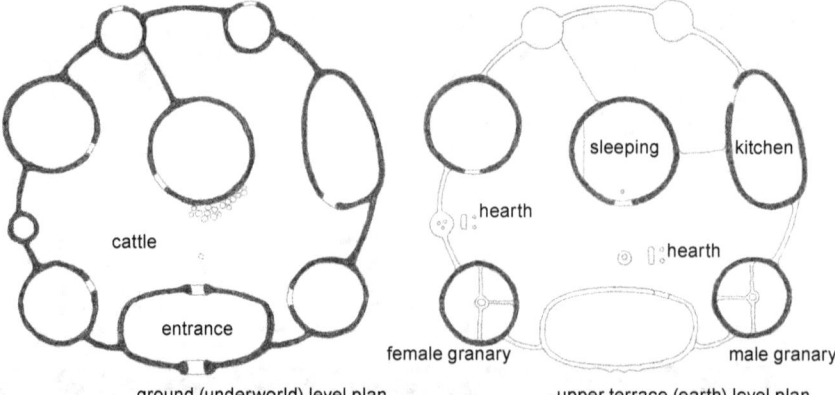

ground (underworld) level plan

upper terrace (earth) level plan

A significant part of the power possessed by the celebrated buildings illustrated below derives from their metaphorical representation of the world/universe, and our relationship with it and each other, and with any gods we believe to exist.

Parthenon on the Acropolis in Athens (5thC BCE)

The temple – the house of the god – on its rocky crag stands high above the city and ordinary life around (see pages 29, 32 and 94). The architecture and its topography establish a framework of relationship between people and their gods – a model of the universe.

Architecture can model not only the structure of the universe but represent social hierarchies on earth too. Spatial structures become metaphors of conceptual organisations. In both buildings below, levels relate to social hierarchy.

Villa Rotonda, Vicenza, Andrea Pallladio (16thC CE)

heaven

nobility

common world (servants)

underworld

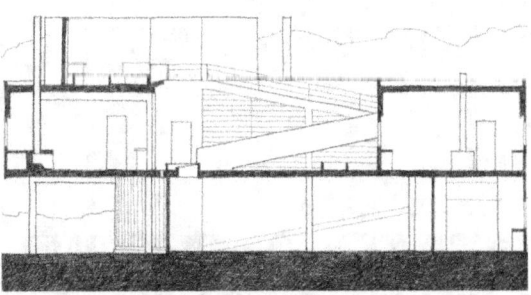

Villa Savoye, Poissy, Le Corbusier (1931)

sky and sun

nobility

common world (servants)

underworld

METAPHOR

ARCHITECT AS GOD
J.G. Ballard – *High-Rise*

The metaphorical reference to God as architect of the world/universe is common, as is discussion of whether architects have a tendency to promote themselves as secular gods. Sinan believed, and demonstrated in his own work, that architects could claim substantial credit for the creation of impressive, technologically astonishing and undeniably beautiful buildings as ornaments to the world and metaphors for Creation. But maybe not all architects have the ability to create work of such quality even though they might think they have. Sometimes they are vilified as creators not of Paradise but of dysfunctional, dystopian Hell.

In 1975 J.G. Ballard wrote a novel called *High-Rise*. It imagined the disintegration of social life amongst residents of an apartment block. Although the details do not exactly match, Ballard's high-rise was inspired by those built by Le Corbusier and his followers in the 1950s and 60s.

Like Le Corbusier's Unité d'habitation in Marseilles (1952, below) Ballard's apartment block aimed at providing everything needed for a community: shops, educational and recreational facilities, including an extensive roof terrace. Le Corbusier's metaphor was the cruise liner. Ballard takes the apartment block (and by implication the liner) as a self-contained world with the architect as creator – a metaphor for humanity at large.

In *High-Rise*, the architect – Anthony Royal – lives at the highest level of the world he has designed. But Royal is an ambiguous god. His building is conceived as an instrument of social order. But that order breaks down because of the unruly nature of the residents. His designing mind is not omnipotent. Eventually Royal is killed by Wilder, the block's most savage resident. ('God is dead... And we have killed him', Nietzsche).

Like a cruise liner, Le Corbusier's Unité d'habitation was conceived as a self-contained human ordained world, detached from the ground, with the architect as its creator. As well as apartments, the building accommodates shopping outlets, a school and recreational facilities including an extensive and sculptural roof terrace – the realm of the (Olympian) gods.

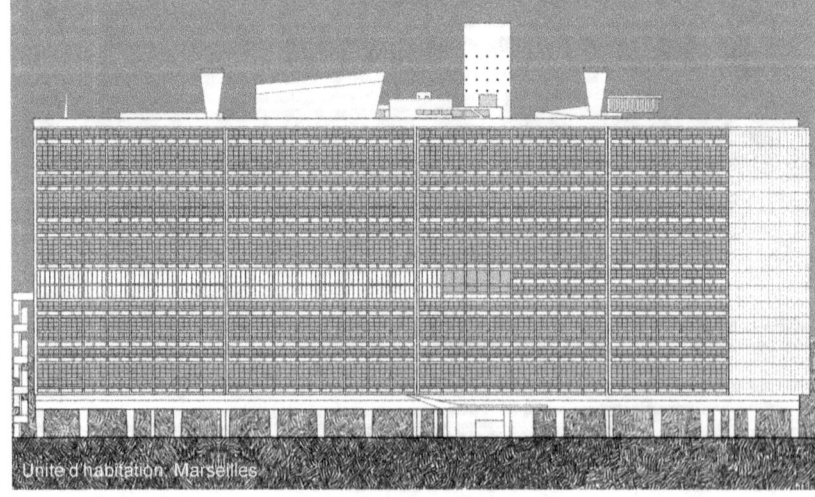
Unité d'habitation, Marseilles

CONTENDING METAPHORS
an illustration of their inherent unreliability

'Now the whole world had one language and a common speech. As people moved eastward, they found a plain in Shinar and settled there. They said to each other, "Come, let's make bricks and bake them thoroughly." They used brick instead of stone, and tar for mortar. And they said, "Come, let us build ourselves a city, and a tower whose top is in the heavens; let us make a name for ourselves, lest we be scattered abroad over the face of the whole earth." But the Lord came down to see the city and the tower which the sons of men had built. And the Lord said, "Indeed the people are one and they all have one language, and this is what they begin to do; now nothing that they propose to do will be withheld from them. Come, let Us go down and there confuse their language, that they may not understand one another's speech." So the Lord scattered them abroad from there over the face of all the earth, and they ceased building the city. Therefore its name is called Babel, because there the Lord confused the language of all the earth; and from there the Lord scattered them abroad over the face of all the earth.'

Genesis 11:4–9.

The words 'architect' and 'architecture' are much used metaphors: politicians are often referred to as 'the architect' of this or that policy; musicologists study the 'architecture' of compositions; computer systems have their 'architectures'; and so on. But what might thwart the idea that God is an architect is the suspicion that the creation operates without any underlying intellectual structure. (Though some believe in 'intelligent design'.) Also, any architect's explicit, tacit or unselfconscious claim to be a 'god' is undermined by the way different architects (professional or not) have different visions about how the world they want to create should be. They operate according to different metaphors, and often find themselves working in contrary or conflicting ways. (Some of those metaphors are illustrated in the following pages.)

'In the center of Fedora... stands a metal building with a crystal globe in every room. Looking into each globe, you see a blue city, the model of a different Fedora. These are the forms the city could have taken if, for one reason or another, it had not become what we see today. In every age someone, looking at Fedora as it was, imagined a way of making it the ideal city, but while he constructed his miniature model, Fedora was already no longer the same as before, and what had been until yesterday a possible future became only a toy in a glass globe.'

The Bible suggests that the Tower of Babel was not allowed to succeed because of God's jealousy. But maybe it failed because the architects could not agree. They sought to promulgate conflicting metaphors; they found themselves 'speaking different languages'.

Italo Calvino, trans. Weaver – *Invisible Cities* (1972), 1974.

METAPHOR

19

ARCHITECTURE INHERENTLY METAPHORICAL
poetry and drama of mediation

Metaphors may be unreliable, especially when stretched beyond plausibility. Their usefulness might depend on certain shared characteristics. But when the boundaries of these shared characteristics are breached metaphors become misleading and treacherous.

Nevertheless metaphors are a vital force of creativity. Products of architecture mediate between us and the world around and represent our being in the world. Literally, the walls and roof of your house mediate between you and your surroundings, identifying (establishing, providing...) a place (a refuge) that is more comfortable, physically and psychologically, than being out in the wind and rain or scorched by hot sun without privacy and vulnerable to assault. Even those who are without homes seek the limited and inadequate (architectural) mediation provided by a cardboard box, a park bench or the archway under a bridge. In these representations, architecture is always metaphorical.

Whether consciously and intentionally or subliminally and unselfconsciously, the architecture we human beings produce may always be seen as a metaphor for our relationship with that which is *not* us: that which we tend to call 'nature' (even though we are 'natural' too); that which we call 'other people', 'society', 'our enemy'... (though we are of course 'other' to 'others'); that which we call 'chance', 'the supernatural', 'divine providence'... (though we might act in ways that are unpredictable even to ourselves).

If I settle under a tree – whether for shade or psychological security – that architectural act (identifying a place to settle) is a metaphor for a relationship between me and the conditions in which I find myself. We might describe it as a poetic manifestation of a relaxed, innocent, mutual relationship with gentle accommodating nature.

If I order my forces (if I had any) to build a fortress to overawe and govern a subjected people then that castle is a metaphor of a very different relationship: a dramatic manifestation of an urge to dominate, to control... and to protect myself from attack.

There are as many metaphorical subtleties in architecture as there are in language, maybe more. The metaphorical power of architecture is inescapable and has many dimensions.

Here my children with a friend are committing an architectural act by sitting under a tree. The actuality, as may the image, can be interpreted as a metaphor for a harmonic relationship with nature.

See also page 45.

A fortress may be interpreted as a metaphor for a very different relationship between those responsible for it (its builders and inhabitants) and their environment, topographical and cultural.

SIMILE, CLICHÉ, METAPHOR?

Metaphor, as its etymology suggests, involves (conceptual/perceptual) transfer. We use metaphor to elucidate the character of one thing by implicit comparison with another. We associate metaphor with verbal language, its use in poetry and everyday communication. But implicit comparison operates in non-verbal communication too: in music, dance, gesture... and in architecture. Not all implicit comparison attains to the status of metaphor. If I was to dance like a giraffe (!) I doubt you would think I was making some metaphorical allusion between myself and the long-necked animal; more likely you would see it, at best, as some sort of non-verbal simile. If, as one girl band once urged, I was to 'walk like an Egyptian', you would probably accuse me of choreographic cliché as well (and of borderline political incorrectness). Alternatively (and dependent on me actually being good at dancing) I might produce movements that you might interpret as a metaphor, expressed in physical movement, for some affecting emotion such as angst, fear, love... These subtle differences apply in architecture too. This section explores how, in architecture, metaphor may be subtly different from simile and the overuse of both as cliché.

METAPHOR OR SIMILE?
what, in architecture, might be the difference?

'Sometimes the building is the sign. The duck store in the shape of a duck... is cultural symbol and architectural shelter.'

Robert Venturi, Denise Scott Brown, Steven Izenour – *Learning from Las Vegas*, 1977.

In architecture, visual resemblance in itself is neither sufficient nor necessary to constitute metaphor. Visual resemblance might be no more than the architectural equivalent of simile.

Building as duck.

In discussing the commercial architecture of Las Vegas (in *Learning from Las Vegas*, 1977) the American architect Robert Venturi famously differentiated those buildings he classified as 'ducks' from those he classified as 'decorated sheds' (right). He derived the term 'duck' from an illustration in Peter Blake's book *God's Own Junkyard* (1964) of a poultry store made in the form of a duck (below).

Two ways in which a building might be a decorated shed.

 Whilst Venturi's term 'decorated shed' is a self-explanatory descriptive label (for buildings whose character and purpose might be blank if it were not for decoration, ornamentation or signage), it is clear (in an unclear way) that his term 'duck' is something else, something more complex. It is a description of the appearance of the Long Island Duckling store. But, as the label for a category intended to include many buildings that do *not* look like ducks, the word becomes a (linguistic) metaphor.

The Long Island Duckling

The Long Island Duckling itself is more a simile than a metaphor – it looks like a duck but is not 'a duck' in any poetic sense. As Venturi says (above), the building is its own sign (symbol, flag, advertisement...). It is a visual cue to customers that they can buy poultry meat inside. If it is a metaphor then it is a metaphor for architecture as a medium for advertising. But Venturi uses his own term 'duck' as a linguistic rather than architectural metaphor, which he applies to other buildings that become their own signs. Thus Sydney Opera House (opposite) is a 'duck'.

PROJECTED SIMILE
unintended consequence

Architectural simile is not always under architects' control. A work of architecture may (or may not) be designed to look like something (a tree, a ship, a human head, a duck...) but the beholder has a view too (the realm of similarities is a shared one) and popular imagination might see in a building a resemblance not intended by its architect.

Both metaphor and simile depend on our innate capacity for seeing correspondences. Such is an essential part of our ability to make sense of the world. Observing (perceiving) that 'this resembles that' (in abstract as well as visible ways) is an intellectual process central to the narratives we spin about our lives, about others, about natural processes, about any spiritual (religious) beliefs we might have. We use this intellectual process seriously in trying to explain things, and unselfconsciously in our everyday language. It is also an essential trait of humour.

Metaphor and simile may both be used as expressions of dislike, as when, in 1984, Prince Charles described Ahrends, Burton and Koralek's proposed design for an extension to the National Gallery in London's Trafalgar Square as 'a monstrous carbuncle on the face of a much-loved and elegant friend' (metaphor) and later Sir James Stirling's Number One Poultry (1997), in the City of London, as looking 'rather like an old 1930s wireless' (simile).

30 St Mary Axe in London (Norman Foster, 2003) is popularly known as The Gherkin (as well as other things). Such popular nicknames have become an important contribution to the advertising power of architecture, by which it connects with public imagination. Nicknames are more often similes than metaphors.

Jørn Utzon's Sydney Opera House (1958-73) is a building that suffers (or enjoys) projected simile.

I shall leave you to decide whether the opera house's resemblance to the spinnakers of sailing boats makes the building an architectural metaphor or a simile (I tend to the latter) and whether the building has always been or later became (in Venturi's metaphorical sense of the word) a duck.

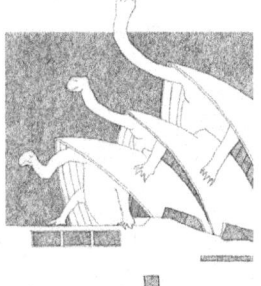

Mischievous cartoonists have seen the opera house not as a duck but rather as a threesome of copulating turtles (an unintended architectural simile rather than a metaphor).

METAPHOR

Titanic Museum, Belfast

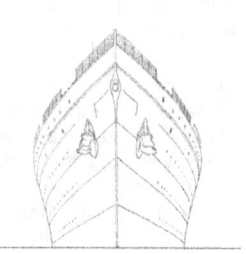
Prow of the Titanic

In some cases architectural simile is intended, as in Eric Kuhne's Titanic Museum in Belfast (2012, the centenary of the 'unsinkable' ship's fatal collision with an iceberg), which manages to look like the prow of the ship and a shimmering iceberg at the same time.

But often architectural simile is unintended, projected onto a building by popular imagination, as in the case of Frederick Gibberd's Liverpool Metropolitan Cathedral (1967), which has been alternatively named 'The (or Paddy's) Wigwam' (tipi) and 'The Mersey Funnel'.

Tipi or wigwam

Liverpool Metropolitan Cathedral

BODY METAPHORS

'During (the Bronze Age), analogies were drawn between the lifecycles of houses, their inhabitants, and certain categories of objects... Houses, pottery and quernstones were treated in similar ways to the human body at critical points in their use-lives, of which "death" is the most archaeologically visible. This suggests that quernstones, pots and houses stood in a metaphorical relationship with human bodies.'
Joanna Brück – 'Body Metaphors and Technologies of Transformation in the English Middle and Late Bronze Ages', in Brück, editor – *Bronze Age Landscapes: Tradition and Transformation*, 2001.

The layout of stones at Callanish (above) resembles a child's drawing of a person. In this it is perhaps more a simile than a metaphor. It is plausible that the stones (on the Isle of Lewis in the Outer Hebrides) were laid out in this way as a representation of a great chieftain, maybe with his remains buried in the cyst found at the heart (or in the stomach/womb) of the arrangement. Since prehistoric times there has been a metaphorical relationship between architecture and the human body. Standing stones are vicarious representations of those who put them in place, as burial chambers are of wombs... Thinking of buildings as metaphorical human bodies has been an important theme in the history of architecture, and not only in prehistoric and Western cultures.

HOUSE AS BODY
Batammaliba house

We have already noted that Suzanne Preston Blier's research into the Batammaliba tribe of west Africa found their houses saturated with metaphor. On page 16 I illustrated the way the Batammaliba build their houses as imagines mundi – models of the world/universe. But the tribe's use of language also demonstrates that they imbue their houses with human attributes and form too, even though that form is not representational.

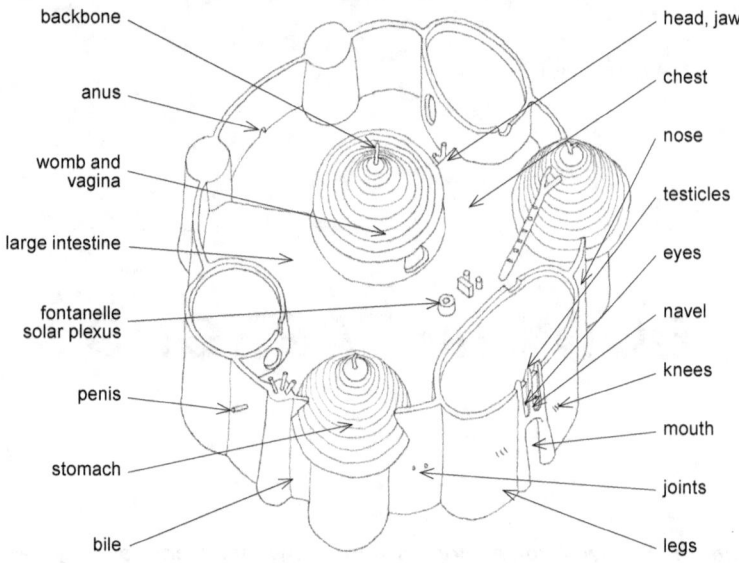

The above drawing shows some of the human attributes and organs Blier found the Batammaliba ascribed to specific parts of their houses. Some are more understandable than others. Most people would probably consider their sleeping quarters as the womb of their home. Similarly, most would be happy with the idea that the front doorway is the mouth; and the places where effluent is discharged or disposed of as metaphors for their equivalent orifices in the human body. A building's structure too can be seen as metaphorically skeletal; and places for food (such as the granaries in the above house) associated with the stomach. Nevertheless, in the above, it is not easy to understand why the head is effectively an entrance onto the upper terrace, nor how parts of that terrace should be interpreted as chest and large intestine, nor for that matter why one of the joining walls should suggest the idea of bile...

The Batammaliba house is conceived and understood as a hermaphrodite human body, with eyes, mouth, stomach, womb, vagina, penis, anus...

HUMAN BODY AS MODEL FOR ARCHITECTURE
the Renaissance view

Passing on his gleanings from the writings of Vitruvius (a first-century BCE architect) and Leone Battista Alberti (an Italian architect working in the fifteenth century CE) the seventeenth-century British diplomat Henry Wotton wrote:

'I had noted, that all Arte *was then in truest perfection, when it might bee reduced to some naturall* Principle. *For what are the most judicious* Artisans *but the* Mimiques *of* Nature? *This led me to contemplate the* Fabrique *of our own Bodies, wherein the* High Architect *of the world, had displaied such skill, as did stupifie, all humane reason. There I found the* Hart *as the fountaine of Life placed about the Middle, for the more equall communication of the vitall spirits. The* Eyes *seated aloft, that they might describe the greater Circle within their view. The* Armes *projected on each side, for ease of reaching. Briefly (not to loose our selves in this sweet speculation) it plainely appeareth, as a Maxime drawne from the Divine light; That the* Place *of every part, is to be determined by the* Use. *So then, from naturall structure, to proceed to Artificiall; and in the rudest things, to preserve some Image of the excellentest... For surely there can be no* Structure, *more uniforme then our* Bodies *in the whole* Figuration: *Each side agreeing with the other, both in the number, in the qualitie, and in the measure of the Parts... (Therefore) passe a running examination over the whole Edifice, according to the properties of a well shapen Man. As to whether the* Wals *stand upright upon cleane footing and* Foundation; *whether the* Fabrique *bee of a beautifull* Stature, *whether for the breadth it appeare well burnished, whether the prinicipall Entrance be on the middle Line of the* Front *or Face, like our* Mouthes, *whether the* Windowes, *as our* Eyes, *be set in equall number and distance on both sides, whether the* Offices *like the* Veines *in our Bodies, be usefully distributed, and so forth. For this* Allegoricall *review may be driven as farre as any* Wit *will, that is at leasure.'*

Henry Wotton – *The Elements of Architecture*, 1624.

According to Renaissance theorists, following hints in the ancient texts left by Vitruvius, architects should seek to emulate in their own work the compositional integrity and physical stability found in products of nature, especially the human form. It was not that buildings should look like people but that they should possess the same axiality, symmetry and coordination of parts found in the human body.

The front (face) of S. Maria Novella in Florence was designed by Leone Battista Alberti and built by 1470.

METAPHOR

DIVINE PROPORTIONS OF THE HUMAN BODY
designing architecture by God's geometric rules

'There is no question but that architectural members reflect the members of man.'

Michelangelo – a letter (1560) in Milanesi – *Le lettere di Michelangelo Buonarroti*, Florence, 1875, translated and quoted in Rudolf Wittkower – *Architectural Principles in the Age of Humanism* (1949), 1952.

'First we shall talk of the proportions of man because from the human body derive all measures and their denominations and in it is to be found all and every ratio and proportion by which God reveals the innermost secrets of nature... After having considered the right arrangement of the human body, the ancients proportioned all their work, particularly the temples, in accordance with it. For in the human body they found the two main figures without which it is impossible to achieve anything, namely the perfect circle... and the perfect square.'

Luca Pacioli – *De divina proportione* (1509), translated and quoted in Rudolf Wittkower – *Architectural Principles in the Age of Humanism* (1949), 1952.

These Renaissance writers and architects took their lead from antique authority – Vitruvius, who himself followed the Greeks and suggested that because the proportions of the human frame seemed based on circles and squares then architecture should be too:

> 'Since nature has designed the human body so that its members are duly proportioned to the frame as a whole, it appears that the ancients had good reason for their rule, that in perfect buildings the different members must be in exact symmetrical relations to the whole general scheme.'

Vitruvius, trans. Hicky Morgan (1914) –*Ten Books on Architecture* (1st C BCE), Book 3, Chapter 1.

The suggestion was that architects could, should, emulate God's finest creation.

Leonardo da Vinci's drawing (c.1490; right) is the most convincing graphic interpretation of Vitruvius's words. Various geometric proportions may be found in the drawing – including squares, circles and Golden Rectangles – some of which I have indicated. Leonardo's circle is centred on the navel; his square on the genitals – the two centres of birth and generation.

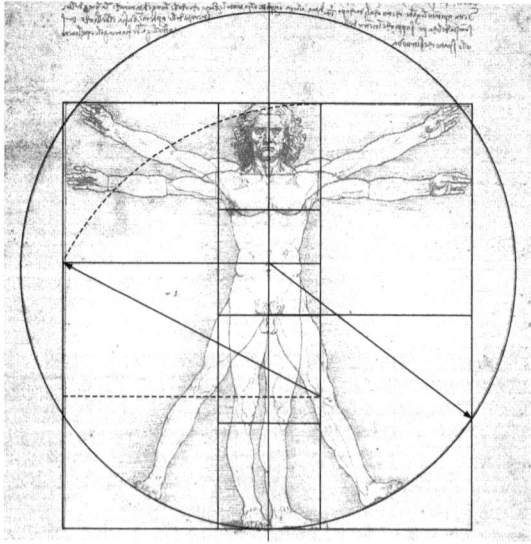

ANTHROPOMORPHIC GEOMETRY
The Parthenon

'On finding that, in man, the foot was one sixth the height, they applied the same principle to the column, and reared the shaft, including the capital, to a height six times its thickness at its base.'

Vitruvius – *Ten Books on Architecture*, Book 4, Chapter 1.

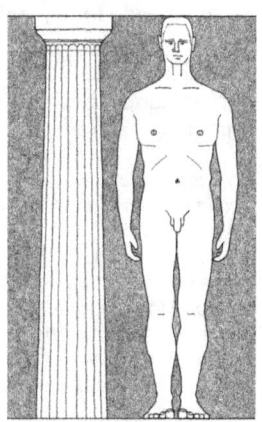

Vitruvius did not provide illustrations, but the inference drawn by Renaissance architects and theorists was that ancient temple buildings were proportioned according to measures and relationships found in human form. The truth of this is uncertain, but some Greek temples, though their proportioning systems vary, can be graphically interpreted to fit the theory. Below is the front of the Parthenon analysed in terms of squares and Golden Rectangles.

Vitruvius said that ancient Doric columns were proportioned according to the ratio of a man's foot to his height, i.e. 1:6. Thus columns could not only be counted as vicarious people but as representing their God-given form too.

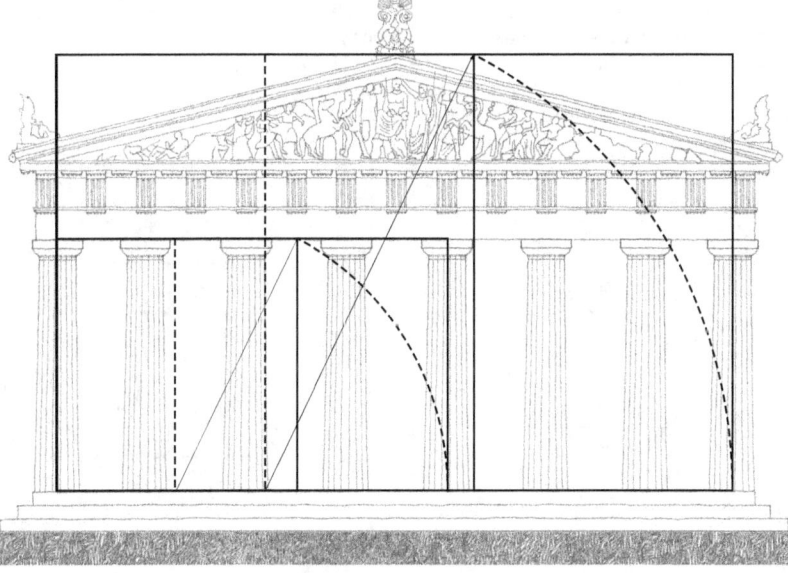

METAPHOR

29

EMULATING THE HUMAN BODY
Villa Rotonda, Andrea Palladio

All this suggests that when Andrea Palladio was designing his Villa Rotonda in the sixteenth century he was not merely engaged in an exercise in geometry but was intent on building a metaphor for the human form manifest in architecture, with geometry as the link (medium) between the two. The villa was realised as a secular temple to the perfect human being as defined geometrically by Vitruvius.

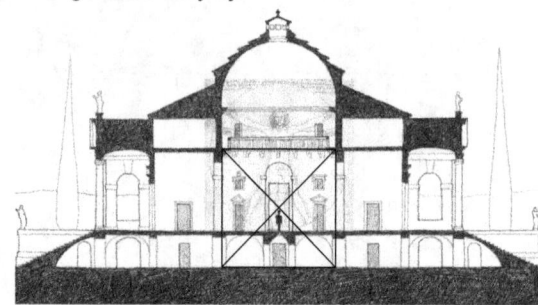

Both in plan (below) and in section (right), Palladio's design is proportioned according to the geometry thought to inform the proportions of the human body. The building is constructed on an armature of squares and circles.

We have already seen some have thought of God as an architect (pages 14–15) and that architects might be considered gods (page 18). Both metaphors centre on creativity and the generation of form. But they also suggest that if architects, as representatives (agents) of the human race, want to create a world apt for human occupation, they might want to do so using the same generative mechanism or language (we shall look at both these two metaphors later in this Notebook) employed by God in the Creation. Geometry, mathematics, being found hidden in nature – such as the human body, gravity, the movement of the planets... – seemed to Renaissance thinkers, artists, architects... to have a claim to be that mechanism or language.

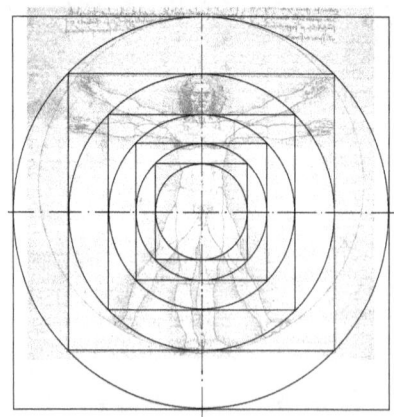
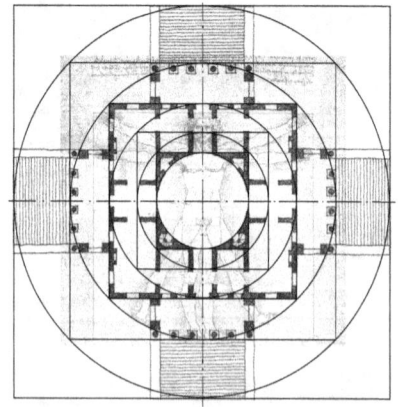

MODULOR
Le Corbusier's version of Vitruvian man

'Geometry is the language of man.'

Le Corbusier – *Vers une architecture* (1923), trans. Etchells – *Towards a New Architecture*, 1927.

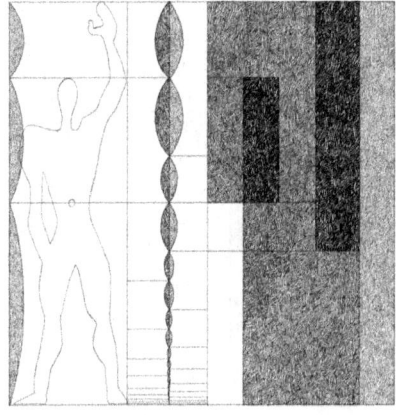
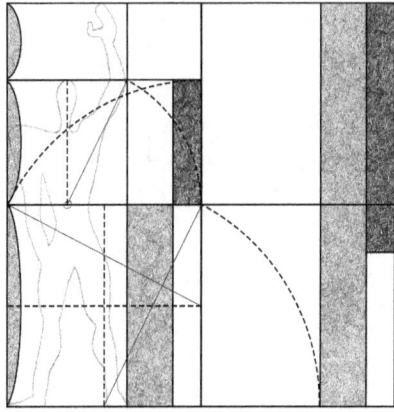

' "What is the rule that orders, that connects all things?" '

Le Corbusier quoting his own rhetorical question, trans. de Francia and Bostock – *The Modulor* (1948), 2004.

It is impossible to say exactly where mathematics resides. It cannot be claimed that it is an invention of the human mind because it is ubiquitous and operates according to laws that are universal. But neither can it be said to be natural because natural things never display the perfection and precision that mathematics promises. Nevertheless mathematics seems a presence underlying their form and operation. This hidden relevance makes it fascinating as a generator for architecture.

Le Corbusier developed a system for design called the Modulor. It is more complicated than Vitruvius's, based on the Fibonacci series as well as circles, squares and the Golden Rectangle. His diagrams (above and right) are more sophisticated versions of that of Leonardo da Vinci. But they too take their origin from human form, and stipulate measurements for application in the architectural frames humans inhabit. With the Modulor as an instrument for design, Le Corbusier felt he was accessing the generative force behind all things, and sought to create spatial harmony between people and the buildings they occupy.

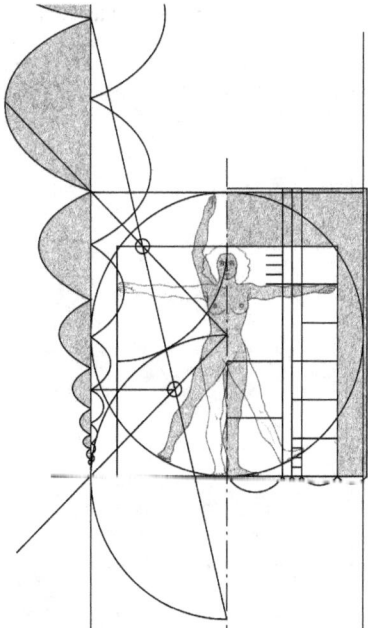

This is my version of a diagram by Justino Serralta and André Maisonnier that Le Corbusier included in Modulor 2 *(1955).*

' *"I am faced with a problem that is geometrical in nature; I am in the very midst of a phenomenon which is visual; I am present at the birth of something with a life of its own."* '

Le Corbusier, trans. de Francia and Bostock – *The Modulor* (1948), 2004.

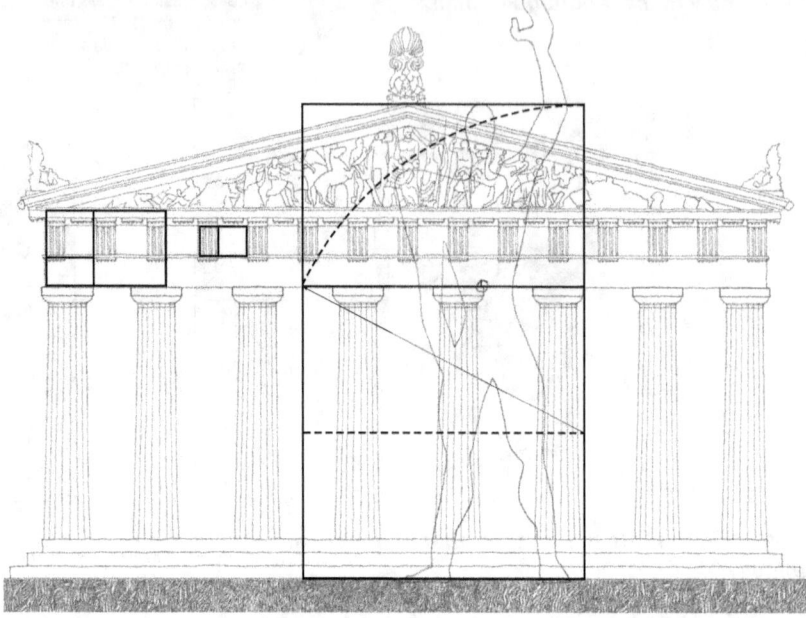

Le Corbusier was influenced too by the geometries said to underpin the beauty of ancient buildings and applied them in his own work. He called these geometries 'les tracés régulateurs (regulating lines), suggesting they constituted rules for beauty.

Le Corbusier employed geometries found in the Parthenon (above) in his own designs, such as the Villa Stein (below; 1927).

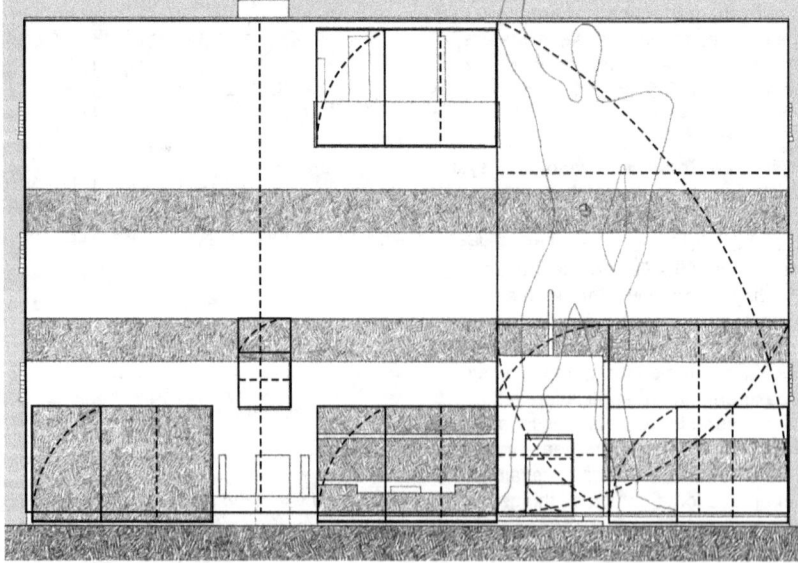

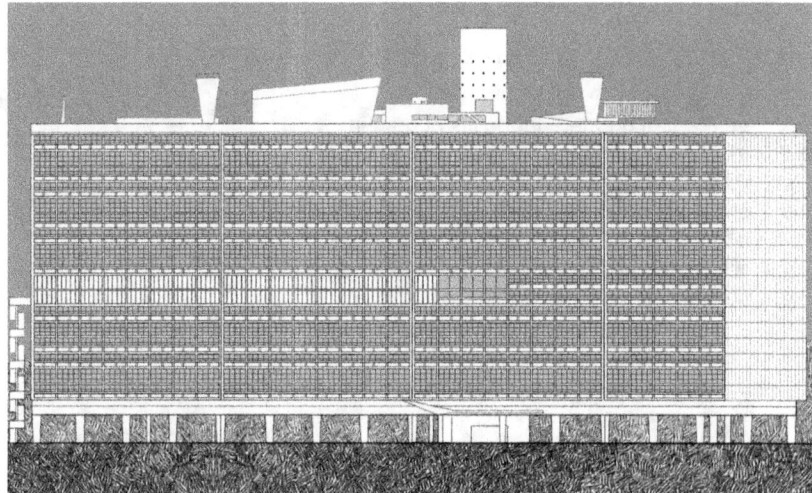

Le Corbusier applied his system to large buildings too. The ideas behind the Unité d'habitation in Marseille date from the same period he was developing the Modulor. Because the building's dimensions are all determined by the architect's scale of measurements related to the Fibonacci series – which as it grows bigger approaches the Golden Mean – the form of the Unité is replete with squares and Golden Rectangles, overlapping and of many different sizes. Just a few are shown in the drawing below. Nevertheless all develops from the geometric interpretation of the human form. This is architecture, or so Le Corbusier claimed, that grows from the same generative origin as human beings themselves.

      The Modulor was a system that Le Corbusier felt could be applied to the design of whole worlds. It was as if it invested him with the power of a benevolent god (as pilloried by J.G. Ballard in *High-Rise*; see page 18).

Le Corbusier's Modulor system of proportions and measurements can be applied at all scales, from the most intimate and human – determining the position of a door handle or the height of a shelf or seat – to the dimensions of large multi-storey buildings – such as the Unité d'habitation – and even to the layout of whole cities. Thus architectural form would derive from that of its creator and its client.

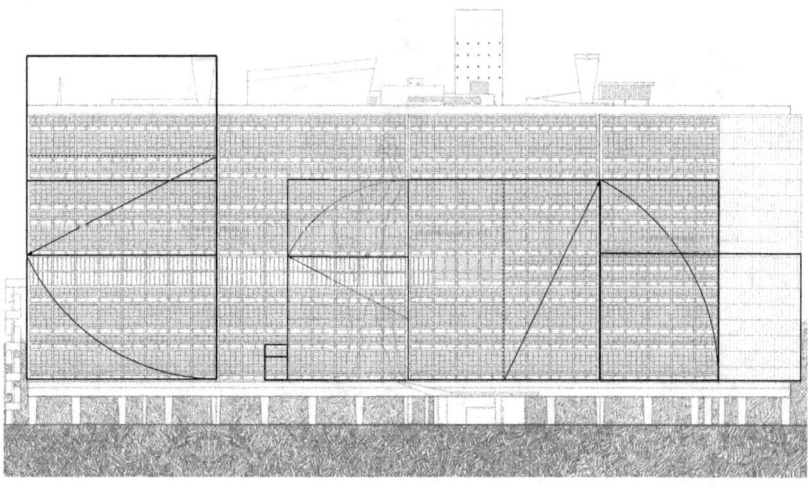

EMBRACING ARMS
Piazza S. Pietro, Gian Lorenzo Bernini

Architecture can be metaphorically human in different ways. Following Vitruvius and Alberti, Palladio, Le Corbusier and many others drew on geometric frameworks thought to underlie (perfect) human form (see pages 28 and 31). Sometimes architecture can be more directly anthropomorphic, as in Bernini's design for the piazza in front of St Peter's in Rome (completed in 1667).

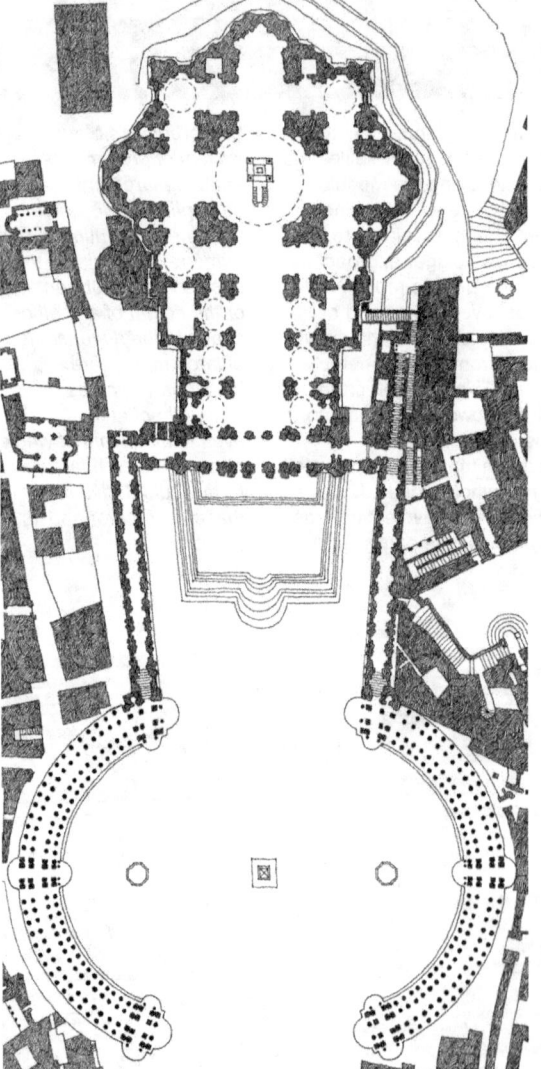

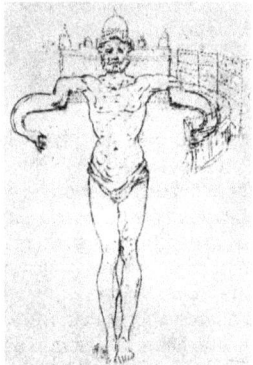

It seems that Bernini himself did a sketch (above) to illustrate his idea of the church as the body of Christ, with the dome of St Peter's as the head and with the arms of his curving colonnades reaching out to embrace the world.

As in Medieval cathedrals and churches, the cruciform plan of St Peter's is an architecturally expressed representation of the body of Christ on the cross. The anthropomorphic metaphor informs much church architecture.

WINDOWS AS EYES
they see outwards… and inwards too

*'How wondrous the Creator, who, from concealment, made Himself manifest
And, from the letters käf and nūn, laid out this pavilion!
Without columns He caused these nine vaults to stand,
And hung suspended the solar sphere.
Kneading clay with [His] hand of power,
He constructed Adam's body.
The eye became the window of the pavilion of the body,
And inscription[s] became its eyebrows.'*

Sinan, trans. Crane & Akin – 'Record of Construction' (1588?), in *Sinan's Autobiographies*, 2006.

Everybody thinks of windows as the eyes of a house. In the film *Mon Oncle* (Jacques Tati, 1958) the windows of a modern house – the Villa Arpel – appear, for comic effect, as eyes revolving.

But the same anthropomorphic idea that windows are eyes can be more sinister too. In the city of Safed (Tzfat) in northern Israel steps were built under the British Mandate to separate the Arab and Jewish communities (right). Any incursions either way across the steps could be monitored from a building at the top, provided with two pairs of 'eyes'.

Windows can be eyes looking inwards as well as outwards. In Bristol, on 7 February 2015, residents of the Bishopston neighbourhood made their front windows into displays (left). The event was called 'Window Wanderland'. It gave people a view into the imaginations of their neighbours.

There are numerous examples of windows as being the eyes of a building. The metaphor provokes the realisation that buildings are there not only to be looked at, but looked out from and in to. The insides of our houses are the insides of our selves, from which we view the world.

METAPHOR

SKELETON AND SKIN
structure and weatherproof membrane

*'That the **Walles** bee most exactly perpendicular to the **Grounde-worke**: for the right **Angle**... is the true cause of all **Stability**; both in **Artificiall** and **Naturall** positions; A man likewise standing firmest, when he stands uprightest... That certain courses or **Ledges** of more strength then the rest, be interlayed like **Bones**, to sustaine the **Fabrique** from totall ruine, if the under parts should decay. Lastly, that the **Angles** bee firmly bound, which are the **Nerves** of the whole **Edifice**...'*

Henry Wotton – *The Elements of Architecture*, 1624.

As can be seen from the above quotation, the metaphorical relationship between a building's structure and a biological skeleton has been around for hundreds of years.

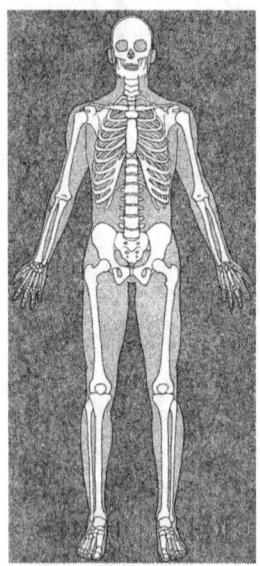
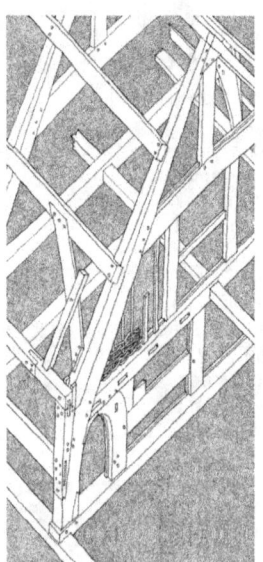
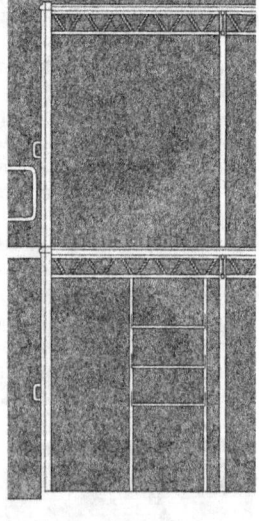

Hopkins House, Michael Hopkins (1976)

The idea that the structure of a building might be a skeletal framework to which a weatherproof skin is attached has been part of vernacular traditions around the world for hundred of years. Nowadays it is the principle metaphor underlying many steel and concrete frame buildings.

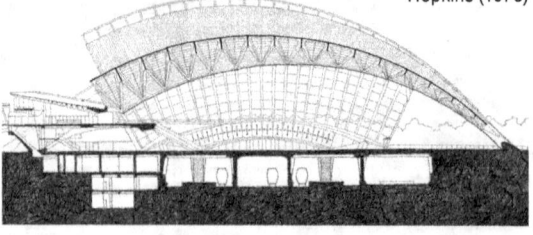

Santiago Calatrava has developed the aesthetic potential of skeletal structure. This is his station at Lyons (1994).

ANALYSING ARCHITECTURE NOTEBOOKS

MIRANDA (in *The Tempest*; of Ferdinand)

> **'There's nothing ill can dwell in such a temple:**
> **If the ill spirit have so fair a house,**
> **Good things will strive to dwell with't.'**

ROMEO (in *Romeo and Juliet*; to Juliet)

> **'If I profane with my unworthiest hand**
> **This holy shrine, the gentle fine is this:**
> **My lips, two blushing pilgrims, ready stand**
> **To smooth that rough touch with a tender kiss.'**

GENDER METAPHORS

Gender metaphors are related to body metaphors, but deserve their own section of this Notebook. In the above quotations, Shakespeare prompts his characters to apply architectural metaphors to the objects of their love. Romeo refers to Juliet as a 'holy shrine' or perhaps, more erotically, to the 'holy shrine' within her – the shrine where new life is conceived. Miranda calls Ferdinand both 'a temple' and 'a house': as a 'temple' he stands strong and handsome, an object of admiration; as a 'house' he is protective, accommodating, kind... In these few short lines, Shakespeare manages to allude to the subtle spectrum of ideas associated with a gendered appreciation of architecture: a 'male' emphasis on the object and presentation to the world; a 'female' emphasis on the receptacle of life and the notion of protective accommodation.

MALE AND FEMALE FORM
Doric and Ionic; tower and dome

'Thus the Doric column, as used in buildings, began to exhibit the proportions, strength, and beauty of the body of a man. Just so afterwards, when they desired to construct a temple to Diana in a new style of beauty, they translated these footprints into terms characteristic of the slenderness of women, and thus first made a column the thickness of which was only one eighth of its height, so that it might have a taller look. At the foot they substituted the base in place of a shoe; in the capital they placed the volutes, hanging down at the right and left like curly ringlets, and ornamented its front with cymatia and with festoons of fruit arranged in place of hair, while they brought the flutes down the whole shaft, falling like the folds in the robes worn by matrons. Thus in the invention of the two different kinds of columns, they borrowed manly beauty, naked and unadorned, for the one, and for the other the delicacy, adornment, and proportions characteristic of women.'

Vitruvius, trans. Hicky Morgan (1914) – *Ten Books on Architecture* (1st C BCE), Book 4, Chapter 1.

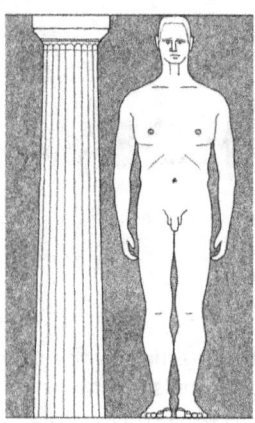

Doric columns are said to have 'male' attributes of strength and straightforwardness whilst Ionic columns are delicate and elegant – i.e. 'female'.

In such simplistic and binary gender characterisations, priapic skyscrapers are 'male' and mammary domes are 'female' (below).

Swiss Re, Fosters (2004)

Dome of the Rock, Jerusalem

SEXUAL ARCHITECTURE
Claude-Nicolas Ledoux

Claude-Nicolas Ledoux (1736–1806) was a French Neoclassical architect. Through his career he designed various buildings to accommodate sexual pleasure. Generally in his work Ledoux was interested in the meaning of architecture. So, in designing his houses of pleasure he used sexual references.

Ledoux's designs (quite obviously) refer to the human genitalia. But they do so in different ways and with different effects.

Hôtel aux Champs-Élysées – House of Bacchus (1802)

The plan of his first design for a House of Pleasure (below) evokes a quasi-mystical symbol comprising a female circle occupied by a male member.

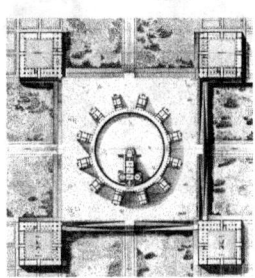

House of Pleasure, 1787

Ledoux's final House of Pleasure design (right) develops the idea of using a simplified drawing of a penis as the basis for the plan. But, visiting the building, it is unlikely you would realise that unless you saw the plan.

It is only his Hôtel aux Champs-Élysées (above right) that seems to offer any phenomenological correspondence between architecture and the sexual organ to which it refers.

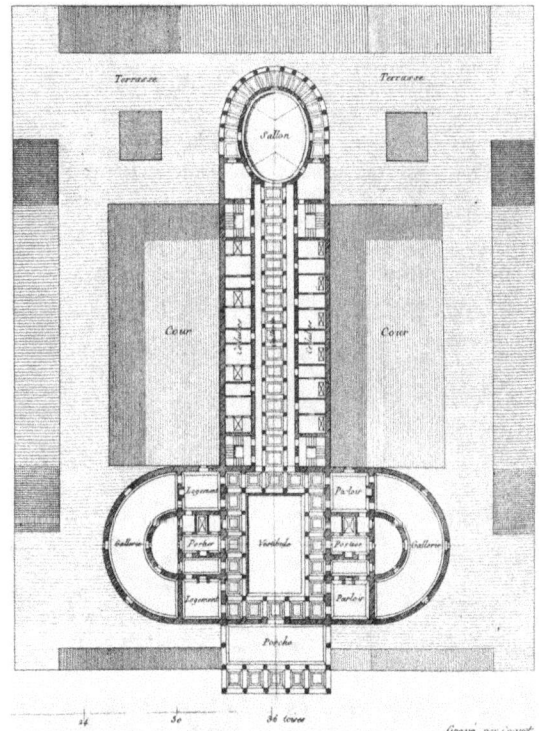

House of Pleasure –Oïkema (1804) – simile more than metaphor

METAPHOR

A FLIP
figure–ground; object–receptacle

But there are other ways in which generalised gender characteristics can contribute to nuanced understanding of the workings and powers of architecture. Pertinent is the dichotomy between the projection of potency characteristic of the opulent object building and the nurturing accommodation offered by the comfortable room.

In technological equipment there are 'male' and 'female' elements. A 'male' jack fits into a 'female' socket. Bolts screw into nuts. The female space receives/accommodates the male object.

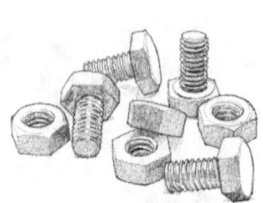

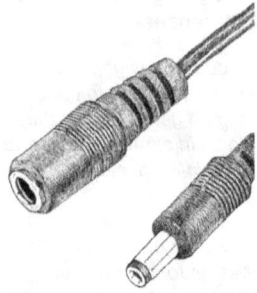

The image to the right is a well known conundrum. You see either the silhouettes of two black faces almost nose to nose or a white chalice against a black background. Unless you see the chalice as fitting exactly between the profiles of the faces, your interpretation flips between the two, with either the white or the black areas being the object of attention. The products of architecture are no mere two-dimensional graphic images, but they can prompt a similar 'flip' in interpretation.

In architecture the dichotomy of the flip concerns place and object: we see buildings – such as the Dome of the Rock (below) – as objects. But they contain (frame) places. In their 'male' presentation buildings are objects, projecting their presence into the world; in their 'female' presentation they are receptacles, places that receive, accommodate, protect and nurture.

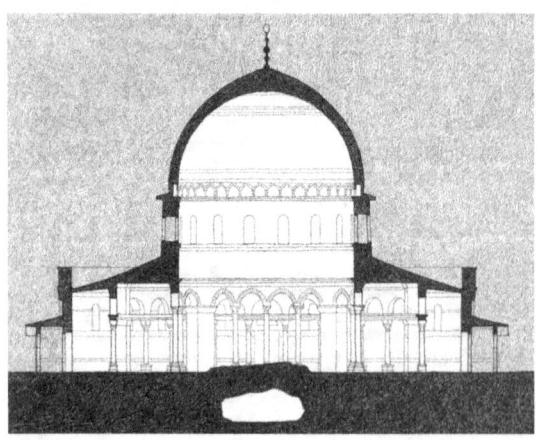

The Dome of the Rock (left and bottom right on page 38) is seen as an object, glistening in the sun, displayed on the platform of Temple Mount in Jerusalem. But the building is a frame. It identifies the circle of presence of the significant place it contains: the large rock at its centre which is claimed (amongst other things) to be the site of Abraham's attempt to sacrifice his son; and the cave beneath, said to be the site of John the Baptist's annunciation.

YIN YANG
complementary opposites

'Thirty spokes meet in a hub;
> *but it is on the hole at the centre that*
> *the use of the wheel depends.*
Turn clay into a pot;
> *it is the space within that makes the*
> *pot useful.*
Build doorways and windows into a room;
> *the spaces where there is nothing*
> *make the room useful.*
So, although what we make is Something,
it is the Nothing that makes it useful.'

Lao Tzu, my translation
(based on those of others) –
Tao Te Ching (c. 6thC BCE).

The yin yang (female–male) image depicts/symbolises the mutual dependency of complementary opposites.

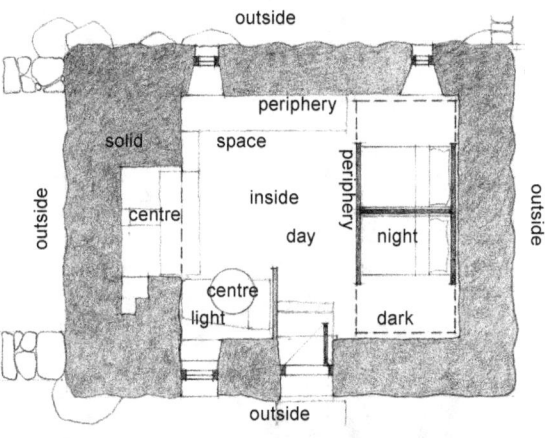

The yin and yang of architecture consists in the opposites of solid and space, object and enclosure. But it can also be between inside and outside, day and night, light and dark, centre and periphery… In the above plan I have labelled these complementary opposites in a small house, Llainfadyn (see page 72–3; and Case Study 3 in *Analysing Architecture*, fourth edition, pages 261–4).

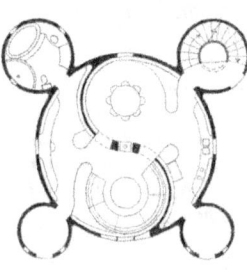

The yin yang symbol has been literally converted into the plan of a house in this example (designed by Mark Clipsham). But 'dining' and 'living' do not convince as complementary opposites. Maybe, if not between space and solid, it could have been between the realms of day and of night, or male and female.

The traditional Mongolian ger (right) has a 'female' and a 'male' side. Similar arrangements are found in other traditional domestic architectures. (See, for example, the Batammaliba house on page 26; and the ancient houses at Skara Brae on Orkney, page 7.)

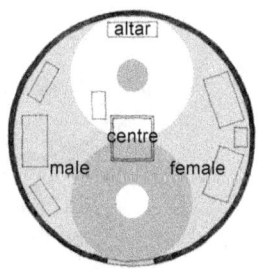

All buildings are a collaboration of the complementary opposites of matter and space, yang and yin. We can see and touch the solid matter but we live in the intangible space, moulding it – by adoption and manipulation – into places for the various things we do.

METAPHOR

YIN YANG OF AN IGLOO
a bump on the ice or a refuge from the cold

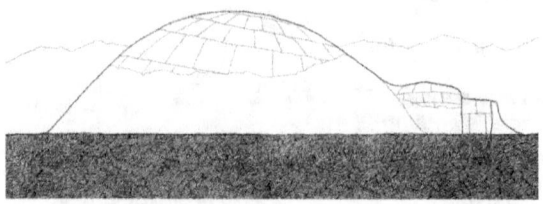

An igloo is a chilly example of yin yang. It cannot be described as an opulent object building. Even so we see it as a built feature (a bump, an object) on an icy landscape.

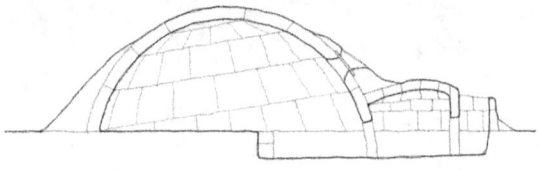

Alternatively we can consider it, and draw it, in terms of the way in which it was built – a spiral dome of ice blocks. But considering it like this does not account for the motive for building it.

The primary motivation for the building is to contain space, to identify a refuge from the cold, snow and wind.

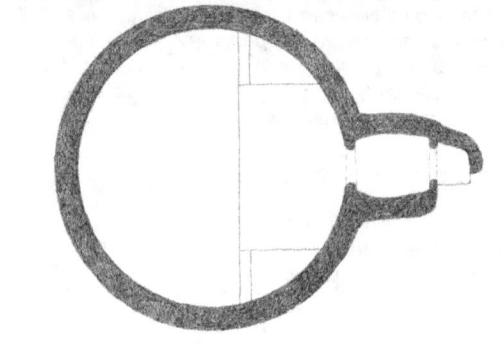

The igloo describes, identifies, a circle of place for inhabitation, and creates a refuge from the cold and wind of the Arctic ice fields.

Though the icy form of an igloo is a 'something' it is in the enclosed 'nothing' (space) that inhabitants keep warm. That place is the temporary datum for their semi-nomadic lives.

TREE METAPHORS

Tree metaphors are related to gender metaphors in that whereas thin vertical trees might be thought of as masculine, trees with wide spreading canopies are generally considered – by Freudian psychoanalysts as well as poets – as feminine, maternal. They shelter, embrace, protect... and provide a datum, a home, a refuge. Architecture can use the tree as a structural metaphor too. Forests can be metaphors for settings in which it is possible to get lost. And lines of trees, arcades, can be metaphors for processional routes, for the road of life.

STRUCTURAL TREE
metaphor or simile?

The tree as metaphorical model for the structure of buildings is so common that a whole Notebook could be filled with examples. If stone buildings – from megalithic burial chambers on – are cave and womb metaphors, then timber (and latterly steel) buildings are, at root, tree metaphors. But there are tree similes in architecture too.

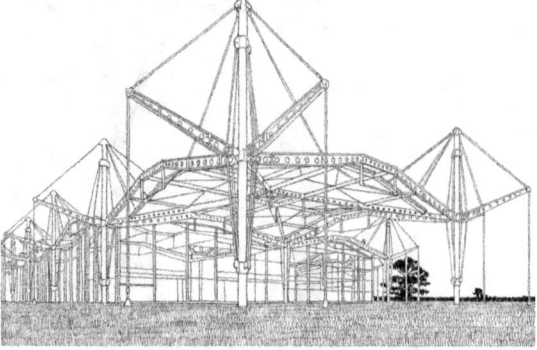

Renault Distribution Centre, Swindon, Fosters (1982)

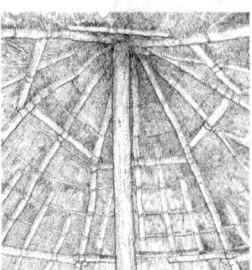

Timber structures have developed from trees, with comparable hierarchical branching of elements.

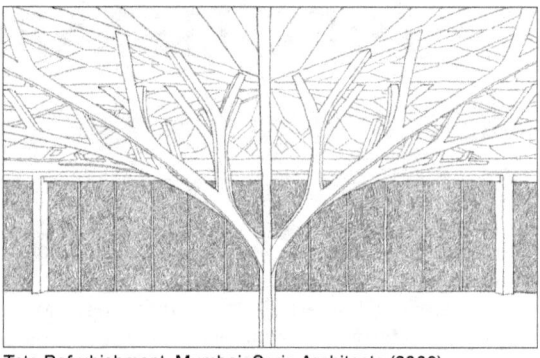

Tote Refurbishment, Mumbai, Serie Architects (2009)

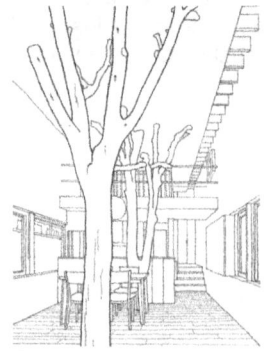

Garden Tree House, Kagawa, Hironaka Ogawa (2012)

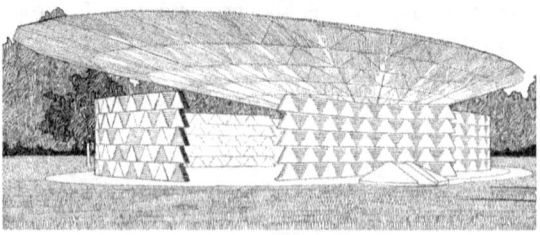

'I was inspired by the big tree in my native village of Gando, The community always gathers in its shade.'

African architect Francis Kéré talking about his design for the 2017 Serpentine Pavilion, London (above).

MATERNAL TREE
home, refuge, datum...

We convert trees into works of architecture merely by adopting them as places to be. But our relationship with the tree is subtle. We sense the tree already identifies a place which offers to accommodate us; it provides psychological protection and a datum, a reference point, by which we know where we are in the world. The tree – its reliable trunk and sheltering canopy – embraces us like a mother. It is understandable that this 'maternal' power has been emulated metaphorically by architects.

The central column in Sigurd Lewerentz's S. Petri Church in Klippan, Sweden (1966; below), may be interpreted metaphorically in different ways. One is as a tree under which the congregation sit.

See also: Simon Unwin – *Twenty-Five Buildings Every Architect Should Understand*, 2015, pp. 175–86.

By choosing the shade of that tree as a place to sit, my children are subliminally recognising and accepting its maternal protection.

The central column and spreading vaults of Westminster Abbey's Chapter House (c.1250; below) constitute a stylised tree, under which the clergy would sit to discuss the business of the abbey.

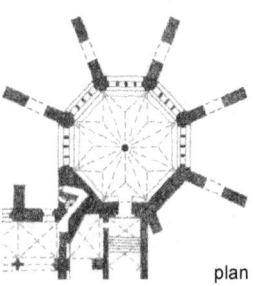

plan

FOREST METAPHOR
a place in which to get lost... or be equal

The forest has no external form; it offers only an interior. We can get lost in a forest and so we may see it as a metaphor for being psychologically lost. We have built forests – probably as realms of uncertainty and confusion – since prehistoric times.

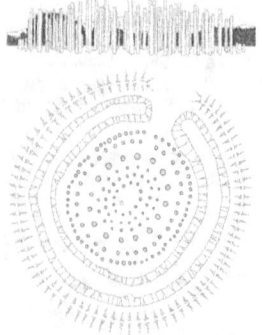

Woodhenge (above) stood on Salisbury Plain more than 4000 years ago. The uncertainty of its forest of columns resolves into a central clearing.

The mosque in Cordoba (from 10thC CE) is a forest of columns.

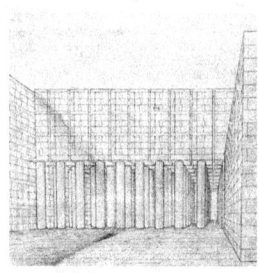

The storyline of Giuseppe Terragni's Danteum (1930s; above) follows Dante's Divine Comedy (14thC CE) by beginning in a dark forest of uncertainty. It culminates in a forest of light – Paradise.

See also: Simon Unwin – *The Ten Most Influential Buildings in History: Architecture's Archetypes*, 2017, pp. 96–109.

In his 1930s Johnson Wax building, Frank Lloyd Wright reinvented the architectural forest as a place of light, openness and egalitarianism.

PATH OF DESTINY
a clear route through confusion

When we encounter a pathway through the forest, especially one that is straight, we know it will lead us somewhere. Finding a path is a metaphor for finding a way forward – maybe from confusion (the general confusion of the disordered forest) to certainty, enlightenment, salvation...

This metaphor has been used by architects since prehistoric times too. Maybe it is the most used metaphor in all of architectural history. Most religions that offer spiritual and moral guidance along a pathway through the forest of confusion replicate (represent) that metaphor in their architecture.

The pathway through the forest can also be interpreted as a way back to the certainty, protection and refuge of the house, home, womb – a place of protection, where you know where you are.

Though grand cathedrals possess many architectural qualities, one way they may be interpreted is as metaphors for a certain pathway through a forest of uncertainty. The pathway leads to a refuge – the cathedral's sanctuary (heaven) and the suggested promise of salvation. Though tacit, and felt subliminally, the architectural manifestation of this metaphor is at least as powerful as any verbal description in scripture.

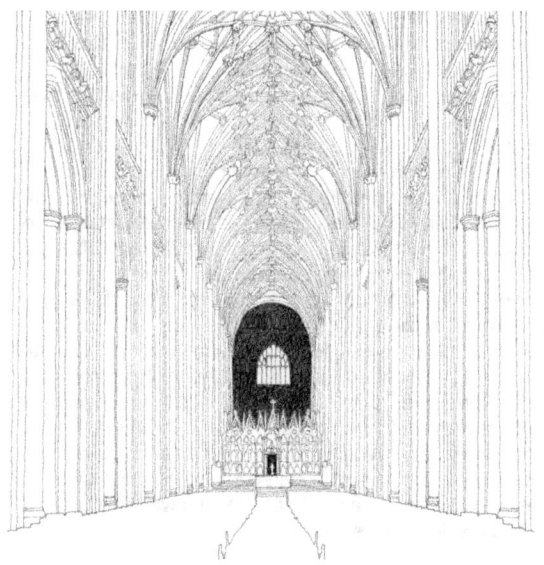

CITY AS TREE (OR NOT)
Aldo van Eyck versus Christopher Alexander

In the 1960s there was a brief spat between the Dutch architect Aldo van Eyck and the Berkeley-based architectural academic Christopher Alexander. Van Eyck was a member of the Congrès internationaux d'architecture moderne (CIAM) and a leader of the loose grouping of architects known as Team 10 (aka Team X). Alexander went on to write A *Pattern Language* (1977) and other books.

At a Team 10 meeting in 1962 van Eyck put forward an argument that involved a comparison between a city and a tree. Alexander, who was present as an invitee at the meeting, countered by writing an essay entitled 'A City is Not a Tree' (*Architectural Forum*, 1965). Then in 1968 when Team 10 published its ideas in *Team 10 Primer*, van Eyck dismissed Alexander's attack as 'neither a valid negation nor a valid affirmation of the truth'.

The idea of a tree in spatial organisation implies discreet elements, each with their own function, connected conceptually by branched links. An example might be an airport where one proceeds through a strict trunk of routes: from check-in and bag-drop to security, and then branch off to your particular boarding gate. There are secondary branches along the trunk: at check-in you might be directed to an airline desk to have your ticket checked; at security you might be diverted to a search room... The spatial arrangement is a tree.

Alternatively a work of architecture might be composed of a more complex arrangement of multifunctional spaces, which overlap and are used in different ways at different times or even at the same time. Alexander termed this a 'spatial lattice'. An example might be an open-plan house or school. Alexander said a city was one of these, more complex and subtle than a tree.

Considering his other writings, which suggest subtlety and complexity in human use of space, it seems likely that van Eyck never intended his tree metaphor to be interpreted so strictly as it was by Alexander. But that is the danger of metaphors: they can be overstretched, innocently or intentionally, as an attempt at polemic or rhetorical advantage.

Nevertheless, thinking of spatial organisation as a tree radically affects how a building might be planned. The Robert Kerr plan on page 112 might be considered a tree, with corridors as branches and individual rooms as leaves. Whereas Donald Trump's desk (page 56, top), with its mutable overlapping zones is not. How would you plan the spaces of a building in such a way that they do not constitute a tree?

> 'tree is leaf and leaf is tree – house is city and city is house – a tree is a tree but it is also a huge leaf – a leaf is a leaf, but it is also a tiny tree – a city is not a city unless it is also a huge house – a house is a house only if it is also a tiny city'
> Aldo van Eyck, in Alison Smithson, ed. – *Team 10 Primer*, 1968.

> 'The city is not, cannot and must not be a tree. The city is a receptacle for life. If the receptacle severs the overlap of the strands of life within it, because it is a tree, it will be like a bowl full of razor blades on edge, ready to cut up whatever is entrusted to it. In such a receptacle life will be cut to pieces. If we make cities which are trees, they will cut our life within to pieces.'
> Christopher Alexander – 'A City is Not a Tree', in *Architectural Forum*, 1965.

DOORWAY METAPHORS

Doorway metaphors are related to both body and gender metaphors. But the metaphorical potential of the doorway deserves its own section in this Notebook too. Doorways are conduits that take us out into the world, or back to the safety of refuge (the womb). A doorway defines transition, and is therefore often the locus for rites of passage marking transition from one state of being (childhood or being unwed) to another (adulthood or marriage). In referring to Himself as a door, Christ suggested the doorway might be a metaphor for salvation. And finally, the doorway is often used as a metaphor for death.

The doorway illustrated above, which I encountered in a Chinese Buddhist monastery, penetrates a patinated naturally side-lit light blue wall. It reads as a doorway through the sky to paradise beyond.

EROTIC DOORWAYS
a sensual and emotional phenomenon

There is a silent dream sequence in Pedro Almodóvar's 2002 film *Talk to Her*. It shows a tiny man curiously exploring a woman's body. The sequence culminates with the man stripping and entering the woman's vagina (right). Dreams are often interpreted as metaphors. This sequence seems to blend man's sexual drive with his desire to return to the womb.

Phenomenologically, architecture draws on those same instincts. On a breezy day campers on a beach gravitate to the maternal refuge of a cave.

Such phenomenological metaphors, manifest spatially (architecturally), have subliminal (Freudian) psychological appeal and effect.

Some architects have sought consciously to exploit this erotic potential.

The Temple of Venus, West Wycombe Park, John Donowell (1748).

Pushing through an archway in a thick shaggy hedge, with the leaves brushing your sides, can elicit an emotional response, provoke a sensual frisson. Such experiences suggest something of the emotional potential of architecture.

Doorways are often copiously decked with plants, symbols of welcome and fertility. They serve to advertise the opening; but they also invite us into the warmth and psychological comfort through the doorway.

DOORWAYS OF TRANSFORMATION
framing transition and change

Because they mark thresholds between places, doorways are apt metaphors for transition. They play their part in rites of passage in almost all human cultures. Doorways punctuate our experience of the world and can act as instruments of transformation.

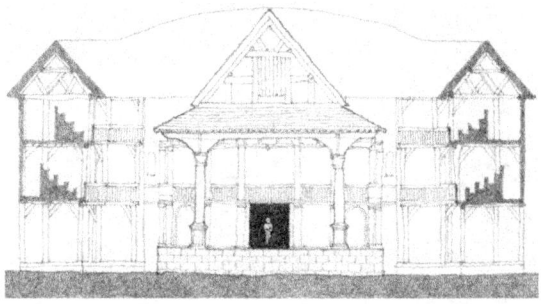

The doorway through which an actor enters a stage (in The Globe for example) frames the moment of her transformation from her everyday self into the character she is playing. The same door acts as the instrument of her 'death' as that character when she leaves.

'It is an instructive sight to see a waiter going into a hotel dining-room. As he passes the door a sudden change comes over him. The set of his shoulders alters; all the dirt and hurry and irritation have dropped off in an instant. He glides over the carpet, with a solemn priest-like air. I remember our assistant maître d'hôtel, a fiery Italian, pausing at the dining-room door to address an apprentice who had broken a bottle of wine. Shaking his fist above his head he yelled (luckily the door was more or less soundproof): "Tu me fais – Do you call yourself a waiter, you young bastard? You a waiter! You're not fit to scrub floors in the brothel your mother came from. Maquereau!" Words failing him, he turned to the door; and as he opened it he delivered a final insult in the same manner as Squire Western in TOM JONES. Then he entered the dining-room and sailed across it dish in hand, graceful as a swan. Ten seconds later he was bowing reverently to a customer. And you could not help thinking, as you saw him bow and smile, with that benign smile of the trained waiter, that the customer was put to shame by having such an aristocrat to serve him.'
    George Orwell – Down and Out in Paris and London, 1933.

A wedding ceremony takes place at the altar, but it is when the couple appear at the church door that they are reborn into the world conjoined. The doorway marks, punctuates, frames that change in their public state of being. In the cartouche above its doorway, this cathedral in Modica, Sicily, is identified as MATER ECCLESIA – Mother Church.

DOORWAYS OF SALVATION
focuses of aspiration; instruments of salvation

Subliminally, we experience doorways as instruments of transformation. As such a doorway can also be used architecturally as the focus of religious aspiration, a promise of salvation and ultimate entry into paradise.

The Mihrab of a mosque (here the Green Mosque in Bursa, Turkey) is a metaphorical doorway indicating the direction of Mecca and promised access to paradise.

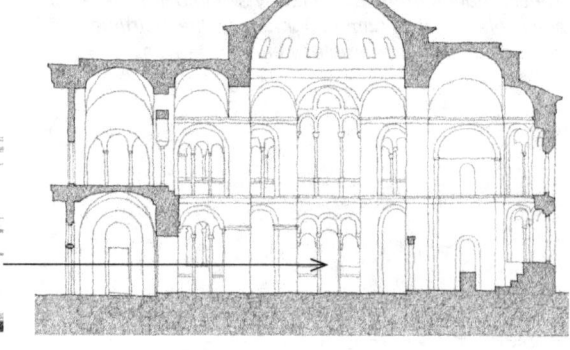

'I am the door: by me if any man enter in, he shall be saved, and shall go in and out, and find pasture.'   John 10:9.

In the monastery church of Hosios Loukas in Greece an image of Jesus is placed directly over the doorway between the narthex and nave (above; and at a, right) so that the opening becomes His body.

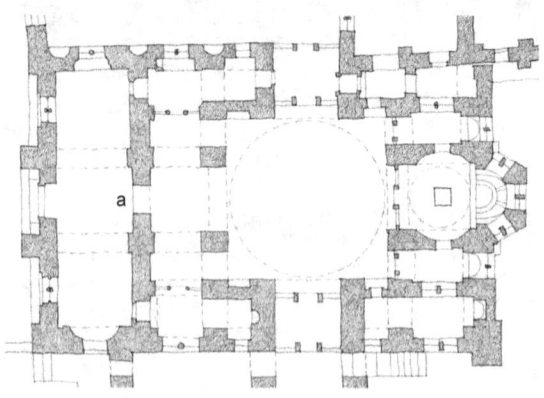

DOORWAYS OF INTERCESSION
where worlds meet

Ettore Sottsass made a series of metaphorical doorways. This one (right) was positioned on the rocky shore of a lake with a view of distant mountains. It was entitled 'There is sometimes a door through which you are meeting your love' and decked with flowers. Sottsass built another doorway, similar to the above but positioned on a shadow line (below). It was called 'Design of a door to enter into darkness'. A third was criss-crossed with string and titled 'There is always a doorway someone doesn't let you through'.

'Blessed is he who shall encounter thee at daybreak, seated before the threshold of thine abode.'
Gilbert of Swineshead, 12thC CE.

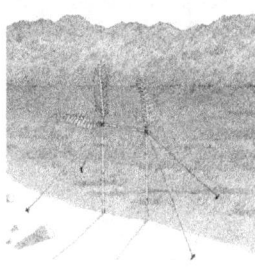

Thousands of years ago Egyptians used doorways as metaphors. Pharaohs might appear before their subjects at dawn, symbolising rebirth.

The doorway of Number 10 Downing Street in London marks the 'births' and 'deaths' of British Prime Ministers. It conceals the private zone from which the Prime Minister emerges to make public statements. The doorway is a picture frame and a symbol of authority. But it is also a mouth through which authority speaks.

DOORWAYS OF DEATH
pyramids, mausoleums and concentrations camps

'All hope abandon ye who enter here. Through me you pass into the city of woe: Through me you pass into eternal pain: Through me among the people lost for aye.'   Dante Alighieri, trans. Cary – *The Divine Comedy* (1321), 1814.

Doorways allow passage in two directions, inwards and outwards; but in some cases there is no escape. Doorways are metaphors of birth and also of death.

Pyramid temples were provided with doorways into the solid matter of the pyramid, the realm of death. The soul of the dead Pharaoh was said to be able to emerge from the blind doorway to receive offerings.

'Work makes you free' on the gate into Dachau concentration camp where hundreds of thousands of people died.

See also: Simon Unwin – *Doorway*, 2007.

The mausoleum section of John Soane's Dulwich Picture Gallery (1817) has, appropriately, blind (false) doorways that are metaphors of death.

Doorways also frame thresholds between different rooms, zones, worlds… They present the challenge of transition from one side to the other, filtering out what (or who) is not allowed to enter (or exit). Doors are valves. They are focal places for defence. They also frame welcomes, and farewells. Doorways are possibly the most potent metaphors in architecture.

METAPHORS OF PERSONALITY

Movie directors and designers understand the power of place to contribute subliminal narrative messages. As metaphors of personality, places represent and reinforce the characters of those who make and inhabit them. The effect operates at all scales, from the vast to the intimate. In Western movies, pioneer cowboys are heroically dwarfed by the volcanic plugs of Monument Valley on the Arizona–Utah boundary. In *The Lady in the Van* (Nicholas Hytner, 2015) a battered transit van filled with rags and dirty bedding houses and metaphorically represents the down-at-heel but feisty character of Mary Shepherd (Maggie Smith) who has settled herself on the driveway of the writer Alan Bennett (Alex Jennings). When, eventually, the lady dies, Bennett observed that the van had become her 'sepulchre'.

PLACE AND IDENTITY
place infused by person

Our character as individuals is not restricted to our selves as persons – bodies, faces, demeanour, posture, gait, expressions, gestures... We move and do things; we occupy, visit, work in and inhabit places. Given long enough, we infect those places not only with our odours and DNA (as hounds or forensic detectives would look for us) but also with our character and other aspects of our general identity. The character of a well-used place becomes a metaphor for the identity of the person who inhabits it.

People's identities fill the spaces they inhabit to the extent that those places become metaphors of their identities. In this instance – Donald Trump's office – identity is expressed through photographs, awards and other affirmations of importance, references to nation and national history, piles of work papers, biographical publications, name stickers... even the absence of a computer. In the expression of identity through inhabitation everyone is, unwittingly or not, an architect.

My own workspace is somewhat untidy. I think of it as geared to my work; but its contents, arrangement, furniture, equipment, the books on the shelves, and the other bits and pieces... all probably say something about who I am and what I do.

The workshop of a craftsman is a metaphorical transfer of the craftsman's technique and skill into place, accommodating work surfaces, light, tools, storage... and pragmatic relationships. Person and place become a symbiotic unit.

PORTRAIT
presentation of self

In this sixth-century CE Egyptian grave stele of Rhodia the temple frame is a metaphor for her Christian sanctity. It also, more generally, recognises that architecture both frames and represents life.

'*Every Mans proper* **Mansion** *House and* **Home,** *being the* **Theater** *of his* **Hospitality,** *the* **Seate** *of* **Selfe-fruition,** *the* **Comfortablest** *part of his owne* **Life,** *the* **Noblest** *of his* **Sonnes Inheritance,** *a kinde of private* **Princedome;** *Nay, to the* **Possessors** *thereof (it is) an* **Epitome** *of the whole* **World...**'
Henry Wotton – *Elements of Architecture*, 1624.

Sanctity is possibly not the word for the autobiographical information provided by Tracey Emin's gallery installation titled 'My Bed'. As a place it is an intimate self-portrait, metaphorically representing the messy vulnerability of the artist's life.

PERSONA
the mask metaphor

In the theatres of Greek and Roman antiquity actors wore masks. These had exaggerated features and mouth openings like megaphones to help them project their voices. But more importantly they established actors' dramatic fictional characters. In Latin such a mask was called a persona. We now use this word when someone adopts a character that is not their own. If I (right) was to don one of these Greek masks (below) it would hide 'me' and change how I am seen by others, projecting a different persona.

Architecture can be the same. Individuals, organisations, national governments... use architecture to present a persona to influence the way in which they are seen by others. Used in this way architecture can be a mask, hiding actuality and modifying interpretation. Ben Pentreath, architect to the Prince of Wales, is quoted as saying of Poundbury, the Prince's neo-traditional village near Dorchester (see pages 78 and 79):
> *'We are engaged in creating a convincing fake... All architecture is essentially wallpaper: underneath it's all the same stuff.'* Touchstone: Architecture in Wales, 2017.

'An ambassador is an honest gentleman sent to lie abroad for the good of his country.' Henry Wotton, in Augsburg, 1604.

CHAPTER III. — PALLADIAN STYLE.

CHAPTER IX. — MEDIÆVAL OR GOTHIC STYLE.

CHAPTER X. — THE COTTAGE STYLE.

CHAPTER XI. — THE SCOTCH BARONIAL STYLE.

When, in the 1860s, Robert Kerr offered the English gentleman a variety of different styles in which to build his country house it was as if he was asking him which mask he wanted to put on, which persona he wanted to adopt.

Images from Robert Kerr – *The English Gentleman's House*, 1864.

And banks tend to adopt masks of classical dependability or of high-tech modernity.

METAPHOR

MASK METAPHOR
what do our cars and houses say about us?

We live in an age of masks. Through history it has always been the case that those in power or who wish to have political power might don masks that bolster democratic support or reinforce dictatorial authority. Consumerism and social media now seduce more and more people into the adoption of masks to manage the presentation of self to the wider world. It is arguable that, for everyone involved, the management of a Facebook profile is in fact the management of a mask. Certainly in selecting the cars we drive, the clothes we wear, the houses in which we live... we are influenced by the personae we wish to present to the world.

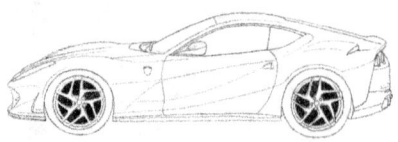

There is an idle pastime that involves asking 'If so-and-so was a car, what car would he or she be?' Motor company marketing departments certainly know that the car we buy says something about who we would like to be seen to be.

Some enjoy using masks to manage presentation of self in more complex ways. For example, a few engage in 'souping up' cars that look sedate so that their impressive performance contradicts their modest appearance.

When in the late eighteenth century William Chambers designed the Casino at Marino just outside Dublin, he was providing his client – the Earl of Charlemont – with an architectural mask of taste and sophistication based in learning drawn from classical times, all underpinned by wealth and assumed nobility.

When the German architect Peter Behrens designed New Ways in 1926 maybe he thought he was designing a house without a mask. But it is arguable that he was merely supplanting the historically derived masks of the adjacent Northampton suburban semis with the mask of Modernity.

And now, in twenty-first century Britain, some new houses are provided with cottage-style elevations that sit, just like masks, only over the front faces of otherwise bland brick boxes. The masks have porches, bay windows with false small panes, and even fake chimneys. These are masks for which buyers are happy to pay.

POET'S HOUSE
Lennon, Larkin, Thomas, Yeats

John Lennon, Liverpool

Philip Larkin, Hull

Dylan Thomas, Swansea

Poets have lived in mundane houses. But sometimes they choose to live in houses that somehow have a metaphorical relationship with the psychological and creative challenges of being a poet. Dylan Thomas, for example, moved to a house on the edge of the sea (a poetic metaphor for death) in contact with distance, the horizon, eternity... W.B. Yeats, by contrast, chose an ancient tower, from the roof of which he had a panoramic and elevated view of the world around.

Dylan Thomas's Boathouse, Laugharne, south-west Wales.

W.B. Yeats's Tower, Ballylee, County Galway, Ireland.

'I pace upon the
   battlements and stare
On the foundations of a
   house, or where
Tree, like a sooty finger,
   starts from earth;
And send imagination
   forth
Under the day's declining
   beam, and call
Images and memories
From ruin or from
   ancient trees,
For I would ask a
   question of them all.'
W.B. Yeats – 'The Tower', 1928.

METAPHOR

POET'S HOUSE IN FICTION
Jean-Luc Goddard – *Le Mépris*; Inspector Montalbano

A house such as the Laugharne Boathouse, inhabited for a time by Dylan Thomas, becomes a metaphor for the state of being of a poet. Adjacent to the ever-changing and romantic sea with its many symbolic associations with memory, with distant lands, with reflection, with travel, with the horizon, with infinity, with death. There may be views of mysterious, unattainable islands across the water that stimulate the poetic imagination to envisage and empathise with their isolation. Such a house is on the edge, precarious, tricky of access, solitary... the dwelling place of an individual with barely a foot in the quotidian world, occupying a transcendent marginal realm. By living in a place like this you can acquire something of the power of architectural metaphor to affect your identity. In such places you seem, or perhaps actually become, more poetic!

Le Mépris (Jean-Luc Goddard, 1963) is a film about machismo and jealousy. Camille Javal (Bridget Bardot) believes her scriptwriter husband (Michel Piccoli) is tacitly offering her to a movie producer (Jack Palance) for commercial reasons. Some of the drama of mistrust develops at the producer's villa on a rocky sea crag.

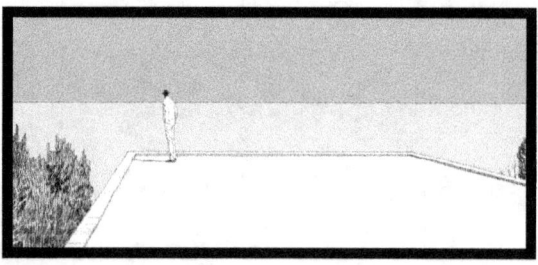

The producer's project concerns Homer's Odyssey. *At one point the scriptwriter stands on the villa's flat roof like Odysseus on the deck of his ship, contemplating the horizon and pondering his predicament (as a poet).*

The dwelling by the sea is a common narrative trope in books and movies. Not only does it usually provide opportunities for picturesque settings but also imputes poet-like mystique to the protagonists that live in them.

Sicilian television detective Salvo Montalbano (played by Luca Zingaretti) – with whom we viewers are encouraged to identify as a person (almost a shaman) able to make sense of confusing situations in a treacherous world (an investigator poet) – lives in a house by the sea and periodically immerses himself in its cleansing waters.

TEMPLE METAPHORS

Architectural metaphor can be incestuous. We have seen that architects may apply masks based on one kind of building on to a different kind of building to evoke a particular persona. These masks are themselves metaphorical. In the next section of this Notebook we shall consider the Cottage Metaphor, but this section focuses on the metaphor of the Temple. This is a metaphor that involves more than the presentation of a persona by the adoption of a mask. It is a metaphor that can evoke associations with other times and with international sophistication. It is a metaphor that suggests architecture can possess an integrity thought to reside in other intellectual disciplines such as mathematics and language.

TEMPLE 1 – DECORATED SHED BECOMES A DUCK
complexities in architectural metaphor

Ducks and decorated sheds (see page 22) are not mutually exclusive concepts. A building type that started out as a decorated shed can become a duck. An example is the generic classical temple.

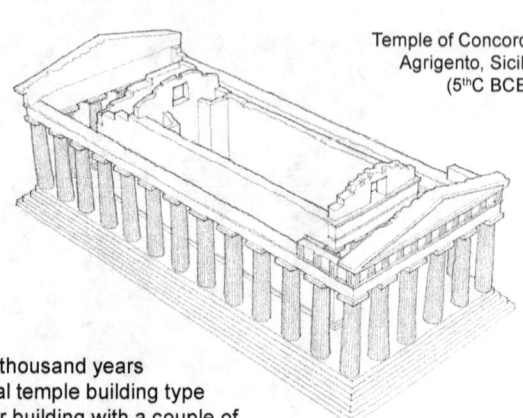

Temple of Concord, Agrigento, Sicily (5thC BCE)

In ancient times, maybe three thousand years ago, what became the classical temple building type started as a simple rectangular building with a couple of columns supporting a porch at its entrance. Gradually, over time and through various iterations, it evolved by the addition of columns, decoration and aesthetic refinements. It remained a decorated shed. Various styles developed – Doric, Ionic, Corinthian... There was never one building that represented a quintessential example. The universally recognisable generic form of the classical temple emerged: columns supporting an entablature and triangular pediment, all symmetrical about a central doorway axis. The decorated shed had developed into a duck. Across the world there are innumerable examples of architects emulating this particular architectural duck, building churches, government offices, banks, grand houses... in the form of the classical temple (e.g. The White House, below).

The Long Island Duckling (page 22) is an architectural simile in that it looks like a duck. But it is also a metaphor for architecture as a medium of commercial advertising. Although many examples of classical buildings are similes in that they look like temples, they also constitute metaphors for authority and for the intellectual and aesthetic achievements we associate with ancient civilisations.

The 'temple' is not any one particular building but an idea; an idea that can be used as a metaphor.

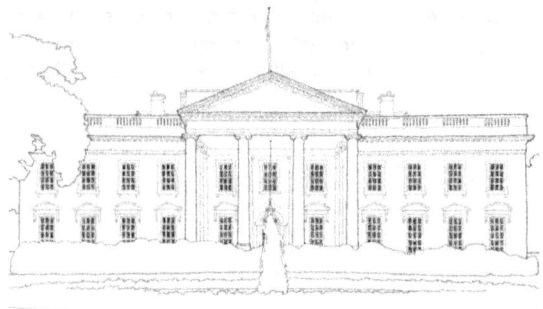

The White House, Washington D.C., (James Hoban, 1800)

For a discussion of the metaphorical potential of the 'temple', and its contradistinction to the 'cottage', see the chapter 'Temples and Cottages', in *Analysing Architecture*, fourth edition, 2014, pp. 117–32.

TEMPLE 2 – MASK
Andalusia Mansion, Thomas U. Walter

Architectural similes are not only matters of public perception; they can be intended too. An architect might want their building to look like something specific (as in The Long Island Duckling) or perhaps to be a replica of a venerable precedent, maybe the 'duck' that is the ancient temple… here presented as an architectural trophy.

Andalusia Mansion, near Philadelphia, PA., Thomas U. Walter (1836)

In the 1830s, Nicholas Biddle wanted to extend his family's house, Andalusia (right), on the banks of the Delaware near Philadelphia. In his youth he had travelled in Greece, and so he asked his architect, Thomas Ustick Walter, to make the house's river front as a replica of the Hephaisteion (or Theseion, Theseum), the well-preserved ancient temple which stands overlooking the agora of Athens (below).

In terms of its spatial organisation, Andalusia is not a temple in any other sense than that it has been made to look like the Hephaisteion. Of course, Biddle may have thought of it as a temple to himself or to his family. Architecturally, however, Walter's extension projects a temple-like architectural composition – style, form and axis – outwards across the river, but not internally into the planning of the house itself (see the plan on the following page). The layout of the pre-existing house made that difficult. The result is a temple front – a replica of the Hephaisteion's – applied to the house in the form of a porch or a veranda.

The Hephaisteion, Athens (5thC BCE)

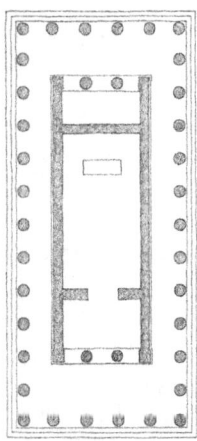

The Hephaisteion, plan

The Greek temple is not just about external appearance. Its axiality informs the whole building, in plan as well as elevation.

METAPHOR

The temple idea does not inform the composition as a whole. For example, in place of the central doorway and main room (cella) of the Hephaisteion (and most other classical temples) there is a not-quite central spine wall (a) dividing two reception rooms. The composition at Andalusia denies (disrupts) the axial progression – from approach, under portico, through pronaos and doorway, into the presence of the god within the cella – which is the essential generating dynamic of the original temple idea (more essential than external appearance).

The building therefore presents a superficial simile of a specific ancient Greek temple, The Hephaisteion. If Andalusia's porch stands as a metaphor, it does so in its representing a particular idea of the nature of architecture, i.e. that architecture is primarily concerned with external appearances. The porch is also a metaphor for an attitude to the architecture of the past. As well as representing the wealth necessary for such an undertaking, it is a hunting trophy, the head of a temple hung on the front of house like the head of dead buffalo on a gentleman's study wall. This Hephaisteion porch may be a duck, but it is not an *architectural* metaphor.

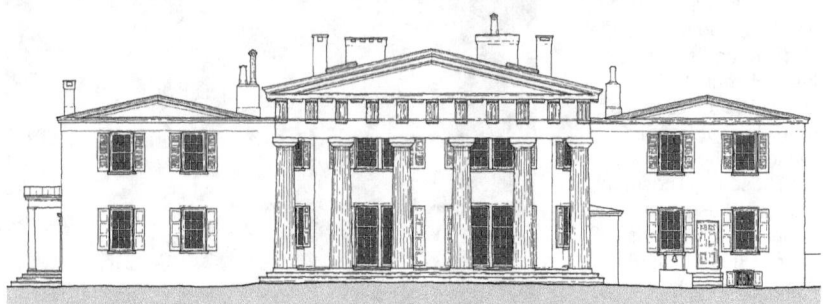

Andalusia, elevation to river with portico by Thomas U. Walter (1836)

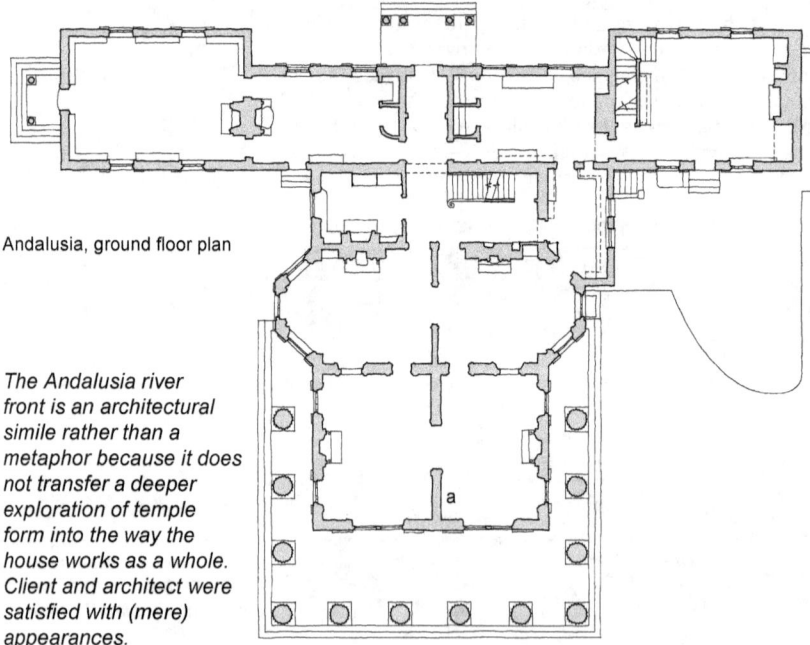

Andalusia, ground floor plan

The Andalusia river front is an architectural simile rather than a metaphor because it does not transfer a deeper exploration of temple form into the way the house works as a whole. Client and architect were satisfied with (mere) appearances.

66 ANALYSING ARCHITECTURE NOTEBOOKS

TEMPLE 3 – CLICHÉ
including the doorway axis and symmetry

Rolls-Royce radiators have grilles in the form of a stylised temple surmounted by the winged figure of Nike, Greek goddess of victory.

The temple portico has become the architectural logo of authority, nobility, responsibility, respectability, cultural sophistication… Like posh radiator grilles they front banks, churches, law courts, government buildings, galleries… as well as grand houses.

In language, some metaphors are so ready to hand that they have become clichés. 'Ticking all the boxes' and 'living the dream' have become easy clichés in every television property and talent show. The troubled detective has become a cliché in crime dramas. The motor car as status symbol has become a cliché of life aspiration. Cliché pervades commercial advertising. And, as buildings may be advertisements, cliché can infect architecture too.

By the end of the nineteenth century (at least) the classical temple front had become an architectural cliché; one of the greatest, or at least most pervasive, in (Western) history. The temple's general interpretation as a metaphor for authority, wealth and cultural status had become so ubiquitous as to be, if nothing else, boring to creative minds, especially those which craved a new, more democratic, order. The temple and the classical style more generally, with its dominant axiality and mirrored symmetry, were associated with class divisions and authoritarian structures that had, in Europe, supported conditions which led to and exacerbated the disaster of the First World War.

If the temple portico – a metaphor for classical virtues – had become the logo of authority (which to some extent it still is) then its axis was the primary architectural metaphor for the projection of power. Near Paris, at Versaille (below) – the home of the great French kings including le Roi Soleil (Louis XIV, 1638–1715) – palace, gardens and city streets were all laid out on axes like the sun's rays shining forth (and rearwards) from the royal residence.

The temple and its axis (the underpinning motifs of the classical style) dominated architecture in Europe and America through the nineteenth century. It became the architectural lingua franca of Western nations and

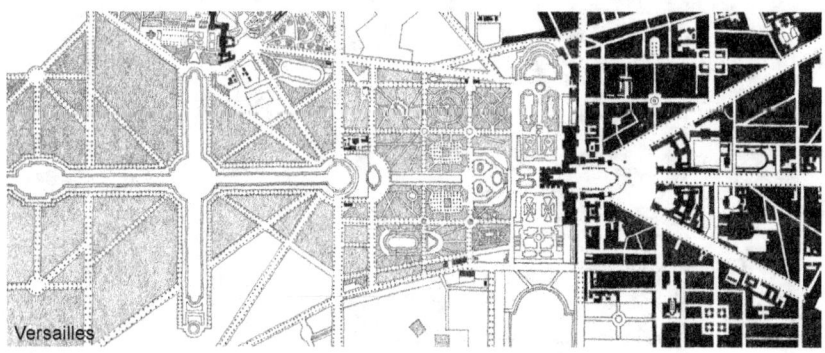

The Pigsty, Fyling Hall (1890)   Venturi, Mother's House (1964)

their colonies. In schools of architecture (the École des Beaux-Arts in Paris was the pre-eminent example) it was the only 'language' taught. Design projects became exercises in arranging axes (below). The axis became less a metaphor for power than a simplistic strategy in sometimes convoluted architectural games.

Modern architecture in the twentieth century expressed itself as radical escape from (avoidance of) such architectural clichés. Someone, somewhere decided that the world had had enough of the temple front and its dominating axiality.

The metaphorical power of the temple front is illustrated by its selection for subversion. In the late nineteenth century a Yorkshire squire used it for a pigsty (far left). In the mid-twentieth century Robert Venturi, designing a house for his mother (near left), chose to deconstruct the temple as a critical subversion of both Modern and Classical architecture and their respective metaphorical allusions.

See also: Case Study 8, in *Analysing Architecture*, fourth edition, 2014, pp. 284–8.

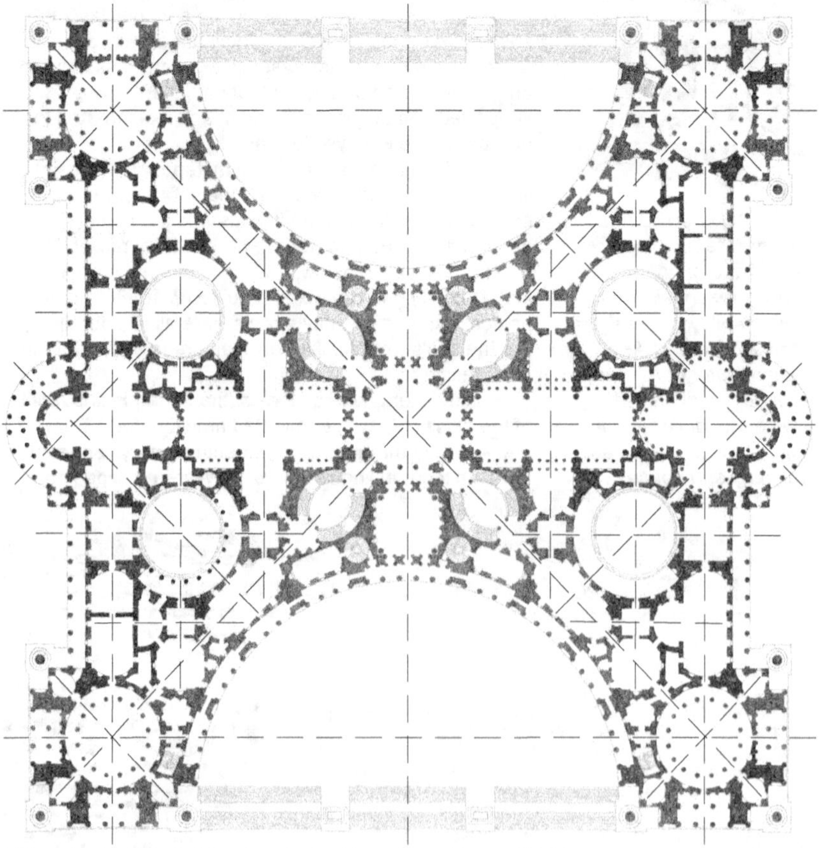

Bâtiment qui contiendroit les Académies, Marie-Joseph Peyre (1756)

TEMPLE 4 – MEGARON
Villa le lac, Le Corbusier

Rejecting simile and cliché some architects have explored the potential of the ancient temple as a basis for architectural metaphor in more subtle ways. In 1923, Le Corbusier built a small house for his parents on the northern shore of Lac Léman near Vevey in Switzerland. The plan of the house can be analysed as a deconstructed, reinterpreted ancient megaron – a domestic temple framing his parents as mythological heroes.

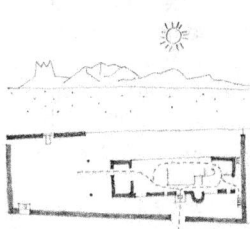

The Villa le lac values the underlying power of the architectural metaphor of the temple but without succumbing to either the simile of the temple front nor the cliché of symmetry and the doorway axis.

The plan of the villa can be analysed as a reinterpretation of ancient precedent. The territory of the house (a) is the temple's temenos with, as in Greek examples, a strong relationship with landscape. The portico is simplified to a sitting porch (b). The pronaos (c), following Homeric narrative, becomes the guest (and music) room. The living room (d) is the cella. And the more complicated arrangements – bedroom, bathroom, kitchen… – necessary for twentieth century rather than antique living are accommodated in back spaces (e). Generally however the temple axis is subverted.

The Villa le lac looks out across Lac Léman (from Vevey, Switzerland) at the grandeur of the Alps.

The villa becomes poetic by virtue of its realisation of metaphor in architectural form.

See also: Simon Unwin – *Villa Le Lac*, 2014; ebook available from the iBooks Store.

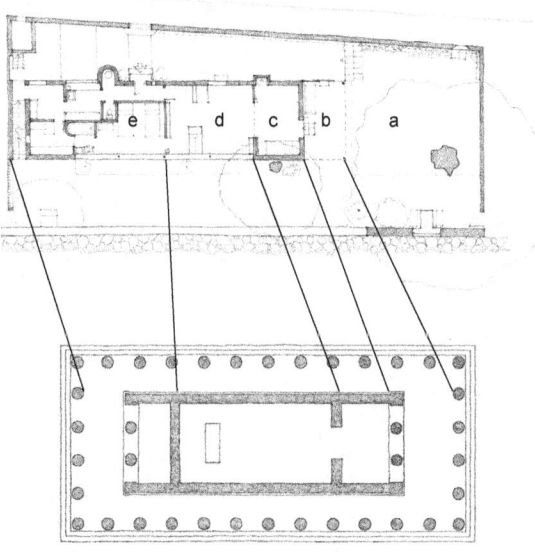

TEMPLE 5 – VITRINE
Farnsworth House, Mies van der Rohe

A quarter of a century later, Mies van der Rohe built a house in steel and glass on the banks of Fox River, near Plano, Illinois. He built it in 1950 for his friend Edith Farnsworth. The friendship faltered, partly because of the difficulty she found in living comfortably in a house with so much glass, so open to its surroundings. It is nevertheless clear that Mies intended the building as a metaphorical temple to her.

Mies's temple is very different from Le Corbusier's. Both the Villa le lac and the Farnsworth House stand side-on to their adjacent bodies of water but the materials and construction methods are very different; as is the attitude to the ground and between inside and out. Mies retains axial symmetry in the entrance and hearth.

The Farnsworth House is more contextual than it seems. It too stands like a temple related to its landscape.

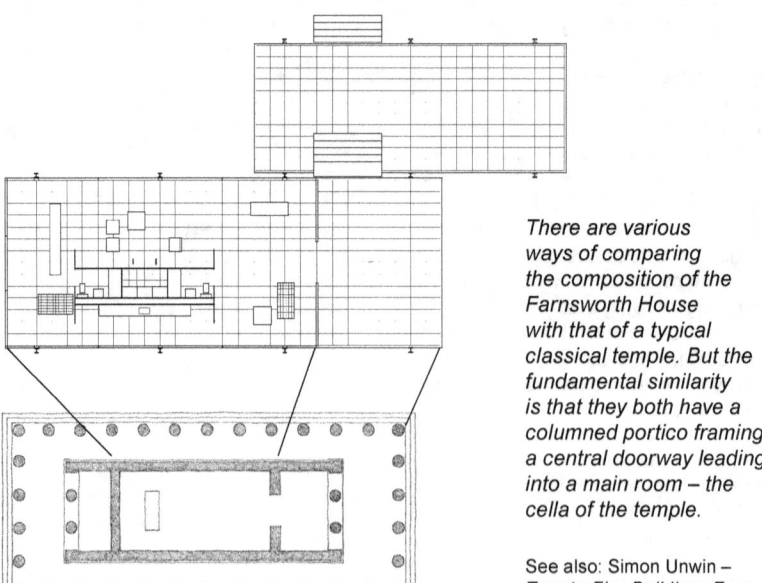

There are various ways of comparing the composition of the Farnsworth House with that of a typical classical temple. But the fundamental similarity is that they both have a columned portico framing a central doorway leading into a main room – the cella of the temple.

See also: Simon Unwin – *Twenty-Five Buildings Every Architect Should Understand*, 2015, pp. 63–78.

COTTAGE METAPHORS

The cottage is another example of an incestuous architectural metaphor. When, towards the end of the nineteenth century, Ernest Gimson designed Stoneywell Cottage (above) he did not have it built merely as basic shelter and was not going to live in it as a subsistence worker on the land. He built it as a poetic architectural expression of the cottage metaphor. Its exaggerated chimney, warm blanket of thatch and the way it nestles into the rocky topography are all aspects of that poetic expression. The cottage metaphor has a long history and continues to be current in our present (the twenty-first century) but it has a variety of different versions, some concerned with imagery, others seeking essential characteristics. Here are eleven of those versions; there are probably more.

COTTAGE 1 – AUTHENTICITY(?)
a 'real' cottage

Llainfadyn – a north-Wales slate-worker's cottage

Metaphor always involves comparison. You want to describe or explain something and do so by comparing it implicitly with something else. Metaphor depends upon our capacity for interpretation. We interpret what we want to explain and find resonance with our understanding of something else. Then by use of metaphor we transpose the characteristics of the latter onto the former (and vice versa) as a vehicle of description and explanation. Our perception of the actuality of each is modified by their mutual contribution to the transaction. In this transaction lies the creative and poetic potential of metaphor; and its potential for treachery (manipulation of the truth) too.

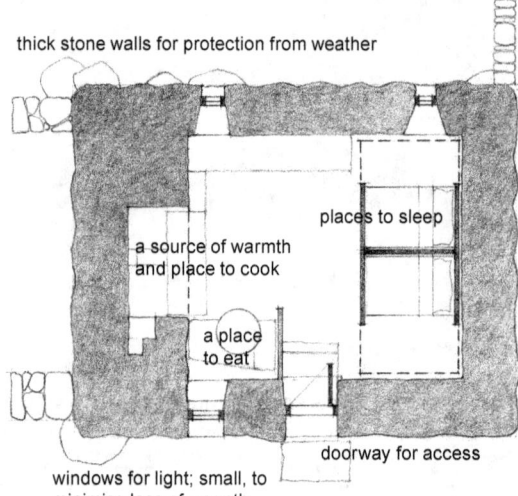

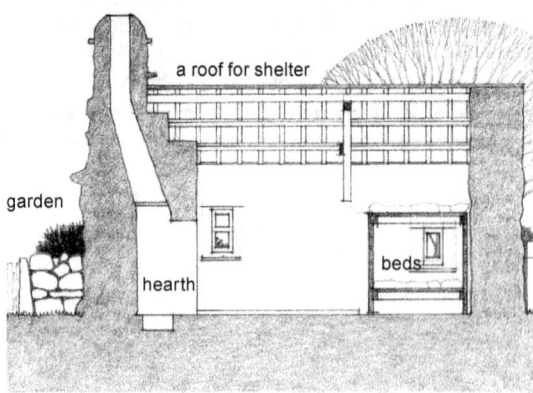

I have analysed the Welsh slate-worker's cottage called Llainfadyn (left) in previous books.* It is a clear example of a building made only to satisfy the basic human need for shelter, warmth and a safe place to sleep.

In our minds it is difficult not to project into such buildings ideas about how they would originally have been inhabited, whether or not those ideas are true. It is difficult also not to imbue such buildings with (romantic) moral worth because we often interpret them as metaphors for a simple life lived close to nature.

* See for example Case Study 3, in *Analysing Architecture*, fourth edition, 2014, pp. 261–4.

Llainfadyn's boulder walls

'The very materials... are used with nature's finger-marks still on them, not obliterated by a precision of workmanship both useless and expensive.' *

This quotation illustrates how difficult it is not to infuse description with the moral/aesthetic interpretation and judgement that informs metaphor and suggests (artificial) emulation might be a good idea.

So what characteristics help us identify Llainfadyn as a real (authentic, quintessential, true) cottage? It was built merely for physical protection from the weather. The builders used readily available inexpensive materials and straightforward construction techniques. There is no suggestion of architectural style or aesthetic refinement. (I am trying to describe these characteristics without any moral or poetic overtones.) Its form and internal space are conditioned by the needs of inhabitation and the constructional possibilities of the materials available. In a cool and damp climate (such as Wales) it provides a place to keep warm by a fire, to cook and eat food, and to sleep. In Llainfadyn, a slate-worker's cottage from north Wales, all these things are accommodated in a simple space bounded by four strong walls and a roof.

    It is probable that the builders and inhabitants of what we see as a 'real' cottage did not see it as metaphorical. But that does not stop us projecting metaphor onto it. We find it hard not to do so; in writing the above bare description of an 'authentic' cottage, even though I had a real example to hand, I found it hard to avoid metaphorical connotations. 'Merely', 'straightforward', 'simple'... are value-laden words. We treat buildings of the past as screens onto which images of an idealised life may be projected. The 'cottage' has come to be a metaphor for a life free of stress, lived in rural surroundings in fresh air and in contact with nature, away from what are seen as the evils of the city... even if life in one was originally poor and hard.

    It may of course be the case that the idea of an authentic cottage is always Platonic – it exists as an ideal that no actual cottage can ever achieve. Llainfadyn is, after all, a reconstruction of a cottage, idealised for exhibition in a museum.**

Llainfadyn's place to eat

This place inside Llainfadyn is simply and pragmatically arranged to benefit from light from a small window and warmth from the hearth (just out of the picture, to the right).

* Harold Hughes and Herbert L. North – *The Old Cottages of Snowdonia*, 1908.
** St Fagans National History Museum, Cardiff.

COTTAGE 2 – SIMPLE PEASANT LIFE
Eumaeus's hut; Laertes' farm

Around three thousand years ago, Homer, in his story of the adventures of Odysseus, implicitly referred to a dichotomy that remains current today. He juxtaposes the life of the king with that of the farmer. The dichotomy involves the architecture that frames their respective lives.

In *The Odyssey* (c. eighth century BCE), Odysseus, one of the heroes of the Trojan War, is delayed by ten years returning to his home. When he finally finds his way back to Ithaca he does not want to be recognised immediately. He has business to attend to – ridding his palace of the suitors pestering his wife – and so he lodges unrecognised with his swineherd, Eumaeus.

Later, Odysseus (again incognito) goes to see his father, who, when his son had not returned from war, retired from the royal palace to live simply on a farm in the countryside.

In both instances, the simplicity and honesty of rural life is presented as an antidote to the cares and challenges of being a king. Odysseus finds temporary refuge, and a chance to plan how to deal with the suitors, in the swineherd's hut. He finds his father on his...

'... rich and well-run farmlands... which he had wrested from their natural state by his own exertions long ago. Here was his cottage.' *

Whether slate workers or farmers, fishermen or swineherds, miners or shepherds, cottages are the homes of people who work directly in and with nature. This gives them a tacit authority not enjoyed by those who through rank and wealth have to worry about political, pecuniary, military matters. The former are free; free of the worries suffered by the latter... or so it seems to the latter.

Such associations are interpreted in and projected onto the forms of farm buildings so they become a metaphor for honesty and simplicity. Eight hundred years after Homer, so the story goes, Christ was born in a Bethlehem stable.

Eumaeus's hut, which may have been even more rustic than this, was simple and unpretentious, built directly with available material – a mere shelter from the elements.

By contrast, Odysseus's palace (below) was more sophisticated, with many rooms centred on a grand axially symmetrical hall with a large central hearth – the megaron and quarters of the king. Rather than a frame for a simple life, the palace was a stage for intrigue, duplicity and struggle.

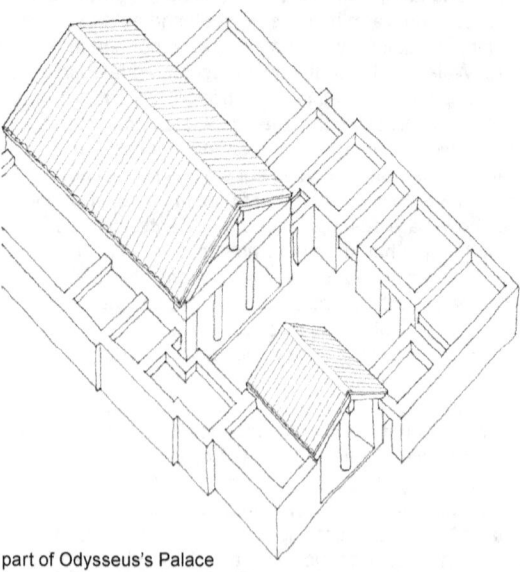

* Homer, trans. Rieu – *The Odyssey* (c. 8thC BCE), 1946.

part of Odysseus's Palace (speculatively based on King Nestor's Palace at Pylos)

COTTAGE 3 – TRUTH TO NATURE
John Ruskin and the Lake District cottage

The cottage is an important and common metaphor. Although an actual cottage is a work of architecture it becomes a metaphor when it is seen as representing a particular way of life – close to nature – and consequently imitated… as if emulating the architecture of a cottage bestows natural honesty and simplicity on both architect and inhabitant.

In *Analysing Architecture* (fourth edition, 2014, page 119) I quoted John Ruskin describing 'the mountain cottage'. He did so in vague and value-laden terms that, rather than accurately describing its form, effectively transformed it into a metaphor:

'Everything about it should be natural, and should appear as if the influences and forces which were in operation around it had been too strong to be resisted, and had rendered all efforts of art to check their power, or conceal the evidence of their action, entirely unavailing… It can never lie too humbly in the pastures of the valley, nor shrink too submissively into the hollows of the hills; it should seem to be asking the storm for mercy, and the mountain for protection; and should appear to owe to its weakness, rather than its strength, that it is neither overwhelmed by the one, nor crushed by the other.' *

As well as being associated with a farming life in direct relationship with nature, the architecture of a cottage is interpreted as demonstrating a similar direct relationship with life, materials and climate.

Ruskin interpreted the cottage anagogically (bringing out associated moral ideals) as the architectural manifestation of (and model for) life lived close to nature (and hence, for him, close to God). The actuality of the life (probably hard) lived in the cottage was (almost) irrelevant.

By contrast with the temple, through writers such as Ruskin, the cottage became a cliché of an alternative attitude to life, one we might describe as being 'away from the rat-race'. If the temple was associated with authority and nobility, the cottage was the architecture of ordinary people, of egalitarianism and community, of general liberty for all. It retains many of these associations in the twenty-first century (as its frequent use in commercial advertising suggests). The problem, for some in the twentieth century, would be that the cottage was also a symbol of the pre-industrial rural idyll. They wanted the moral virtues of honesty and simplicity but without the romantic imagery.

* John Ruskin – *The Poetry of Architecture* (1837), 1893.

COTTAGE 4 – ORIGINAL VIRTUE
Jean-Jacques Rousseau

Ruskin, like others in the nineteenth and twentieth centuries, was influenced in his attitude to nature, appreciation of life lived close to nature and of the architecture and crafts associated with those lives, by the mid-eighteenth-century work of the French philosopher Jean-Jacques Rousseau.

In his *Discourse on the Arts and Sciences* (1750), written in response to the question 'Has the restoration of the sciences and arts contributed to the purification of morals?' To condense his argument, Rousseau answered, 'Non!', life was better when we lived close to nature. And he included architecture in his argument. In doing so he evoked the ghost of an early Roman – Gaius Fabricius Luscinus –whom Dante had mentioned in his *Divine Comedy*, referring to him as 'O buon Fabrizio, con povertà volesti anzi virtute che gran ricchezza posseder con vizio'*.

Rousseau, Maurice Quentin de La Tour, 1753

* 'O good Fabricius, who preferred poverty with virtue to wealth with vice.'
Dante (my translation) – *Commedia* (*The Divine Comedy*; 1308–20), 'Purgatorio', Canto XX 24–7.

> 'What would the great soul of Fabricius have felt, if it had been his misfortune to be called back to life, when he saw the pomp and magnificence of that Rome, which his arm had saved from ruin, and his honourable name made more illustrious than all its conquests. "Ye gods!" he would have said, "what has become of those thatched roofs and rustic hearths, which were formerly the habitations of temperance and virtue? What fatal splendour has succeeded the ancient Roman simplicity? What is this foreign language, this effeminacy of manners? What is the meaning of these statues, paintings and buildings? Fools, what have you done?" We cannot reflect on the morality of mankind without contemplating with pleasure the picture of the simplicity which prevailed in the earliest times. This image may be justly compared to a beautiful coast, adorned only by the hands of nature; towards which our eyes are constantly turned, and which we see receding with regret. While men were innocent and virtuous and loved to have the gods for witnesses of their actions, they dwelt together in the same huts; but when they became vicious, they grew tired of such inconvenient onlookers, and banished them to magnificent temples.'

Jean-Jacques Rousseau, trans. Cole – *Discourse on the Arts and Sciences* (1750), 1973.

Rousseau set 'pomp and magnificence' against 'thatched roofs and rustic hearths', 'fatal splendour' against the 'simplicity which prevailed in earliest times', 'magnificent temples' against communal 'huts'. The cottage became a metaphor not only for natural honesty and simplicity, but for the lost paradise. Adam and Eve's dwelling would undoubtedly have been a cottage. It is hard to overstate the ubiquity of this dichotomy – sophisticated = bad/ simple = good.

COTTAGE 5 – FORMAL IRREGULARITY
the artificial cottage, James Malton

Such are the vagaries of our minds' relationship with metaphor that sometimes we are content with the appearance rather than the essence. As with the temple, some architects, beguiled by the cottage as metaphor for a life lived close to nature have produced architectural similes.

One of the first was James Malton, an architectural draughtsman, who in 1798 offered guidance and designs as...

> '...hints to those Noblemen and Gentlemen of taste, who build retreats for themselves, with desire to have them appear as cottages...'

Cottage design, Malton

Malton defined a cottage as:

> 'A small house in the country; of odd, irregular form, with various, harmonious colouring, the effect of weather, time, and accident; the whole environed with smiling verdure, having a contented, chearful (sic), inviting aspect, and door on the latch, ready to receive the gossip neighbour, or weary, exhausted traveller.'

Furthermore, it should have:

> 'A porch at entrance; irregular breaks in the direction of the walls; one part higher than another; various roofing of different materials, thatch particularly, boldly projecting; fronts partly built of walls of brick, partly weather boarded, and partly brick-noggin dashed; casement window lights, are all conducive, and constitute its features.'

Malton was aware that he was not designing 'true' cottages, which he thought had been 'originally the effect of Chance', but artificial ones. He may have given a more precise description of the architectural forms of cottages, but like Ruskin, he too viewed them primarily as an architectural metaphor for habitation offering escape from care:

> 'The greatly affluent in sumptuous equipage, as they pass the chearful dwelling of the careless rustic or unambitious man, who prefers agrestic pleasures to the boisterous clamour of cities, involuntarily sigh as they behold the modest care-excluding mansions of the lowly contented; and often from the belief of solid comfort can be found only in retirement, forsake their noisy abodes, to unload of their oppressing inquietudes in the tranquil retreat of the rural shelter. Often has the aching brow of royalty resigned its

James Malton – *An Essay on British Cottage Architecture: Being An Attempt to perpetuate on Principle, that peculiar mode of Building, which was originally the effect of Chance*, 1798.

crown, to be decked with the soothing chaplet of the shepherd swain.'

These ideas are far from having been confined to the history of the eighteenth and nineteenth centuries. The romantic associations of the cottage remain powerful in the twenty-first.

In the early twentieth century the desire for honesty and simplicity in architecture drove the design of 'garden' villages and cities inspired by the ideas of Ebenezer Howard in 1899. One of these, laid out by Barry Parker and Raymond Unwin – the principal architects of the Garden City Movement – is at Rhiwbina near Cardiff in Wales (right; and on page 84).

Rhiwbina, Cardiff (1910s)

The Garden City Movement, inspired by the British Arts and Crafts Movement and by urban design ideas in the USA, influenced housing design in European countries other than Britain.

House developers picked up on the idea that people wanted to live in 'cottages' and covered many acres on the outskirts of cities with their artificial versions (right).

Suburban cottage (1930s)

Enthusiasm for the 'cottage' has continued into the present, reinforced in Britain at least by the views of Charles, Prince of Wales. As well as in his own developments, at Poundbury near Dorchester for example, garden village ideas have influenced British government housing policy in the second decade of the twenty-first century. Loftus Garden Village (Newport; right) is currently in development as I write.

At least since Rousseau in the eighteenth century the cottage has become an architecturally expressed metaphor for past times longed for as a lost paradise. In the nineteenth century – as expressed by Ruskin and others – the cottage was interpreted as a manifestation of honesty and simplicity and became a metaphor for life lived close to nature.

Core to the metaphorical moral value ascribed to the cottage was its claim to honesty and simplicity: in its use of materials, the construction methods employed and in its relation to regional conditions and the everyday lives lived by ordinary people. It is ironic therefore that in latter day 'cottages' we see this classic metaphor for honesty and simplicity architecturally expressed with pretence and sham. The chimneys at Loftus Garden Village, as at Poundbury, are false, provided only for ornamental effect. They have windows with false glazing bars. The cottage appearance of the Loftus houses is superficial, being confined to their street elevations. And certainly inhabitants do not work close to nature. The cottage metaphor holds more valence than the essence.

'Garden village' cottages built in 2016 (Loftus Garden Village, Newport, Gwent; Pobl Housing Association).

Here the cottage imagery is applied only to the street elevations (see also page 60), and the chimneys are false – the houses have no hearths. Their attraction relies on the common visual metaphor of cottage imagery.

COTTAGE 6 – HOMELINESS
the advertisers' metaphor

It is the general valence of the cottage metaphor that underpins its widespread use in advertising. In this arena, actual virtues are irrelevant. All depends on perception, on our susceptibility to suggestion.

A Hovis bread advertisement from the 1970s. The television version was directed by Ridley Scott (who later directed the 1982 film Blade Runner) *for Collett Dickenson Pearce advertising agency. Filmed on Gold Hill, Shaftesbury, Dorset, it has (apparently) been voted Britain's favourite advert of all time.*

In places such as Poundbury (top) and Portmeirion (by Clough Williams-Ellis) the cosmetic application of cottage and village imagery make them feel like stage sets on which residents can pretend to live village/cottage/peasant lives.

See also: Simon Unwin – 'The Vernacular', in *The Ten Most Influential Buildings in History: Architecture's Archetypes*, 2017, pp. 200–21.

Although the backdrop to the Hovis advert depicted above is a real place (see caption), it would have worked just as well had it been a stage set – painted flats with no dwelling accommodation behind.

The cottages on this steep street represent, to the eye only (we the viewers do not need to experience their actuality), a simple, settled, mutually supportive… way of life in a traditional (timeless) village. Here that architecturally expressed metaphor has been extended to include physical health as well as mental well-being.

Such observations help us understand twenty-first-century garden villages such as Loftus (opposite) and their influences (Poundbury, for example), where cottage imagery is applied as a stage set, so that the houses become advertisements for themselves.

COTTAGE 7 – HONESTY AND SIMPLICITY
the Holy Grail

In the preceding examples, concern to replicate the cosmetic appearance of 'the cottage' has, ironically, led to pretence and sham. Some architects in the nineteenth and twentieth centuries have been more concerned to follow the essential lessons of the cottage as a metaphor for honesty and simplicity. Even in their work there is variety. It seems either that there is no one route to honesty and simplicity or that those virtues are protean and elusive. (Such is more evidence of the treachery of metaphor.)

Imitation cottages are rarely blessed with the honesty and simplicity interpreted as informing their originals. Emulating those virtues of primitive architecture, and escaping romanticism and cosmetic imitation, has been something of a Holy Grail for architects. This was one of the guiding principles of what has been called 'Modern' architecture.

    Two examples from many... Frank Lloyd Wright and Mies van der Rohe were two leading architects associated with Modern architecture. Their buildings were very different but they both professed admiration for primitive architecture. In 1910, Wright wrote:

> 'The true basis for any serious study of the art of Architecture still lies in those indigenous structures; more humble buildings everywhere being to architecture what folk-lore is to literature or folk-song to music.'

In 1938, on taking up the post of Director of the Armour Institute in Chicago, Mies urged:

> 'Let us lead (students) into the healthy world of primitive building methods, where there was meaning in every stroke of an axe, expression in every bite of the chisel. Where else can we find such unity of material, construction and form?'

I have already identified Mies's Farnsworth House as a 'temple' (page 70) but it is arguable that Mies himself also saw it as a 'cottage'. As I have suggested in *Twenty-Five Buildings Every Architect Should Understand* (2015, page 71) his enthusiasm for primitive architecture, such as the African hut (right), led him to try to emulate its honesty and simplicity in his own work, particularly in the assembly of materials.

    The influence Wright drew from 'cottage' or 'vernacular' architecture was different. His promotion of ideas associated with the organic metaphor in architecture will be discussed and illustrated later in this Notebook, but here it is sufficient to note his interest in the spatial composition and social inhabitation of space. One illustrative example is the composition of hearth, screen and settle, which he repeated in various houses.

In Indiana Jones and the Last Crusade *(Steven Spielberg, 1989) the Holy Grail (from which Christ drank at the Last Supper) was depicted as a simple cup made of clay. The implication, far from being exclusive to this film, was that Christ stood not for opulence but for honesty and simplicity.*

Frank Lloyd Wright – Preface to *Ausgeführte Bauten und Entwürfe*, 1910.

Mies van der Rohe – Inaugural address as Director of Architecture at Armour Institute of Technology, 1938.

COTTAGE 8 – DOMESTIC PLACES
Robie House, Frank Lloyd Wright

The Robie House (1910) was designed in the same period that Wright wrote the quotation opposite. It is reasonable to assume it incorporated some of the lessons he had learnt from the 'more humble buildings everywhere' (but perhaps especially Wales, the land of his mother).

The clearest instances where Wright learnt lessons from cottage architecture seems to have been around the fire – source of warmth and symbolic centre of family life. In the Robie House, as in other of his Prairie House designs, this became a complex composition of: hearth (set in its chimney stack); stair (benefiting from the structural stability offered by the strong core given the house by the chimney); a draught screen, which also provided the back rest for a bench seat (a settle, where you could warm yourself by the fire and talk with family and friends).

This is a composition of elements common in Welsh vernacular houses. Everyone responds to a place that offers a frame for social as well as physical warmth.

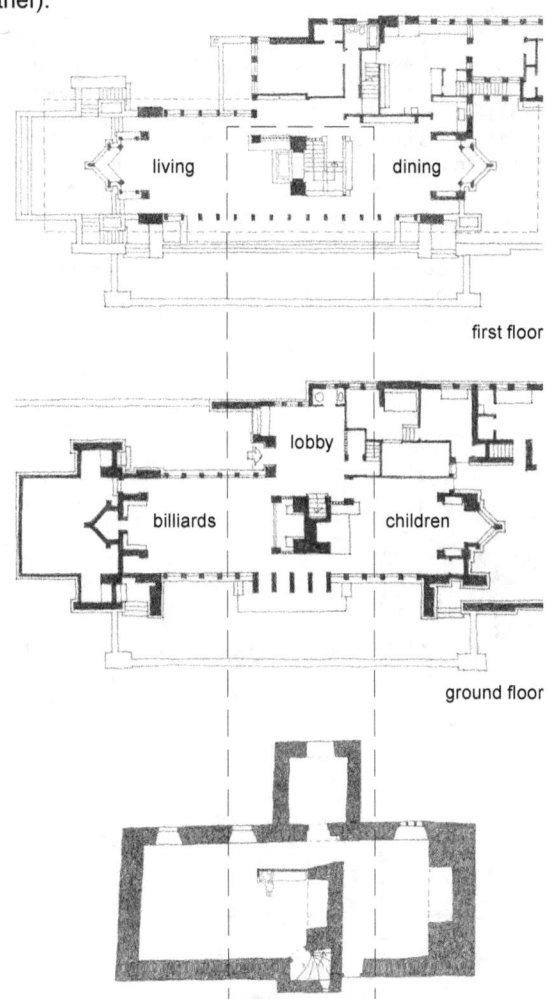

first floor

ground floor

As in the Robie House, these traditional Welsh houses (left and above) have: strong central masonry chimney stacks; entrances approaching one side of the stack; stairs built into the stack; and draught screens cum settles alongside the hearth. By replicating this timeless composition of fire, built form and people, Wright was evoking the powerful cottage metaphor.

COTTAGE 9 – DIRECT PRAGMATISM
Chamberlain Cottage, Breuer and Gropius, 1940

Some architects have responded to the cottage metaphor by seeking to emulate the honesty and simplicity that lies at its core.

Chamberlain Cottage is an attempt to follow the virtues of honesty and simplicity in the design of a weekend house, whilst avoiding stylistic imitation of the appearance of old cottages. Here, readily available materials – including modern ones such as plate glass and flat roofing – are used in direct ways where construction is visible and easy to understand. Note that the lower floor is built of stone; the upper in board-clad timber frame – light over heavy. Both floors are pinned together by the stone chimney stack; the hearths identify social sitting places on both floors.

In designing this house, Marcel Breuer and Walter Gropius (refugees to the USA from Europe, where they had both worked at the Bauhaus) sought to achieve a fresh and modern approach to architecture by following the lessons of honesty and simplicity found in traditional cottages whilst at the same time rejecting romantic associations with the past.

Breuer and Gropius's approach combines straightforward construction using readily available materials in simple ways with a sense of identification of place – using architecture primarily to frame personal inhabitation.

perspective view

Chamberlain Cottage was an exercise in honesty and simplicity; in using readily available materials in straightforward ways to construct an architecture that's prime purpose was to frame the unremarkable events of everyday life: cooking, eating, washing, sleeping, sitting by a fire chatting... These are aspirations central to the cottage metaphor. But here those ideas, expressed in the New World of pioneers, are also distanced from a past that had led to devastating war in Europe.

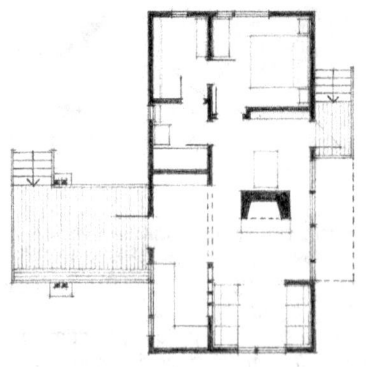
upper floor plan (living)

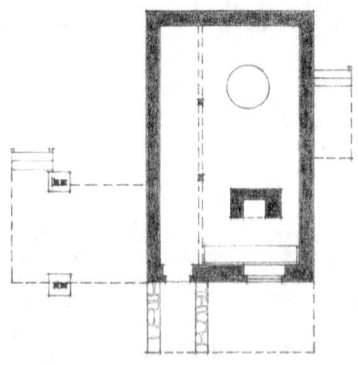
lower floor plan (workshop, storage, den)

COTTAGE 10 – LOCAL CONSTRUCTION
Sea Ranch, Charles Moore and others

Charles Moore's attempt to propagate a living community by building a unified (though irregular) condominium of 'cottages' at Sea Ranch (1965) did not succeed. But it did follow the cottage/village metaphor in its evidently straightforward attitude to its timber frame construction and to identification of places for the unremarkable events of everyday life. Rather than establish a community, it is mainly used for vacation visits.

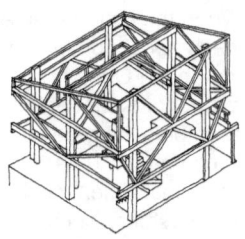

Like some nearby timber barns, the condominium units at Sea Ranch are constructed simply and honestly in timber. The interiors (below) clearly identify places for life.

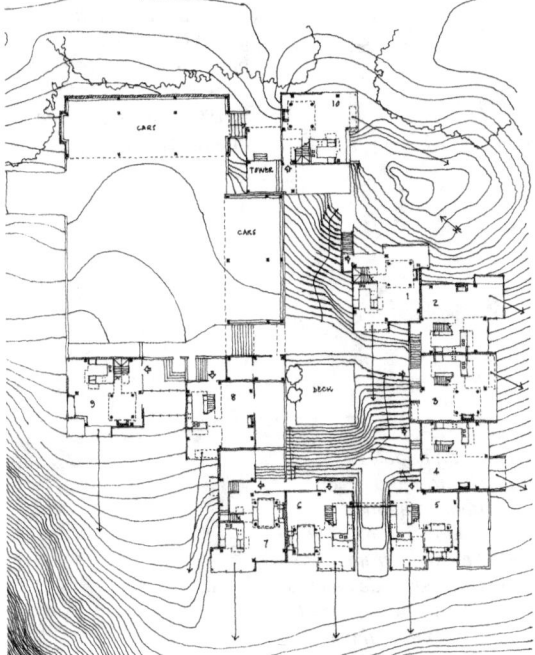

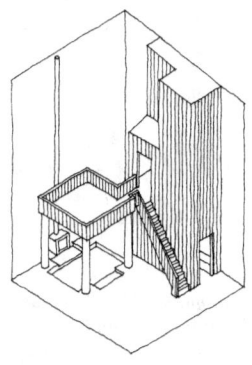

The village of ten units is built around a garage court and a small green (left), as if architectural form could in itself stimulate community

See also: Simon Unwin – *Twenty-Five Buildings Every Architect Should Understand*, 2015, pp. 153–62.

COTTAGE 11 – COMMUNITY
Rhiwbina Garden Village, Parker and Unwin

When the cottage metaphor is extended to include ideas about community it becomes the village metaphor. One particularly powerful associated metaphor is that of the village green. In original examples the green is read as a manifestation of community. In artificial examples it is intended as an instrument of community. Whether it is successful as such is a moot point.

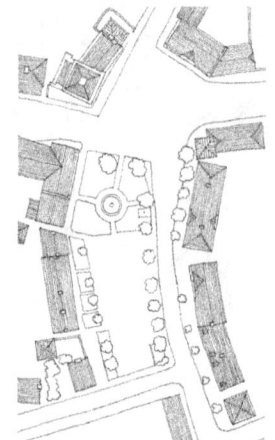

An authentic village green is irregular because it has been built incrementally over time by different people with no predetermined formal plan.

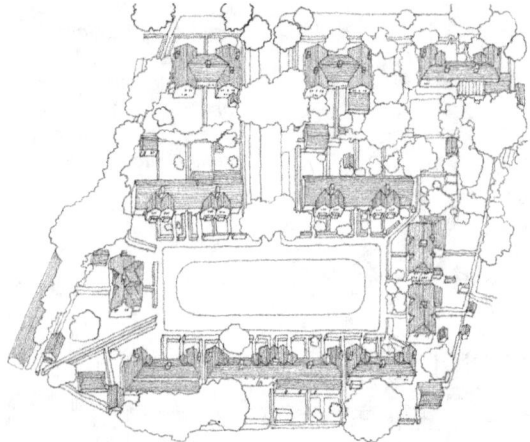

I mentioned Rhiwbina Garden Village on page 78. Twenty-two of its houses are grouped around a green (above and below). The green is a manifestation of their unity as an architectural composition, but as an architectural metaphor it is intended as an instrument of community too. Although you can see modest deviations from the regular, its layout is formal. To make it artificially irregular would have been to deviate from the principles of simplicity and honesty.

Some recent village greens have been built as irregular compositions (e.g. Poundbury, above), even though laid out by a single architect's mind. In such examples it is the picturesque simile of a village that is followed, rather than the principles of simplicity and honesty.

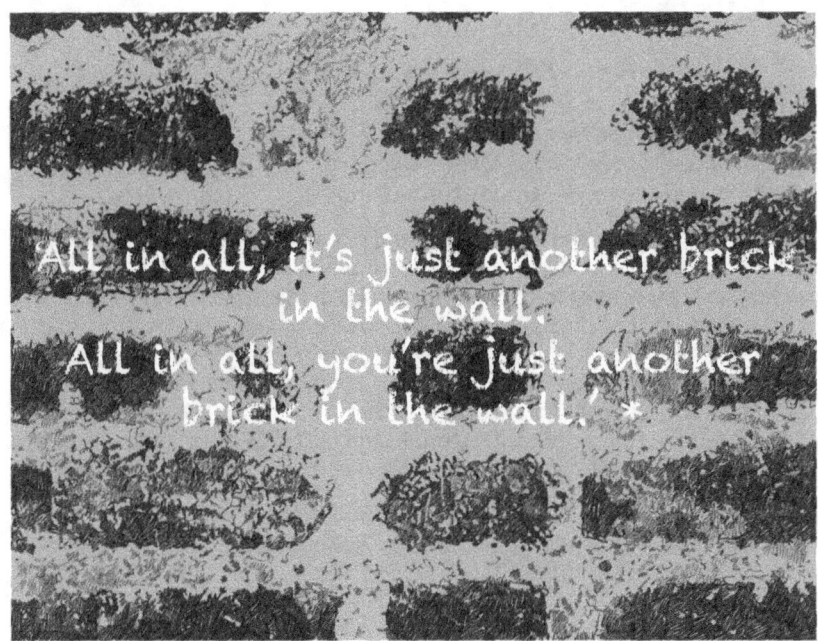

ARCHITECTURE-RELATED WORD METAPHORS

This Notebook is concerned primarily with metaphors expressed in architecture. But architecture is also one of the common sources of metaphor expressed in language – in short phrases we use in everyday speech as well as in poetry and songs. The above lyrics from a 1970s song by Pink Floyd use the wall as a metaphor for formal schooling perceived as suppressing individuality – i.e. the other side of Abbot Suger's suggestion (see pages 12–13) that the stones of a church constitute a metaphor for social cohesion under the guidance of religion**. The use of architecture as a source of verbal metaphor is not a one-way trade; metaphors in common verbal use can prompt, maybe subliminally, architectural ideas. Metaphors seem to swirl around in our conscious and subconscious imaginations, fertilising ideas at the same time as conditioning understanding.

* Pink Floyd – 'Another Brick in the Wall', on *The Wall*, 1979.
** The bricks behind the lyrics are from the church of S. Petri, Klippan, by Sigurd Lewerentz (1963–6) where, in accord with Suger's suggestion, bricks are metaphors for people brought into coherent form by religion (architecture).

ARCHITECTURE-RELATED WORD METAPHORS
in literature and everyday language

'Once our language has been declared insufficient, room is left for others; allegory can be one of them, like architecture or music.'

Jorge Luis Borges, trans. Allen – 'From Allegories to Novels' (1949).

Metaphors can be expressed in words and in architecture; the same metaphor can be expressed in both. Architecture, in a broad sense (as the interventions we human beings make to organise the space of the world and identify place), provides many metaphors used in everyday language, literature and song. As an architect it is valuable to consider what these verbally expressed metaphors indicate about the metaphorical potential of architecture itself. Language owes a debt to architecture for some of its common metaphors, but architecture can reciprocate by producing built versions of metaphors expressed verbally. Here are some common verbal metaphors drawn from architecture:

find a window of opportunity	on the threshold
the eyes are windows of the soul...	borderline
the mouth its door	push the boundaries
close/open the door to	on the edge
the wolf is at the door	over the edge
climb the ladder/slippery pole	find a route through
a step up	up the road
hit the ceiling/roof	on the road
hit/break through the glass ceiling	the long road to recovery
hit the wall	the path to self-destruction
run into a brick wall	turn the corner
stonewall	meet a fork in the road
sit on the fence	light at the end of the tunnel
beyond the pale	reach the end of the road
go over the wall	keystone/cornerstone/foundation
go up the wall	built on sand
climb the wall	in the gutter
wall of silence	over the hill
wall of sound	corner office/window seat
the writing is on the wall	on the table
Chinese walls/firewalls	under the counter/table
walls have ears	church (congregation of worshippers)
build walls	house (family; body of elected politicians)
build bridges	theatre of war
ring fence	ring-side seat
hedge/shelter (find a tax haven)	on the throne
fall through/into a trap door/elephant trap	inner circle
the body/mind is a temple	inside/outside the tent
bats in the belfry	pillar of society
cottage industry	its curtains for...

The following pages illustrate three examples – 'stairway to heaven', 'all the world's a stage' and 'city of God' – where word metaphors have a reciprocating relationship with metaphors expressed in architectural form. I shall leave you to explore other word metaphors that have the potential to be expressed in architectural form.

'STAIRWAY TO HEAVEN'
Led Zeppelin

'And (Jacob) dreamed, and behold a ladder set up on the earth, and the top of it reached to heaven: and behold the angels of God ascending and descending on it.'
Genesis 28:10.

'There's a lady who's sure All that glisters is gold And she's buying a stairway to heaven... To be a rock and not to roll. And she's buying a stairway to heaven.'
Led Zeppelin – 'Stairway to Heaven', 1971.

Stairways to high places, which are considered closer to heaven, are a common feature of religious architecture. Stairways lift a place on to a higher, transcendent level. They prompt aspiration; they offer routes to sacred places; they pose physical challenges as metaphors of moral struggle.

Stairways are associated with Christian religion too. At Pollença on the island of Mallorca, 365 steps (above) lead up to a chapel on Calvary Hill.

At Petra in Jordan there are many stairways cut into the rock. These steps (above) lead up to the Place of Sacrifice, a stone platform on the top of one of the higher crags.

Mayan pyramids have steep steps reaching to platforms where sacrifices were performed, and heads rolled back down. This pyramid is at Chichen Itza in Mexico.

At Meteora in Greece, strenuous steps lead tourists up to monasteries perched on huge natural monolithic pillars.

Most churches have an ascent to the high altar. Burton Dassett Church, Warwickshire (left) is built on a hill. 21 steps lead from the west door to the altar. The rise in levels is a metaphor for pious aspiration.

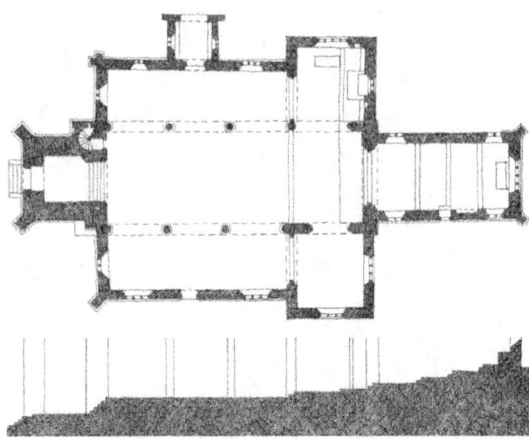

Burton Dassett Church, Warwickshire

METAPHOR

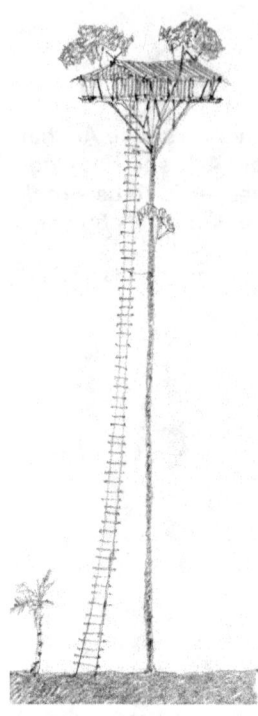
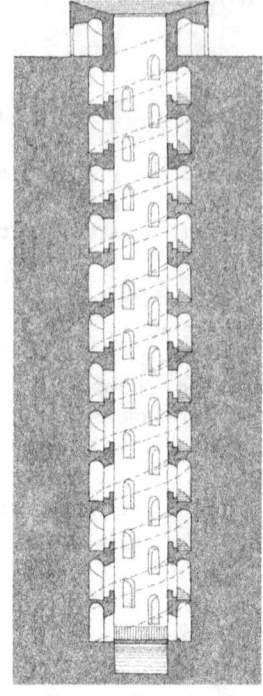

The Glacier Museum in Norway (Sverre Fehn, 1991) has stairways onto the roof that seem to reach for the peaks of adjacent mountains (whether or not they are places of sacrifice).

In the New Guinea jungle, Korowai tree-houses can be 140 feet up, reached by rickety ladders. Such tree-houses offer refuge from the dangers of standing on earth.

St Patrick's Well in Orvieto, Italy, (Antonio da Sangallo the Younger, 1537) is 175 feet deep. (Imagine the climb from the depths back towards the daylight.)

Resembling a Mayan pyramid, the Casa Del Ojo de Agua (below; Ada Dewes and Sergio Puente, 1990) has a stairway from the stream below up to the bedroom. It continues up to a living platform open to the canopy of trees.

Casa del Ojo de Agua, Mexico

See also: Simon Unwin – Twenty-Five Buildings Every Architect Should Understand, 2015, pp. 9–16.

'ALL THE WORLD'S A STAGE'
Shakespeare

'Buildings are used as a popular stage. They are all divided into innumerable, simultaneously animated theatres. Balcony, courtyard, window, gateway, staircase, roof are at the same time stage and boxes.'
Walter Benjamin, trans. Jephcott and Shorter – 'Naples' (1924), in *One-Way Street and Other Writings*, 1985.

Generals talk of the 'theatre' of war but war has no authoritative script. Even so, the world provides the setting for all aspects of human drama. Like the clown performing in a field (right) people identify their own place in which to act. Architecture – in wilderness, urban and domestic situations – defines such places physically, if only with a circle drawn on the ground. A city square (below right) provides the arena for battles between civil protesters and the assertion of authority. If all the world is a stage, and everyone a player, then architects are the set designers. But their sets are not merely pictures painted on flat panels. They identify places, frame the drama of life.

'In their swift advance across the plain, their marching feet had raised a cloud of dust, dense as the mist that the South Wind wraps around the mountain tops.'
Iliad, trans. Rieu, III.

When a clown performs on a patch of ground it becomes a stage.

People find their own stages, however small, for impromptu performances in the sunlight. But everyone, all the time, in public or in private, is acting on their own stage.

The streets and squares of cities are the arenas not only of everyday life but also for the drama of demonstration and the tragedy of terrorist attacks.

Even in the privacy of our homes the rooms are the stages on which we perform the quiet rituals and dramas of domestic life.

METAPHOR

Life in the palazzi of the Renaissance nobility must have been generally theatrical. A Duke's or Queen's bed might be framed by a proscenium arch (as well as a canopy). This one (left) is seen from the Galleria dei Quadri (or Painting Gallery) in the Borromeo family's palazzo on Isola Bella – one of the Borromeo Islands in Lake Maggiore, northern Italy. The theatrical proscenium arch places nobility in a special realm separated from that occupied by lesser mortals, whilst also allowing them audience.

Architecture provides the stages for the everyday performance of domestic events such as family meals (right). They might take place in public or in private. Every activity has its stage. A bed can even be a stage for the act of sleeping (see Sleep; *Andy Warhol, 1963).*

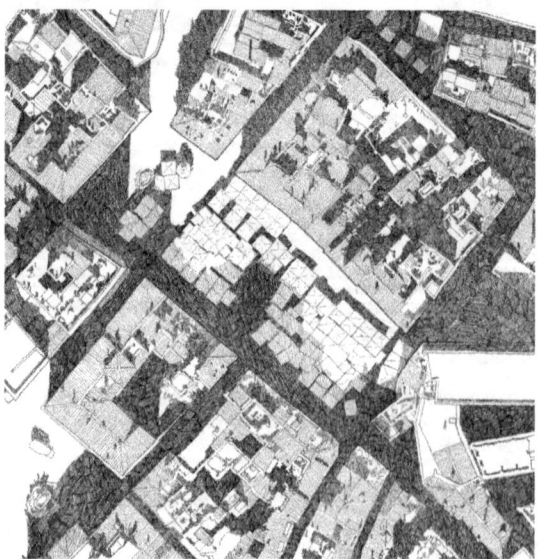

Apartments around a city piazza are spectators of the dramas that happen in that square. Around the Campo de' Fiori in Rome (left) residents can watch the performance of the flower markets. The proliferation of satellite dishes does however suggest that our relationship with performance on the world stage has changed from that before television... or the movies, when cities like Rome became the stage sets for romances such as Roman Holiday *(starring Audrey Hepburn and Gregory Peck, above; William Wyler, 1953).*

A RUDIMENTARY THEATRE
Anton Chekov – *The Seagull*

'The blue distance that never gives way to foreground or dissolves at our approach, which is not revealed but only looms more compact and threatening, is the painted distance of a backdrop. It is what gives stage sets their incomparable atmosphere.'

Walter Benjamin, trans. Jephcott and Shorter – 'One-Way Street' (1925–6), in *One-Way Street and Other Writings*, 1985.

An architectural metaphor is implied by Anton Chekov in the first act of his drama *The Seagull* (1898). It takes the form of a rudimentary theatre erected in a garden for a play written by one character Konstantin Gavrilovich Treplev to be performed by another, his love and muse Nina Mikhailovna Zarechnaya.

The drawing below is my visualisation of Chekov's ad hoc garden theatre. It stands on a pathway amongst trees with a lake as backdrop. Treplev himself says of it:
> 'That is a theatre for you. A curtain, one wing and another, and then empty space. No embellishments at all. Only a view over the lake to the horizon.'

And when the play-within-a-play is about to start...
> 'The curtain rises, revealing the view of the lake with the moon above the horizon reflecting in the water.
> NINA ZARECHNAYA, in white, is sitting on a rock.'

The metaphorical connotations of this rudimentary theatre are rich. Chekov used the play to reflect on the nature of theatre and of being a playwright. Both having

wings, the eponymous seagull can be interpreted as a metaphor for the theatre in general. It can be raucous and strident, with a transcendent view of the world below, swooping and diving to snatch morsels selfishly to devour.

More particularly, the theatre's simple proscenium arch creates what in French is called a *solution de continuité*, a fault line, a rupture, a threshold between the everyday world in which we live and the special make-believe or intensified world of scripted and performed drama.

Positioned on a pathway, Chekov's rudimentary stage identifies theatre as occupying just a moment on the continuum of time which stretches into the indeterminate future, the oblivion of the lake (death again) and the eternity of the horizon. The moon stands for the female principle, personified by the character of Nina.

The table Chekov mentions in his stage directions can be interpreted as an altar, imbuing the theatre with the status of a church. The chairs seat the audience as a congregation gathered to witness the performance as a religious service in which there is the possibility of a crucifixion of both actor and playwright.

In *The Seagull* it seems Chekov was struggling with the validity and continued relevance of theatre as a vehicle for poetic expression. The play encompasses a battle between the playwright Treplev and a novelist, Boris Alexeyevich Trigorin, for the love of the muse Nina. Eventually Nina confirms her greater love for the novelist and the playwright commits suicide.

Chekov is not celebrating the theatre as a temple to divine spirits. Dramatically his narrative kills the playwright, the seagull, the theatre... and perhaps himself as the author of them all.

The rudimentary proscenium arch Chekov asks to be mantled in the fictional garden of *The Seagull* stands as both a frame and a metaphor for the theatre in general. Its eventual dilapidation is seen to mirror the degeneration Chekov felt afflicted theatre in his time.

That proscenium frame is also a metaphor for the juxtaposition of that which is on display and that which is hidden. Chekov's word for the wings – кулиса (pl. кулисы), represented in my drawing by a pair of old doors used as side screens or wings of the rudimentary theatre – is used, in Russian, in reference to the 'life behind the scenes' of theatre, opera, ballet... In some instances such a life is seen as a privilege – being part of a clique – but it can also be experienced as negative – as in not being able to cope with the gossip and back-stabbing of Thespian life.

In these ways, a simple architectural construction – Chekov's stage-within-a-stage – can be imbued with rich, many faceted, metaphorical dimensions. It is a poetic device.

'CITY OF GOD'
St Augustine

'From (the) world's city there arise enemies against whom the City of God has to be defended.'
Augustine, trans. Bettenson – *Concerning the City of God Against the Pagans* (5thC CE), 1972.

'I will not cease from Mental Fight, Nor shall my Sword sleep in my hand: Till we have built Jerusalem, In Englands green & pleasant Land.'
William Blake – 'Jerusalem', 1808.

In some of its semblances the 'cottage' metaphor (pages 71–84) suggests that goodness originates in nature, and that our response, in architecture as in other aspects of life, should be to act according to nature (kata phusin – an idea that dates back to the ancient Greeks, and the pseudonym used by John Ruskin when he first published the passage quoted on page 75). By contrast, both St Augustine and William Blake (quoted above) imply that if we, generally, are left to our own devices (i.e. follow our own nature) the world goes awry. We build cities of impiety (the 'world's city' – specifically Rome) and 'dark Satanic Mills'. If we want to emulate (establish the metaphorical physical manifestation of) the 'City of God' we have to take special care, make special efforts to follow (what we see as or determine to be the right) moral precepts. This is an architectural challenge in which moral philosophy is promulgated in built form. Such 'ideal' cities are usually identified by their ordered form, which distinguishes them from the irregularity of the quotidian world around.

Sigurd Lewerentz's S. Petri Church in Klippan, Sweden (1966), seems to have been conceived as a fragment of an austere City of God. It too is clearly separate from its surroundings.

See also: Simon Unwin – *Twenty-Five Buildings Every Architect Should Understand*, 2015, pp. 175–86.

Richelieu is an 'ideal' town in the Loire Valley, France. It was laid out on a formal geometric grid by the architect Jacques Lemercier for his client Cardinal Richelieu. It was built in the first half of the seventeenth century. As can be seen from the plan (right) the layout incorporates the Christian symbol of the cross, but its general geometric order and axiality is a metaphor for moral rectitude, and distinguishes it from the irregular disorder of nature (and more recent adjacent development). This is (or was conceived as) a 'City of God'.

METAPHOR

Acropolis (ἀκρόπολις – from ákros and pólis) means high or upper city. Many cities, especially from the world of ancient Greece, have them. They are thought to have developed from secular citadel palaces built on rocky crags for defence. But as cities expanded, their heights became sanctuaries from which gods could watch and bestow protection on the settlements around. They became cities within cities, cities devoted to the gods, who were provided with grand temples.

The best known example of an acropolis is the one in Athens. Separated from the ordinary world around by its position on top of a rocky crag, it accommodates a transcendent city of the gods.

Dedicated primarily to Athena, the protector goddess of Athens, the principal temple on the Athenian acropolis – the Parthenon – looks down, benevolently and judgementally, on the city below and its mortal inhabitants.

In his famous photograph of Pierre Koenig's Stahl House (Case Study House #22; built in 1959; right), Julius Schulman develops the image of a modern metaphor for the ancient temple of the gods. With the street lights of Los Angeles twinkling below, Schulman portrays Koenig's cantilevered living room as a glass-sided temple, inhabited by its own benevolent goddesses (or maybe they are angels).

'ARCHITECT/ARCHITECTURE OF...'
metaphor for instigator/intellectual structure

We have already touched on the metaphorical relationship between architect and god or God and Architect (see pages 14 and 18). But the word 'architect' is widely used, especially in journalism, as a metaphor for the person (often a politician) responsible for giving intellectual structure to a policy or initiative. Thus the UK politician Aneurin Bevan may be referred to as having been 'the chief architect of the National Health Service' in the late 1940s (Geoffrey Rivett – nhshistory.net); and Paul Wolfowitz (US President George W. Bush's Deputy Secretary of Defense, 2001–05) identified as 'one of the architects of the Iraq War' (Zachary Pleat – *Media Matters for America* website, September 11, 2016). Other examples are too numerous to cite.

Likewise, the word 'architecture' is applied as a metaphor to intellectual structures that are not buildings, gardens, places, cities... Musicologists refer to the 'architecture' of a symphony; computer hardware designers refer to a computer's 'architecture'; teachers of creative writing refer to the 'architecture' of a novel or play; military strategists refer to the 'architects/architecture' of war. They are not referring to melodic representations of buildings, nor the application of architectural features such as doors and windows to computers, nor the physical stage/setting of a play or novel, nor the devastated ruins of bombed cities. They are referring to that which an architect's mind gives to any creative work – its intellectual structure. In all these instances and many others, the word 'architect' refers to the mind that conceives, and 'architecture' to the intellectual structure that the mind generates (or attempts to generate). Thus those of us who plan our careers carefully attempt to give 'architecture' to our lives. When we plan a route from one place to another we give our journey 'architecture'. Even when we go to the beach we make architecture by laying out our towel and protecting it with a wind shield... And always, we can of course be 'architects' of our own misfortunes. Some people refer to the biological 'architecture' of the human body or of the geological 'architecture' of a cliff face. Such might be taken to infer a designing mind (God the Architect) behind both; but it could also refer to the empirical/epistemological sense the analytical minds of scientists make of them.

Does referring to the 'architecture' of a cliff face mean:

... it was designed by God the Architect of the world and universe, as part of the grand Creation?

... the forces that shaped it have been determined analytically and described cogently by geologists?

... people (or even birds and other creatures) have adopted and amended it as a place to live?

Depending on your beliefs, point of view and what you want to say, it can mean any of these things. (I would be inclined to suggest the last is not a metaphor.)

'A TEAR DROP ON THE CHEEK OF TIME'
Rabindranath Tagore sees the Taj Mahal

'You knew, Shah Jehan, life and youth, wealth and glory, they all drift away in the current of time. You strove, therefore, to perpetuate only the sorrow of your heart... Let the splendor of diamond, pearl, and ruby vanish like the magic shimmer of the rainbow. Only let this one tear-drop, this Tajmahal, glisten spotlessly bright on the cheek of time, forever and ever.'

Rabindranath Tagore

Rabindranath Tagore's word metaphor seems to be quoted every time the Taj Mahal is mentioned. So much so that it has become a cliché. But the Taj Mahal is also a powerful manifestation of an architectural metaphor, one wholly appropriate to its purpose as a tomb for a much-loved wife. With the four towers that pay homage to the dome, the Taj Mahal juxtaposes male and female architectural forms. Its gardens represent eternal paradise.

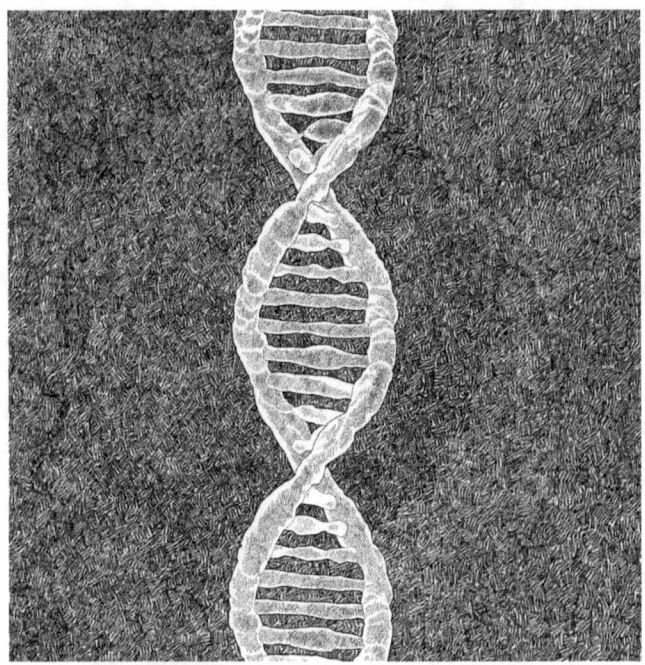

THE GENETIC METAPHOR

There is a large literature related to an organic metaphor in architecture. Some is listed alongside. Much of this literature questions the validity of organic as a concept relevant to architectural design, some labelling it a 'fallacy', others as 'mischievous'. Even so, the idea that human creativity can be imbued with the same integrity as results from the natural operation of genes is a seductive one. At root it suggests that architects might emulate the natural processes of growth to form and the profound integrity of natural creation. This idea can be applied to various aspects of architecture – representation, organisation, construction... The genetic metaphor has been influential throughout the history of architecture, from prehistory to the present. Incidentally, the two stairways of St Patrick's Well in Orvieto (see page 88) make a double helix but that does not mean they constitute a genetic metaphor.

Peter Collins – 'The Biological Analogy', in *Changing Ideals in Modern Architecture* (1965), 1967.
Geoffrey Scott – 'The Biological Fallacy', in *The Architecture of Humanism* (1914), 1924.
John Summerson – 'The Mischievous Analogy', in *Heavenly Mansions* (1948), 1963.
D'Arcy Wentworth Thompson – *On Growth and Form* (1917), 1961.

GENETIC INTEGRITY
order in natural form

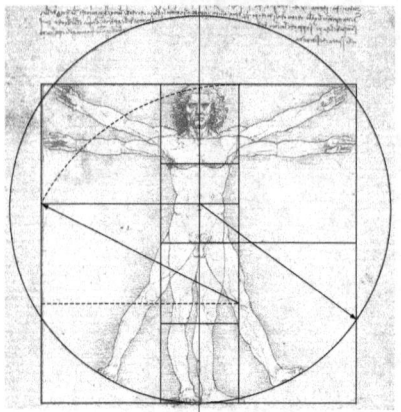

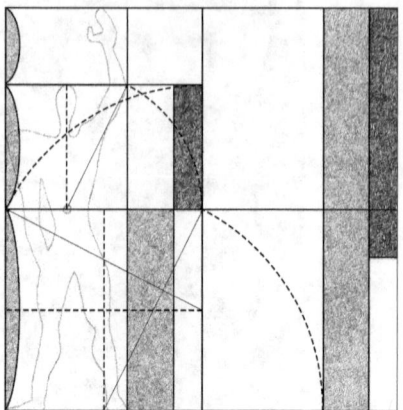

Earlier in this Notebook we saw that part of the metaphorical contribution of the human form to architecture involves trying to imbue architectural form with the same geometric integrity thought to inform the perfect body (see pages 30–31). Both Leonardo da Vinci, following the ancient author Vitruvius, and Le Corbusier sought to codify this (above). Their attempts, and those of others, imply that something of the generative process behind admired human form might be employed in producing good architecture, suggesting the possibility of genetic integrity in architecture as in natural form.

Genetic integrity is not confined to the form of the human body. Formal integrity based in geometry and geometric means can be found in other natural creations too (right and opposite).

Spiral shells such as that of the Nautilus are clearly formed from geometric principles bedded in the mollusc's genetic code. But the exact principles are difficult to identify. Some have suggested they derive from the Golden Mean (see opposite) but measurements suggest not in a simple way. Discussion of possible geometric formulae for the spiral can be found at:
goldennumber.net/nautilus-spiral-golden-ratio/

But now, in the twenty-first century, it has become possible to use computer software to generate forms that emulate the genetic integrity of natural creations in form if not in construction. Understandably, such parametric forms resemble shells; as in the case of the work of architect Zaha Hadid (left).

Heydar Aliyev Cultural Centre, Baku (2012)

GENETIC GEOMETRY
the Golden Mean

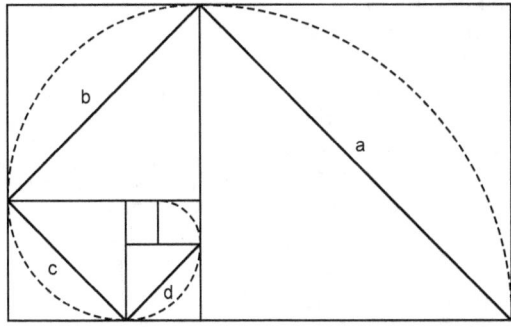

The Golden Rectangle (left), based on the Golden Section or Mean, seems to possess its own genetic integrity because it replicates itself and grows by the addition of a square to one of its longer sides. This means the proportions of diagonals remain constant.

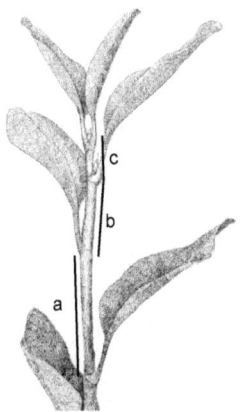

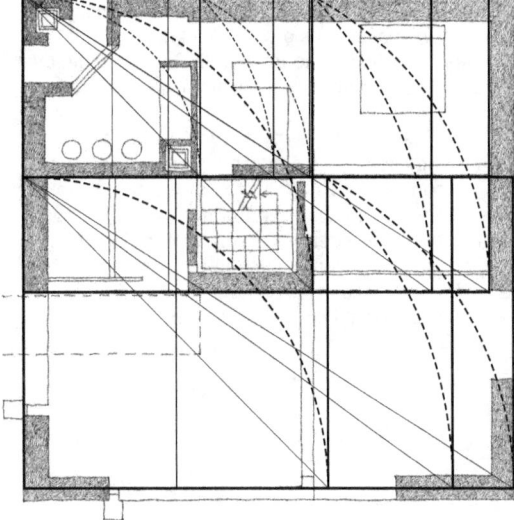

The Golden Mean appears relevant to growth and form of some plants (above) and even the human hand (below).

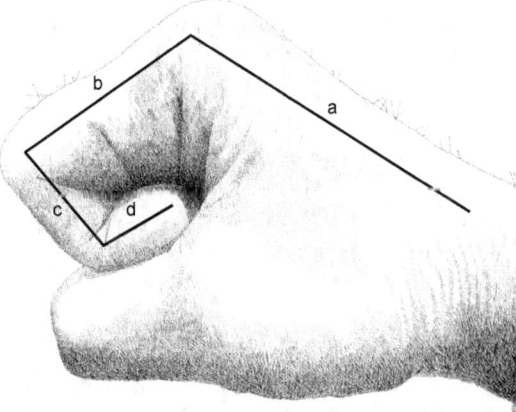

If an architect wants to imbue a design with genetic integrity she or he, like Mario Botta in this design (above) for a house at Riva San Vitale overlooking Lake Lugano in Switzerland, might turn to the Golden Mean. Of course the validity of the genetic metaphor in architecture is disputable because buildings do not grow thoughtlessly but are determined by the will of the architect.

ORGANIC INTEGRITY
Frank Lloyd Wright's driving principle

'(My) designs have grown as natural plants grow... (This method provides) a framework as a basis which has an organic integrity, susceptible to the architect's imagination and at once opening to him Nature's wealth of artistic suggestion, ensuring him a guiding principle within which he can never be wholly false, out of tune, or lacking in rational motif.'

Frank Lloyd Wright – 'In the Cause of Architecture', in *The Architectural Record*, Volume XXIII, March, 1908.

That is certainly what Frank Lloyd Wright thought.

The above quotation is only a small fragment from Wright's extensive writing on this theme of genetic (his word was 'organic') integrity. His aim was not so much to give form the same irregularity seen in natural forms such as plant tendrils or wending streams, but rather to give his designs a consistent disciplined wholeness. He did this geometrically, by designing over a square grid. Two from many examples are illustrated here.

In designing his early houses, Wright found it conducive to overlay his drawings over graph paper. Such a technique helps the architect decide positions and relationships; placing window mullions and door jambs on grid lines seems more 'right' than an arbitrary arrangement. It also lends the design, especially when used in the vertical as well as horizontal dimension, an integrity which Wright could claim as 'organic'.

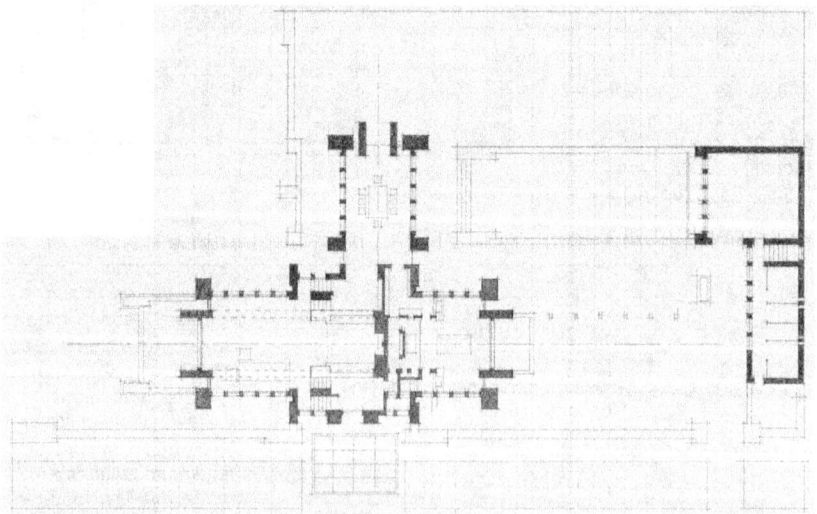

This is my reconstruction of Wright's plan of a house for H.J. Ullman (1904, unbuilt). Drawing over graph paper, even if replicating someone else's design, gives you the feeling of following (or at least interacting with) the (geometric) will of some transcendent power. This must have contributed to Wright's desire for organic integrity.

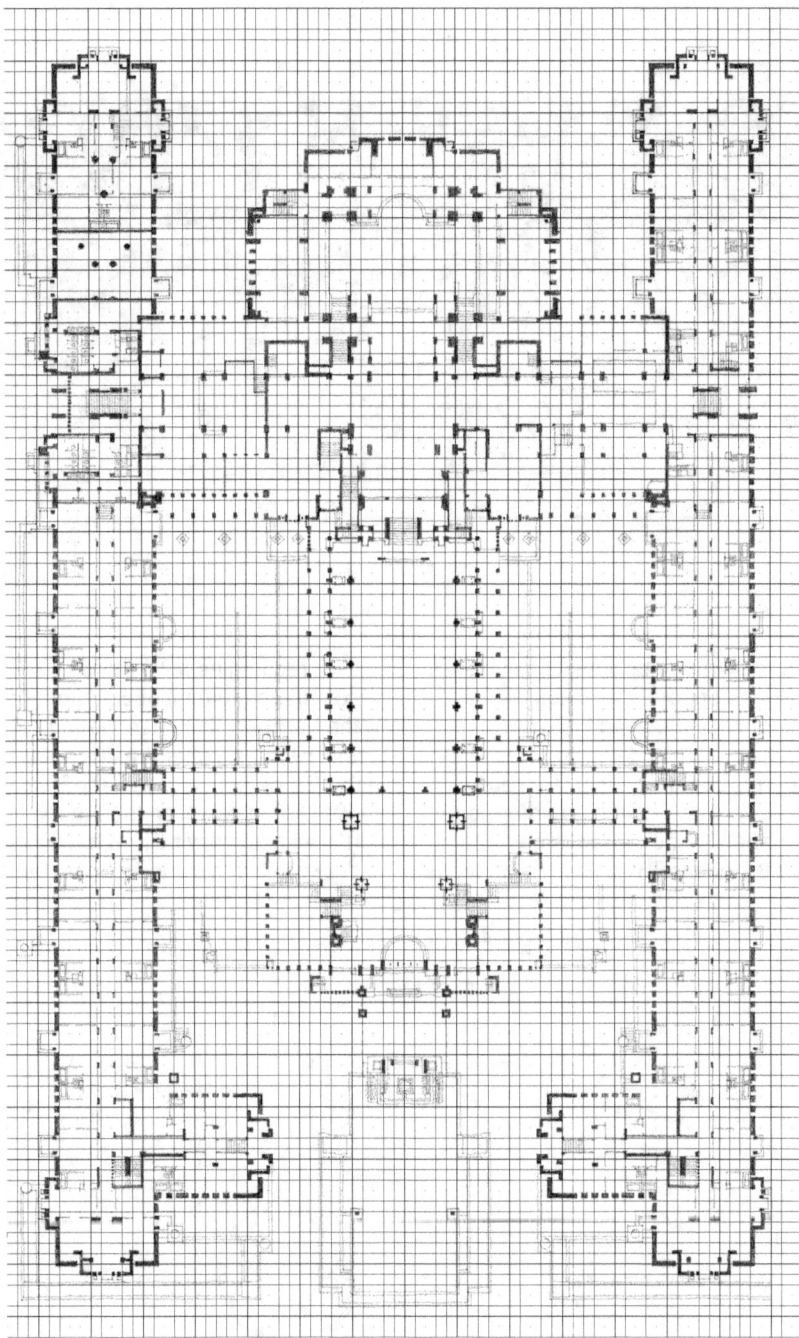

The plan of Wright's Imperial Hotel, Tokyo (1915–22, demolished 1968) overlaps the letters I and H. Every line and element of the plan was held together (integrated) by alignment with an underlying grid. The tiling (not shown) in the public spaces was in accord with this grid too. The grid provides the 'genetic' structure of the 'organism'.

GENETIC CODE
Glass House, Philip Johnson

elevation

Philip Johnson built his Glass House in 1949, apparently influenced by a model of Mies van der Rohe's Farnsworth House, which was not realised until 1951. Both are examples of architecture informed by a 'genetic code' based in geometry; not the geometry of Golden Sections and √2 rectangles but geometry based on an element of construction. In the Farnsworth House the module was a 33" x 24" travertine floor slab; in the Glass House it was apparently an 8½" floor 'tile' (even though the house was actually built with a floor of bricks laid in herring-bone pattern).

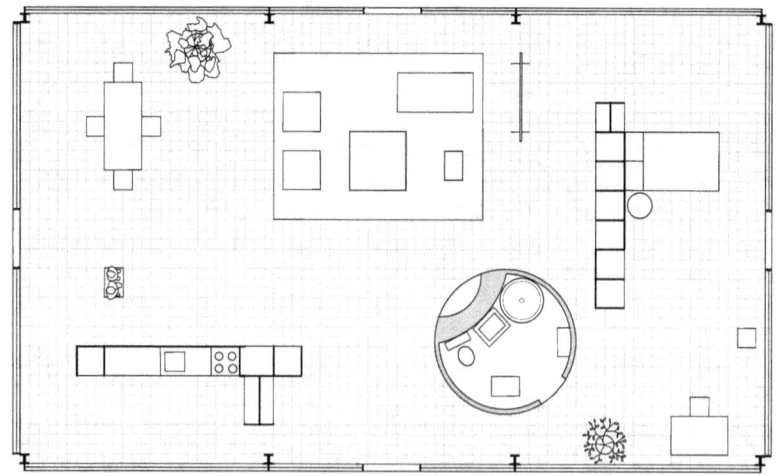

plan

The Glass House does not look like it is a product of a process akin to that which produces natural creatures. But just as the growth and form of creatures is determined and controlled by their hidden genetic code so too is the form of the Glass House controlled by a hidden code based in constructional geometry. Of course the architectural 'genetic' code is nowhere near as complex and subtle as the genetic code of natural creatures, but it nevertheless gives a basis on which formal decisions may be made. It may well be that, as with natural genetics, if the vital components and rules of generation of the Glass House were known, a 'clone' or a 'close biological relative' could be engineered.

As will be seen in the following pages, there have been various attempts by architects to establish a genetic code for architecture. As I have said, that used by Philip Johnson in the Glass House, and his friend Mies van der Rohe in the Farnsworth House, was based on a module derived from one of the building's smaller yet pervasive elements, a unit of floor finish – a floor tile. The dimensions of this unit determines a module that conditions the dimensions of most parts of the house and, aggregated into 11x11 squares, determines the form and dimensions of the house as a whole, in both the horizontal and vertical planes.

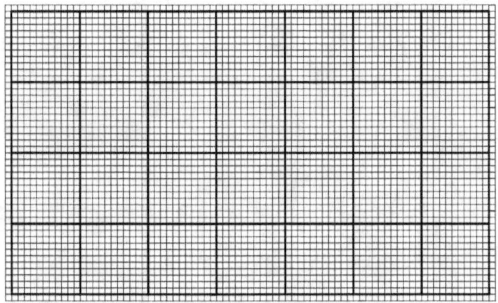

The underlying proportions of the floor plan are based on a 7-wide by 4-deep square grid set inside the structural columns. Each square is 11x11 'tiles'. There is an extra row of 'tiles' on each side to accommodate the width of the columns. Notice that the columns do not sit on this 7x4 grid but at the third points along the front and back.

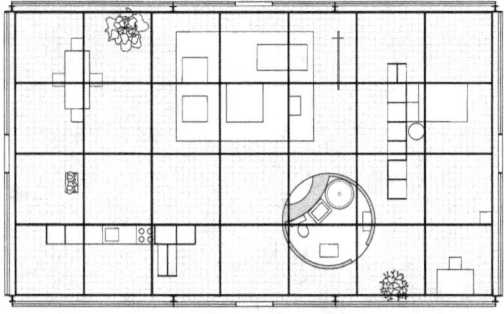

There are twenty-five 'tiles' between columns. Adding one tile for the width of each column means the house is 79 'tiles' wide and 46 deep.

The 11x11 'tile' square accounts for the sizes of the larger wall panes in the vertical dimension too (below).

METAPHOR

GENETICS OF CLASSICAL ORDERS
examples analysed to codify their genomes

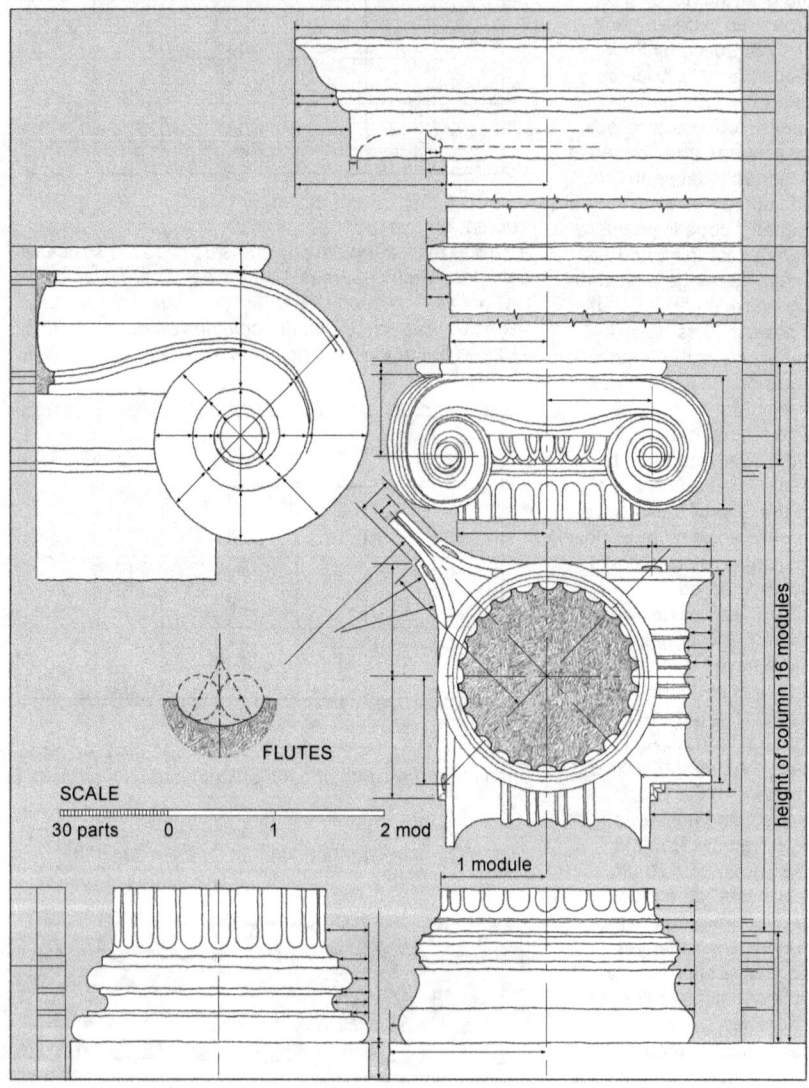

This is an analysis of the Attic Ionic Order based on the Temple on the Illissus near Athens (after Wooster Bard Field, 1922). I have omitted most dimensions but all those indicated with arrows are given in terms of modules and parts of modules.

Since the Renaissance, examples of antique classical buildings, seen to be beautiful, have been analysed to codify their architectural 'genomes'. Drawings such as the above, giving the dimensions of a significant representative sample of a building – all in fractions of a module based on half a column's diameter at its base – are presented as containing the information needed to regenerate (or clone) a whole building.

RE(DE)FINING THE GENOME
standardised versions of classical orders

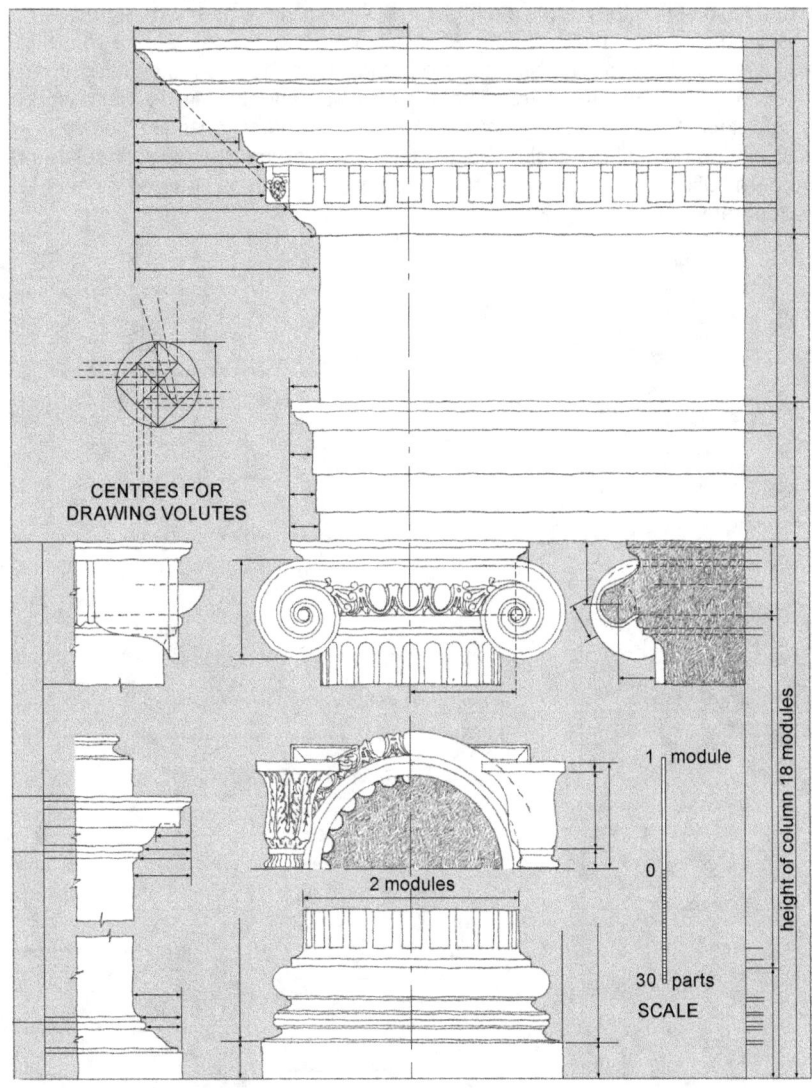

This is Vignola's Renaissance version of the Ionic Order (after Wooster Bard Field, 1922). For each Order, rules were proposed that would produce consistency in design.

Some architects have engineered their own 'genetic' codes. Above is a version of Ionic created by Giacomo Barozzi da Vignola in the sixteenth century. Such standardised versions meant that architects were provided with patterns that they could use in their own designs (without the stress of having to be inventive) in the belief that they described the genome of classical architectural beauty.

CLONING OR REGENERATING
from a fragment of architectural DNA

When I was a young architectural lecturer, we used to set students an exercise in which they were each given a photograph of a small fragment of a building. From this they were asked to generate the design of a whole building. It did not matter that they did not produce the original building from which the fragment was taken. The exercise was about realising that a work of architecture can have a genetic code informing all its parts at all scales. This was the case in Classical buildings. It can also be true of vernacular and modern buildings too. Consider how each of the illustrated fragments might be regenerated into a complete building.

It is interesting to consider too where the DNA of each of these examples, and of any integrated architecture, resides. There are the characteristics of the materials, the construction methodologies and traditions, the styles that are fashionable... But also there is the determination provided by the conscious designing mind of the architect. This is what, ultimately, undermines the genetic metaphor for architecture. It is not natural.

METAPHORS OF SENSE AND NONSENSE

Metaphors are a device by which we try to understand and explain things by implicitly drawing attention to corresponding characteristics between different entities, phenomena... But architecture can be a metaphor for sense itself. One of the ready examples available to me when lecturing was the lecture theatre itself, which, with its tiered seats facing a platform, makes physical and spatial sense of the relationship between lecturer and an audience of disparate students. Just as a book attempts to frame its argument and make sense of its subject, so too does architecture make sense of and frame a setting and an event. To have the members of the audience facing in random directions, or the lecturer behind a screen may not be nonsense, but it would certainly constitute deviation from sense.

MAKING SENSE
Sherlock Holmes, 'a loose thread'

'Can't stand it, never can! There's a loose thread in the world.'

We all feel uncomfortable when things do not make sense: when a politician dissembles; when assembly instructions do not achieve the expected result; when a sentence ***** a verb.

Sherlock Holmes (Benedict Cumberbatch), in *Sherlock*, 'The Six Thatchers' (Rachel Talalay, written by Mark Gatiss), BBC, January 2017.

And yet, at the same time, we all enjoy the challenge of making sense of things: solving a puzzle or predicting the outcome of a detective story.

Sense, however, is (as I suggested in the Introduction to this Notebook) not the same as truth. If a girl completes a complicated Lego model, she has made sense of the primeval chaos of small pieces received in the box. Even so, the model is not 'true' in the sense of having an exact relationship with reality.

In many aspects of life it seems we often confuse sense with truth. Politicians and internet bloggers play on this confusion to further their own agenda. Stories are unsatisfactory if they do not make sense and yet, even when they do, they remain fictions.

Authors are the architects of fictions. Composers are the architects of symphonies. Architects are the architects of works of architecture. They all, usually, deal in sense. But truth is a different matter.

The fragments of a circular disk (right) make sense from only one point of view.

Jack McCulla – 'Red Disk' (2015)

PHILOSOPHER AS ARCHITECT
René Descartes

'There is very often less perfection in works composed of several portions, and carried out by the hands of various masters, than those on which one individual alone has worked. Thus we see that buildings planned and carried out by one architect alone are usually more beautiful and better proportioned than those which many have tried to put in order and improve, making use of old walls which were built with other ends in view. In the same way also, those ancient cities which, originally mere villages, have become in the process of time great towns, are usually badly constructed in comparison with those which are regularly laid out on a plain by a surveyor who is free to follow his own ideas. Even though, considering their buildings each one apart, there is often as much or more display of skill in the one case than the other, the former have large buildings and small buildings indiscriminately placed together, thus rendering the streets crooked and irregular, so that it might be said that it was chance rather than the will of men guided by reason that led to such an arrangement.'

René Descartes, trans. Haldane and Ross – *Discourse on the Method* (1637), 1997.

In the twenty-first century, we might read Descartes' argument as supporting autocracy (in philosophy, creativity and perhaps also, by extension, politics). We live in post-Victorian times, when John Ruskin and William Morris (amongst others) argued in favour of the aesthetic value of 'old walls' and 'streets crooked and irregular', seeing them not as products of chance but as (a metaphor in architectural form) for a rich and complex society generated and governed by free and equal people living and working together rather than under the dominion of an autocrat – whether aristocratic or intellectual.

The layout of Richelieu (left; see also page 93) is a metaphor for the integrity of a individual designing mind (Lemercier's). The irregularity of a village is a metaphor for contributions by many individuals over time. Descartes felt one was better. Others disagree.

THE CARTESIAN WORLD
'Equivalents', Carl Andre

Descartes saw more sense in geometric regularity than in serendipitous irregularity. In 1637 he published a way of making sense of the world using a geometric grid on which any point could be identified using coordinates. It was a way of giving the world an abstract geometric architecture.

On a Cartesian grid every point is equivalent to every other. There is no variation in value; no differentiation of places. This gives it its value in identifying points on irregular terrain for military or scientific purposes.

In the 1960s the artist Carl Andre produced a number of works called Equivalents. Though composed of standard bricks arranged grid-wise (right, top), these illustrate something of the effect Descartes' way of making sense of the world can influence architecture. Some versions were pits of space in a sea of bricks (middle); others were islands of bricks in a sea of space (bottom).

You can see how this might translate into an architectural metaphor that imposes order irrespective of local conditions. The gridded American city may be interpreted as a product of the Cartesian view of the world and a metaphor for consistency and order.

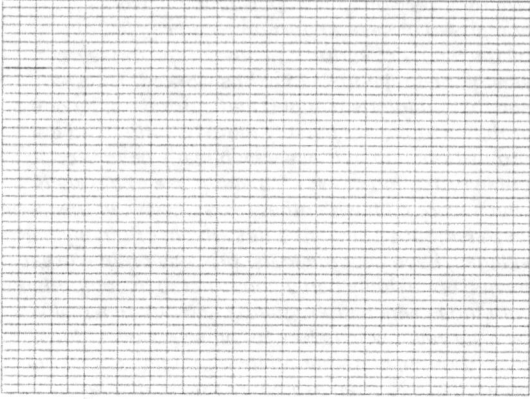

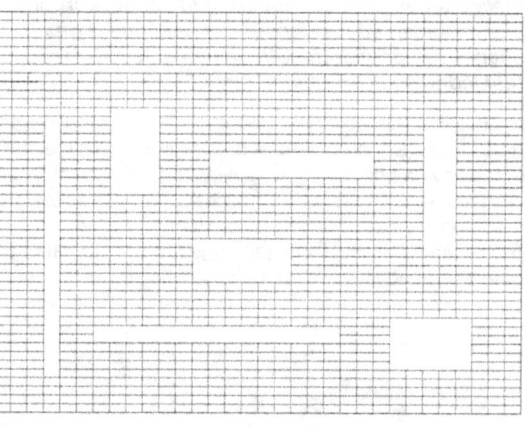

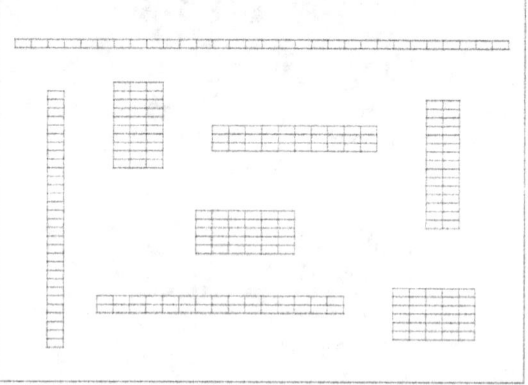

ANALYSING ARCHITECTURE NOTEBOOKS

MAKING AND GIVING SENSE
mapping, and function

Aspiring London taxi-drivers have to study 'The Knowledge'. It involves learning all the street names of the city labyrinth, and being able quickly to plot routes from any point in the city to another. Obviously it makes them better taxi drivers. But they also report psychological satisfaction in mastering 'The Knowledge'. There is achievement in passing the stringent tests involved. But there is also (and perhaps greater) satisfaction in feeling that the labyrinth has been solved, totally. Sense has been made of the daunting confusion of streets. The city (London) has been given an architecture; an architecture of sense in a taxi driver's mind. An architecture that underpins the service the taxi driver provides to the customer.

Generally (although, as we shall see, there have been exceptions) an important part of any architect's challenge is to make sense of the design brief (program) and to realise that sense in the form of a work of architecture. To do this we generate metaphors. In some cases, as is seen in the many examples included in this Notebook, we find a metaphor in linguistic, mathematical or other artistic source. Sometimes the metaphors we choose (see as being appropriate to the task in hand) are abstract (spatially, formally, geometrically...). In all cases there is a metaphorical relationship between the design proposition, realised in the architectural project, and the brief (program) set by the architect's client.

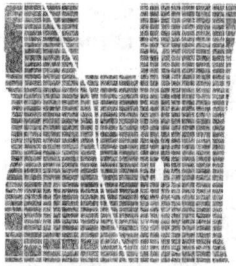

It is rather easier for New York taxi drivers to find their way around Manhattan because it has already been 'architected' into a Cartesian grid of numbered streets and avenues. The 'sense' is there; taxi drivers do not have to learn it (make it for themselves in their own memories).

Between 1922 and 1926 the German architect Hugo Häring designed a complex of farm buildings – Gut Garkau – near Lübeck. The plan of the cowshed is alongside. Rather than being a simple large rectangular shed, in which functions might be freely accommodated, Häring has carefully designed the form to match the function. The bull has his own pen at the focus of the arrangement – the Sultan presiding as a patriarch over his harem. All other functions have their specific places. The architecture makes sense of the processes housed in it. The whole plan becomes an architectural metaphor for the management of milk production and the breeding of cattle.

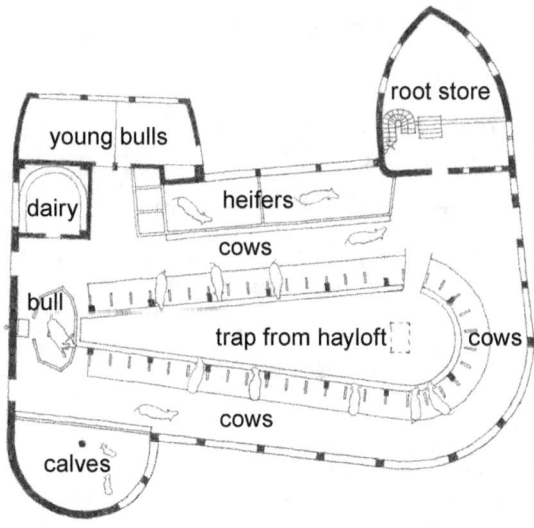

DOMESTIC AND SOCIAL SENSE
Robert Kerr – *The English Gentleman's House*

'Le plan est le générateur.'
'The plan is the generator.'

Le Corbusier – *Vers une architecture* (1923), trans. Etchells – *Towards an New Architecture*, 1927.

Architecture may be thought of as philosophy explored through the medium of space (rather than words). This makes architects philosophers of space, making sense of the arrangement of places to accommodate life. Just as verbal philosophy conditions our beliefs, attitudes to life and behaviour, so too does architecture, but in the generally tacit medium of space.

Robert Kerr's hypothetical plan for an English gentleman's house (below) is a physical expression of the hyper-organised hierarchies and functional arrangements of a wealthy family's household in Victorian England. It is an exemplar of the dictum 'a place for everything and everything in its place' (which might also be extended to 'a place for everyone and everyone in their place').

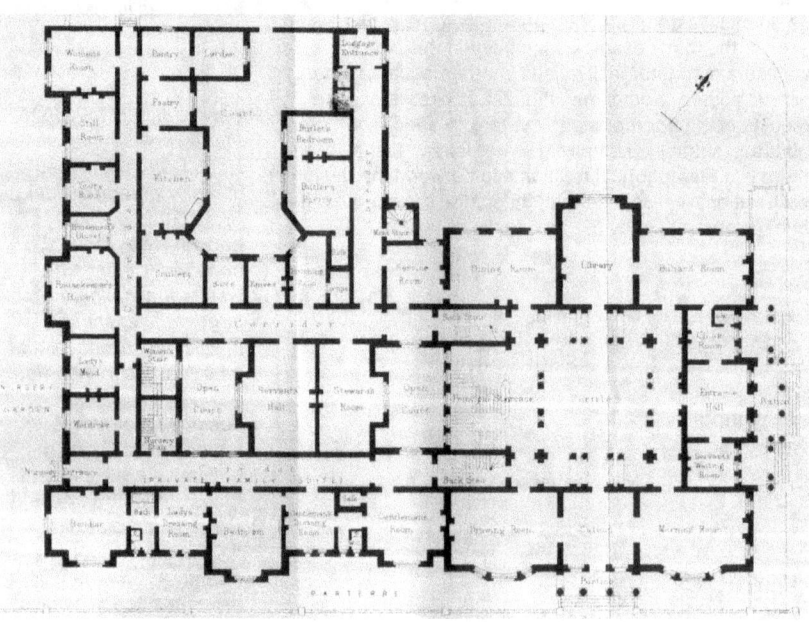

The organisational philosophy of an English gentleman's household is evident in the plan of his house. There is a clear division between the reception areas, the private family quarters, and the 'backstage' areas for the servants. The organisation is itemised down to maids, knives, boots, lamps… with each item having its own room.

A LITURGICAL BATTLE
Christopher Wren's battle for St Paul's

Philosophies of religious liturgy are expressed in architecture too. The celebrated seventeenth-century battle Christopher Wren had with the church authorities when designing the new St Paul's Cathedral in London illustrates some of the factors involved.

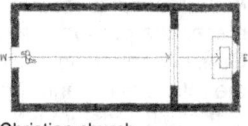
Christian church

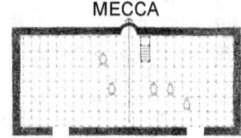
Islamic mosque

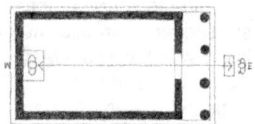
Greek temple

The plan of a place of worship makes sense of the relationship between worshippers and their religion. The architecture of different types of religious buildings places worshippers in subtly different relationships with their God, their priests, each other... the world (right).

The church authorities rejected Christopher Wren's early designs for St Paul's, including the Greek Cross plan (below), because they were not in accord with the Church of England's liturgy. They persuaded Wren to make the cathedral's plan longer and less centralised. The Greek Cross suggests a place that is spatially static; implying that the worshipper is of central importance and stands in confrontation with God. By contrast the longitudinal plan is spatially dynamic, implying, for the worshipper, the possibility of moving towards God, towards salvation. In such ways, the architecture (spatial organisation) of a religious building can be read as a metaphor in spatial organisation for a person's relationship with his or her God. In the case of St Paul's the client authorities disagreed on this matter with their architect.

Religious buildings of different kinds place us in different relationships with our Gods and each other.

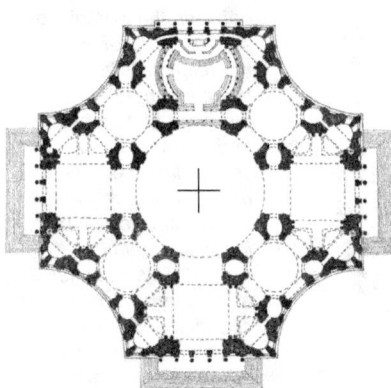

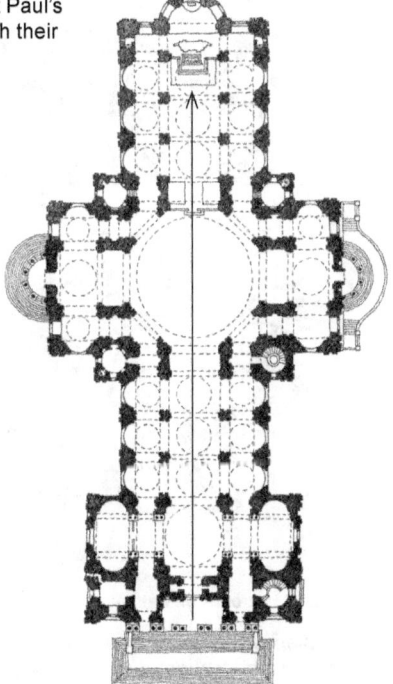

The plan of Wren's second (of five) design (above) compared with the plan of St Paul's as built (right). The key difference is that the above plan is centralised and therefore spatially static while the built cathedral has a long processional axis and is spatially dynamic. In contrast to the former, the latter implies aspiration towards salvation.

METAPHOR

SECOND VATICAN COUNCIL
Liverpool Metropolitan Cathedral, Frederick Gibberd

A church building is an instrumental frame that places the person in a particular relationship with God, heaven, fellow worshippers, religion, and the religious organisation of the church. Which of these is most important is not clear. But it is understandable that the church organisation, as client commissioning the church building, would want to influence those relationships.

Between 1962 and 1965 the Roman Catholic Church held the Second Vatican Council, known as Vatican II. It discussed many aspects of the church, seeking to modernise its relationship with its congregation. The guidance that emerged affected the design of subsequent Catholic churches. One of the largest of these was Liverpool Metropolitan Cathedral (which we have already seen as 'The Wigwam' on page 24). Vatican II asked that barriers between the congregation and the altar and performance of the sacrament be reduced or removed. Designing Liverpool Metropolitan Cathedral, Frederick Gibberd placed the altar at the centre of the building and of an amphitheatre of congregation.

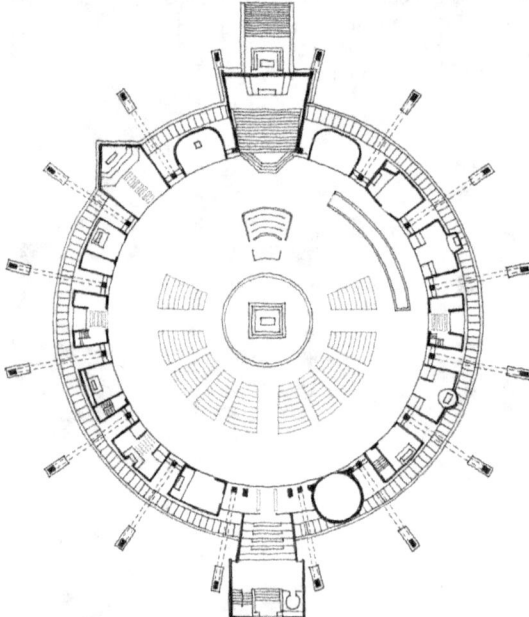

Liverpool Metropolitan Cathedral

This plan is a clear example of the power of centre and circle as a metaphor for a relationship between dominion and subjection, Father and children, God and flock.

The plan of Liverpool Metropolitan Cathedral (left) is centralised and radially symmetrical like Wren's Greek Cross plan (previous page, bottom left). But here the altar is placed at the centre, creating yet another different relationship between the worshipper and the focus of his or her religion. Whereas Wren attempted to place the human being at the centre, almost in confrontation with God, here God is firmly at the centre with worshippers forming an audience around. This arrangement, and its metaphorical connotations, contrasts too with the dynamic progression towards salvation implied in the realised plan of St Paul's (previous page, bottom right). So which is right? Who can claim certainty? Architecture can offer alternative metaphors expressed in spatial organisation.

THINGS FALL APART, THE CENTRE CANNOT HOLD
mere anarchy is loosed upon the world

If the exactness of the circle, the square and the cross are metaphors for certainty and perfection – sense of a sort – then what happens when you fracture them, break them apart? Do you produce metaphors for the more realist uncertainty of the world in which we live – i.e. non-sense.

Remember when your itinerary falls apart, you fail to reach the airport in time for your flight. The knock-on effect is chaos. The architecture of your journey is disrupted, ruined. Or when the recipe depicted with a photograph of perfection in the recipe book turns out a mess. Or, more seriously, when some enemy force insists on bombing your city into chaos.

We yearn for sense. But maybe the truth is that the world, the universe, is characterised by its complex chaos. Maybe it is the sense that architecture proposes, whether of journeys or of recipes or of buildings (places, cities, gardens, houses...), that is the illusion. Rejecting geometric regularity and the geometry of making, some architects have sought to express complexity and chaos metaphorically with complex fragmentary architectural forms.

The sense of being lost, without certain place, not knowing exactly where you are, can be engineered by the creation of a maze.

Chaos prevails when order is not imposed or maintained.

The space under a bridge can be a place for habitation; maybe a home for abject members of society. But it loses that capacity when it is filled with a jumble of rubbish.

Natural disasters turn ordered houses into a jumble of broken pieces.

METAPHOR

Crazy Houses, as fairground attractions, break order deliberately to challenge our assumptions that houses have straight walls, flat floors, and rectangular windows and doorways.

Crazy House, Butlin's Amusement Park, Felixstowe

Some architects have explored similar disruption of ordered geometry for sculptural effect.

Merz School Extension, Coop Himmelb(l)au (1981)

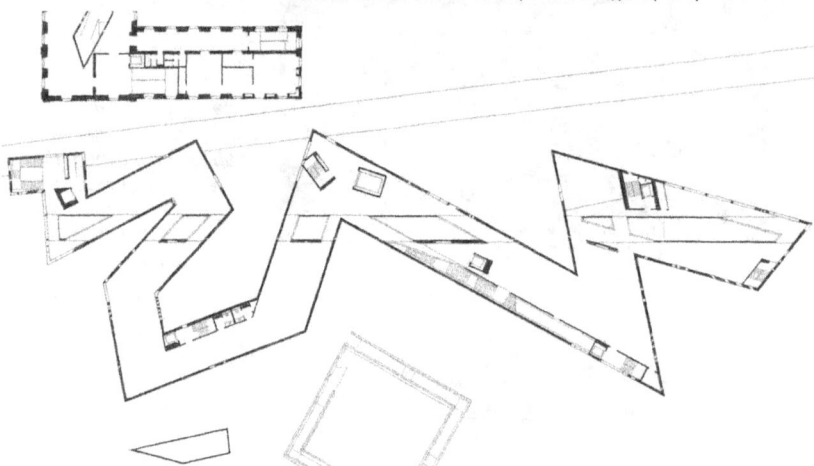

Jewish Museum, Berlin, Daniel Libeskind (2001)

Broken geometry can be an expression of profound trauma, as has been inflicted on the Jewish community through history.

Oscar Finch *(Patrick McGoohan) –* **'The little house you have built has no foundation.'**
Columbo *(Peter Falk) –* **'But it's made of glass. You are inside and can't get out.'**

Columbo, 'Agenda for Murder' (Patrick McGoohan, written by Richard Levinson, William Link and Jeffrey Bloom), 1990.

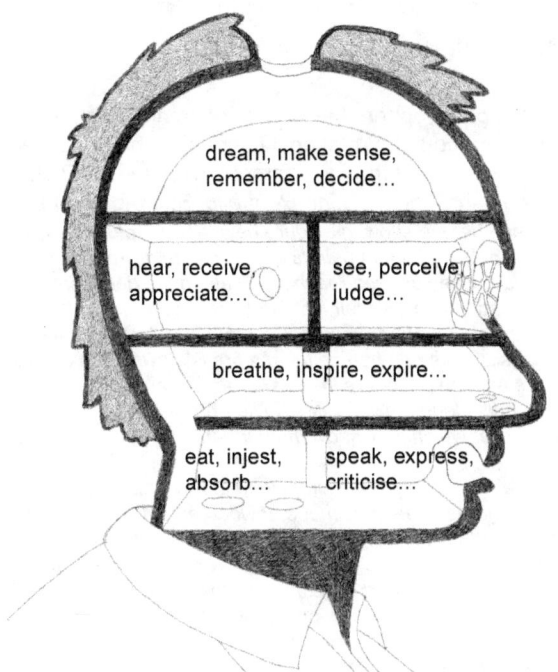

MIND METAPHORS

That the head has 'rooms' is implied by cartoon strips such as 'The Numskulls' (originally drawn by Malcolm Judge in D.C. Thomson comics *The Beano*, *The Dandy* and *The Beezer* in the 1960s and 70s, and here reinterpreted by me, complete with an oculus – an eye to the heavens – in the skull's dome). Judge's cranial architecture was intended as light humour, but serious philosophers (Plato and Descartes are just two of many examples) as well as twentieth-century psychologists (such as Jung and Freud) have also resorted to architectural metaphor to describe the structure of human thought and the psyche. Such metaphors inspire an intriguing realm of the imagination, where architecture, philosophy, psychology – literature too – find themselves mutually dependent and influential. Architecture is considered by some to be an intellectual poor relation to philosophy, psychology and literature; but the frequency with which exponents of those three noble disciplines use architecture as a source of metaphor suggests they owe that 'poor' relation a significant debt!

ARCHITECTURE OF PERCEPTION
Plato's metaphor of the cave

Since ancient times philosophers have resorted to architecture for metaphors to help them theorise about the relationship between human consciousness and the world around. One of the most famous examples is Plato's metaphor of the cave. It occurs in Book 7 of *The Republic*. Socrates addresses Glaucon:

' "And now", I said, "let me show in a figure how far our nature is enlightened or unenlightened: – Behold! human beings living in a underground den, which has a mouth open towards the light and reaching all along the den; here they have been from their childhood, and have their legs and necks chained so that they cannot move, and can only see before them, being prevented by the chains from turning round their heads. Above and behind them a fire is blazing at a distance, and between the fire and the prisoners there is a raised way; and you will see, if you look, a low wall built along the way, like the screen which marionette players have in front of them, over which they show the puppets."
' "I see."
' "And do you see", I said, "men passing along the wall carrying all sorts of vessels, and statues and figures of animals made of wood and stone and various materials, which appear over the wall? Some of them are talking, others silent."
' "You have shown me a strange image, and they are strange prisoners."
' "Like ourselves", I replied; "and they see only their own shadows, or the shadows of one another, which the fire throws on the opposite wall of the cave?"
' "True", he said; "how could they see anything but the shadows if they were never allowed to move their heads?"
' "And of the objects which are being carried in like manner they would only see the shadows?"
' "Yes", he said.
' "And if they were able to converse with one another, would they not suppose that they were naming what was actually before them?"
' "Very true."
' "And suppose further that the prison had an echo which came from the other side, would they not be sure to fancy when one of the passers-by spoke that the voice which they heard came from the passing shadow?"
' "No question", he replied.
' "To them", I said, "the truth would be literally nothing but the shadows of the images."
' "That is certain."
' "And now look again, and see what will naturally follow if the prisoners are released and disabused of their error. At first, when any of them is liberated and compelled suddenly to stand up and turn his neck round and walk and look towards the light, he will suffer sharp pains; the glare will distress him, and he will be unable to see the realities of which in his former state he had seen the shadows; and then conceive some one saying to him, that what he saw before was an illusion, but that now, when he is approaching nearer to being and his eye is turned towards more real existence, he has a clearer vision, – what will be his reply? And you may further imagine that his instructor is pointing to the objects as they pass and requiring him to name them, – will he not be perplexed? Will he not fancy that the shadows which he formerly saw are truer than the objects which are now shown to him?"
' "Far truer."
' "And if he is compelled to look straight at the light, will he not have a pain in his eyes which will make him turn away to take and take in the objects of vision which he can see, and which he will conceive to be in reality clearer than the things which are now being shown to him?"

' *"True", he said.*
' *"And suppose once more, that he is reluctantly dragged up a steep and rugged ascent, and held fast until he's forced into the presence of the sun himself, is he not likely to be pained and irritated? When he approaches the light his eyes will be dazzled, and he will not be able to see anything at all of what are now called realities."* '

Plato, trans. Jowett (1888) – *The Republic*, VII (514a–520a), c.370 BCE.

I have illustrated Plato's (Socrates') metaphor on the right, using a cat as the object. Its shadow is cast on the wall of a cave, where it is seen by the 'chained captive'. The metaphor may be transferred directly into a model of the human head, with 'shadows' of objects outside 'cast', through the eyes, onto the inner surfaces of the brain.

Plato's (Socrates') argument was that it is the role of philosophy (education) to free minds, to help them break the chains, emerge into the light and to see the world as it really is rather than accept the mere shadows projected on the walls of their prison-cave.

The metaphor is, however, ironic in that through it Plato is presenting us with his architecture of the relationship between our consciousness and the world (expressed in the architectural form of a cave). It is the philosopher who holds up the constructed cat to cast a shadow on the cave wall.

All architecture is, metaphorically, a shadow cast on a cave wall. Architecture is a version of the truth – a version of sense – proposed by the architect and realised in the physical form of buildings and the identification of places for inhabitation.

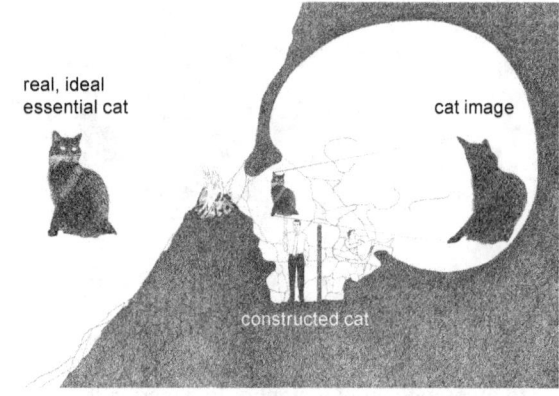

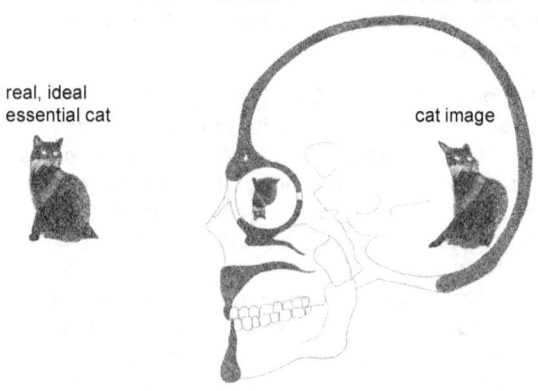

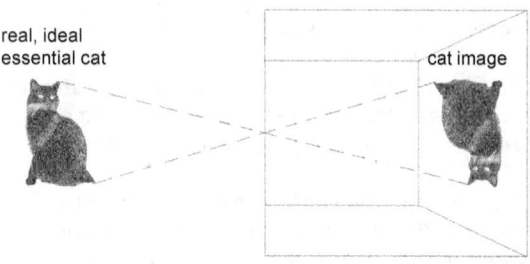

A camera obscura is similar to Plato's cave, except that the cat is transformed into an image by natural phenomenon – the effect of light passing through a small hole – rather than by mental construction.

EMPTY ROOM
Chuang-Tzu

Almost a contemporary of Plato, the Chinese philosopher Chuang-Tzu (aka Zhuang Zhou) also used an architectural metaphor to describe the relationship a mind should have with the world outside.

Chuang-Tzu suggested that, if it was to achieve peace, a mind should be passive, like an empty room.

' **"Look at that window. Through it an empty room becomes bright with scenery; but the landscape stops outside. Were this not so, we should have an exemplification of sitting still and running away at the same time.** *[An empty room would contain something, – a paradox like that in the text.]*
' **"In this sense, you may use your ears and eyes to communicate within, but shut out all wisdom from the mind.** *[Let the channels of your senses be to your mind what a window is to an empty room.]*
' **"And there where the supernatural…** *[Something which is and yet is not, like the landscape seen in, and yet not in, a room.]*
' **"… can find shelter, shall not man find shelter too? This is the method for regenerating all creation."** *[By passive, not by active, virtue.]*'

Chuang-Tzu, trans. Giles – *Chuang-Tzu: Taoist Philosopher and Chinese Mystic* (4thC BCE), 1889, 1926 (with Giles's interjections).

' **"Be empty, that is all. The Perfect Man uses his mind like a mirror – going after nothing, welcoming nothing, responding but not storing. Therefore he can win out over things and not hurt himself."** '

Chuang-Tzu, trans. Watson.

And so, it is suggested, peace and perfection will be found not by interrogation but by acceptance.

ROOM OF UNDERSTANDING
John Locke

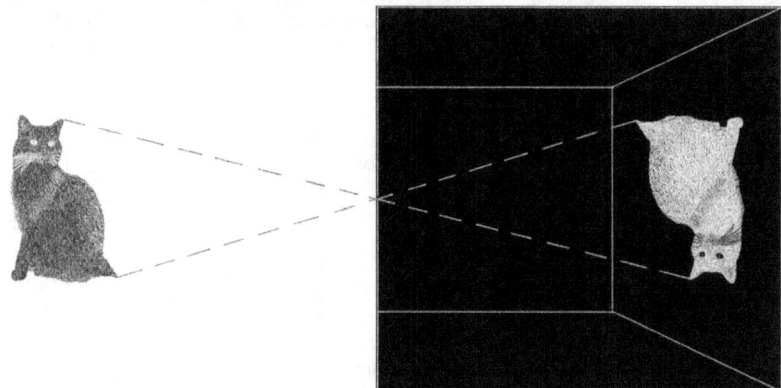

The seventeenth-century English philosopher used the architectural metaphor in a different way from either Plato or Chuang-Tzu. For him the mind was a storeroom of knowledge and understanding.

Understanding a cat by allowing its image to lodge in the dark storeroom of the mind.

'I don't claim to teach, only to enquire. So let me say it again: external and internal sensation [= "sensation and reflection"] are the only routes I can find for knowledge to enter the understanding. These alone, as far as I can discover, are the windows through which light is let into this dark room. The understanding strikes me as being like a closet that is wholly sealed against light, with only some little openings left to let in external visible resemblances or ideas of things outside. If the pictures coming into such a dark room stayed there, and lay in order so that they could be found again when needed, it would very much resemble the understanding of a man, as far as objects of sight and the ideas of them are concerned.'

John Locke – *Essay Concerning Human Understanding*, II xi 17, 1689.

The brain is described by Locke as being a library. Its windows, doorways and any other openings through which 'visible resemblances or ideas' might enter are the eyes and ears. In this metaphor, Locke did not include discussion of the mechanisms by which resemblances and ideas might be analysed, interpreted, classified, indexed (or forgotten) ... during the processes by which the librarians or curators of the mind may manage its collection.

ARCHITECTURE OF MEMORY
Frances Yates – *The Art of Memory*

In *The Art of Memory*, Frances Yates explored memory techniques that originated with orators in ancient Greece and Rome. Many use imagined architectural settings, and imply a metaphorical relationship between the structure of memory and the spatial organisation of buildings.

'In order to form a series of places in memory, (Quintilian) says, a building is to be remembered, as spacious and varied a one as possible, the forecourt, the living room, bedrooms, and parlours, not omitting statues and other ornaments with which the rooms are decorated. The images by which the speech is to be remembered… are then placed in imagination on the places which have been memorized in the building. This done, as soon as the memory of the facts requires to be revived, all these places are visited in turn and the various deposits demanded of their custodians. We have to think of the ancient orator as moving in imagination through his memory building whilst *he is making his speech, drawing from the memorized places the images he has placed on them.*'

Frances Yates – *The Art of Memory*, 1966.

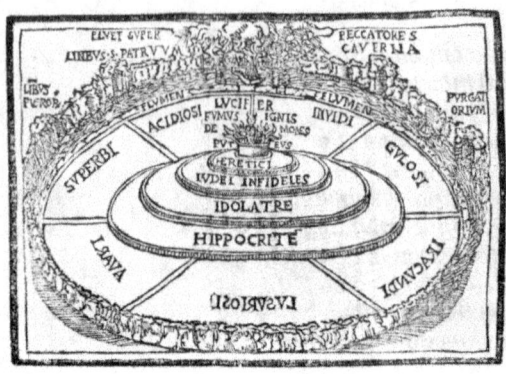
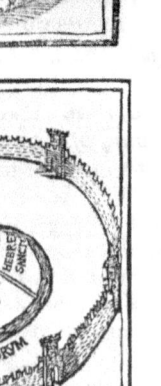

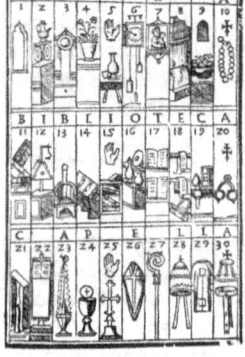

In Medieval times imagined architectural models were used too. Here (left) Hell and Heaven, and (right) an imagined abbey were proposed as frames for memory.

HOUSE AS PSYCHE
Jung and Freud

Many thinkers – in science, philosophy, literature and the arts – have used architecture to provide metaphors to illustrate their ideas. Though such might help their audiences understand what they were trying to say, rarely if ever have those thinkers explained why they find architecture such a useful metaphorical device. Carl Gustav Jung and Sigmund Freud both theorised about the structure of the psyche. Both resorted to architecture to help them explain their theories. Using architectural metaphors they modelled the structure of the psyche, allowing their readers to assimilate psychological theory by relation to common spatial experience.

Throughout his career Jung repeatedly referred to a dream he remembered from 1909:

> 'This was the dream. I was in a house I did not know, which had two storeys. It was "my house". I found myself in the upper storey, where there was a kind of salon furnished with fine old pieces in rococo style. On the walls hung a number of precious old paintings. I wondered that this should be my house, and thought, "Not bad". But then it occurred to me that I did not know what the lower floor looked like. Descending the stairs, I reached the ground floor. There everything was much older, and I realised that this part of the house must date from about the fifteenth or sixteenth century. The furnishings were medieval; the floors were of red brick. Everywhere it was rather dark. I went from one room to another, thinking, "Now I really must explore the whole house". I came upon a heavy door, and opened it. Beyond it I discovered a stone stairway that led down into a cellar. Descending again, I found myself in a beautifully vaulted room which looked exceedingly ancient. Examining the walls, I discovered layers of brick in the mortar. As soon as I saw this I knew that the walls dated from Roman times. My interest by now was intense. I looked more closely at the floor. It was of stone slabs, and in one of these I discovered a ring. When I pulled it, the stone slab lifted, and again I saw a stairway of narrow stone steps leading down into the depths. These too, I descended, and entered a low cave cut into the rock. Thick dust lay on the floor, and in the dust were scattered bones and broken pottery, like remains of a primitive culture. I discovered two human skulls, obviously very old and half disintegrated. Then I awoke.'

C.G. Jung, trans. Winston and Winston – *Memories, Dreams, Reflections* (1963), 1977.

Jung analysed his own dream:

> 'It was plain to me that the house represented a kind of image of the psyche – that is to say, of my state of consciousness, with hitherto unconscious additions. Consciousness was represented by the salon. It had an inhabited atmosphere, in spite of its antiquated style. The ground floor stood for the first level of the unconscious. The deeper I went, the more alien and the darker the scene became. In the cave, I discovered remains of a primitive culture, that is, the world of primitive man within myself – a world which can scarcely be reached or illuminated by consciousness. The primitive psyche of man borders on the life of the animal soul, just as the caves of prehistoric times were usually inhabited by animals before men laid claim to them.'

Jung reciprocated this metaphorical relationship between psychology and architecture by being effectively the architect of two houses. One of these was the refuge he built for himself, in stages, on the banks of Lake Zurich – the Bollingen Tower (right). The form of this house he felt had in some way been generated directly – 'built in a kind of dream' (an implicit reference to the 1909 dream) – from his inner self, as 'a symbol of psychic wholeness'.

> 'From the beginning I felt the Tower was in some way a place of maturation – a maternal womb or a maternal figure in which I could become what I was, what I am and will be. It gave me a feeling as if I were being reborn in stone. It is thus a concretisation of the individuation process, a memorial *aere perennius*. During the building work, of course, I never considered these matters. I built the house in sections, always following the concrete needs of the moment. It might also be said that I built it in a kind of dream. Only afterwards did I see how all the parts fitted together and that a meaningful form had resulted: a symbol of psychic wholeness.'

In this analysis of his own behaviour in building his house, Jung inferred that architecture – which we might think of as the epitome of the conscious mind exerting its will on the physical world – could alternatively be considered an externalisation of the subconscious. That despite ourselves, our inner feelings, beliefs, neuroses... might all find expression in the form of our architecture; even to the extent that architecture – the creation of refuges and burial chambers – may well have originated in an agoraphobic tendency deep-seated in the human psyche since birth.

The Bollingen Tower house stands on the banks of Lake Zurich. Jung designed and built this house for himself as a refuge from the world. He claimed its design was influenced strongly by his dream of 1909. This means the house is (intended as or subconsciously) a metaphor for Jung's own psyche. Its relationship with its inhabitant is more profound than merely providing shelter and physical comfort. Although Jung's primary interest was in psychology, his dream and the Bollingen Tower house also say something about the power of architecture. Metaphor is not only an implicit comparison, it is also (to use another architectural metaphor) a bridge – between our inner and outer worlds – which not only mediates but explains and stimulates too. The house's role as metaphor invests it with additional power.

'At Bollingen I am in the midst of my true life, I am most deeply myself. Here I am, as it were, the "age-old son of the mother"... At times I feel as I am spread out over the landscape and inside things... Here everything has its history, and mine; here is space for the spaceless kingdom of the world's and the psyche's hinterland.'

C.G. Jung, trans. Winston and Winston – *Memories, Dreams, Reflections* (1963), 1977.

See also: Gaston Bachelard, trans. Jolas – *The Poetics of Space*, 1964.

Freud too used architecture to provide metaphors for his model of the psyche. Here he uses the spatial layout of a (rather grand) house to explain the mental mechanism of repression.

> 'Let us therefore compare the system of the unconscious to a large entrance hall, in which mental impulses jostle one another like separate individuals. Adjoining this entrance hall there is a second, narrower room – a kind of drawing room – in which consciousness, too, resides. But on the threshold between these two rooms a watchman performs his function. He examines the different mental impulses, acts as a censor, and will not admit them into the drawing room if they displease him.'

Sigmund Freud – nineteenth lecture of *Introductory Lectures on Psycho-Analysis* (1916–17), quoted in Cosimo Schinaia, trans. Lo Dico – *Psychoanalysis and Architecture: the Inside and the Outside*, 2016.

A scene from the film The King's Speech *(Tom Hooper, 2010; right) illustrates Freud's architectural account of repression. Lionel Logue (Geoffrey Rush), after falling out with Prince Albert, Duke of York (who will become George VI, played by Colin Firth), has come to apologise. But the future king does not want to see Logue who, as his therapist, is challenging him to overcome a speech impediment. He instructs his equerry (the 'watchman/censor', played by the appropriately named Robert Portal) to send Logue away. The scene is mediated and framed by the architecture of the entrance hall. We foreground the interaction between the people involved but the architecture provides the frame for the interaction and hence gets used, by people like Freud, as an explanatory metaphor.*

So what does the fact that theorists in many other disciplines use architecture as a metaphor to describe or illustrate the workings of their own subject say about architecture? Even if we accept the validity of the architectural/spatial metaphor as a way of explaining the structure of the psyche (which is questionable at the least) what sort of different (morally as well as analytically) idea about that structure would we have if the journey in Jung's dream (for example) was inverted, i.e. not a descent into the realm beneath but an ascent into a realm above, or, alternatively, one of travelling further and further into the distance? The same differences – moral and ideological differences – apply in the products of architecture itself. Indeed there they are probably the origin of the metaphorical connotations. A descent into hidden darkness of a cellar is emotionally different from an ascent into exposed light at the top of a tower, or from a journey across a featureless expanse of desert towards the horizon.

'Freud sees the unconscious as a narrative stage on which these archetypal constructs, the superego and the ego, work out, not to mention the Oedipal Complex.'

J.G. Ballard, interviewed by Phil Halper and Lard Lyer – 'The Visitor', in *The Hardcore 8*, 1992, published in J.G. Ballard, eds. Sellars and O'Hara – *Extreme Metaphors*, 2012.

MIND AND UNIVERSE
Newton Mausoleum, Étienne-Louis Boullée

The preceding pages have illustrated examples of philosophers and psychologists resorting to architecture for metaphors to explain/describe their theory of the relationship that does or should pertain between the mind and the world. Each uses the room or cave as a metaphor for the mind contained in the chamber of its cranium but with various windows on the world around. Architects can reciprocate the compliment (that philosophers unwittingly pay architecture) by producing actual rooms that philosophise non-verbally about the possible relationships between the person/mind and the world/universe.

When the neoclassical French architect Étienne-Louis Boullée designed a memorial in honour of Isaac Newton (in 1784) he did so in the form of huge spherical mausoleum on the inner surfaces of which would have twinkled the stars of heaven, conjured by perforations in the dome (below).

The metaphor Boullée intended is clear. The enormous spherical space contained by the dome is Newton's mind contained in its cranium. And it is big enough to accommodate, assimilate and understand the vastness and complexity of the universe. The shadow of the universe is projected on the walls of the cave of Newton's intellect. (Plato's abiding metaphor can be applied in multifarious ways.)

Boullée's proposed spherical memorial to Isaac Newton is a metaphor for the scientist's capacious brain, big enough to contain the universe, and explain the laws that govern its workings.

BURROWING FOR MEANING
Williamson's Tunnels

'My instinct tells me that my head is an organ for burrowing, as some creatures use their snout and forepaws, and with it I would mine and burrow my way through these hills.'

Henry David Thoreau – *Walden* (1854), 1962.

There are some strange tunnels hidden under Liverpool. They were excavated for Joseph Williamson (below) in the early nineteenth century; but no-one knows why. Maybe he was driven by philanthropy, to provide gainful work for the unemployed. Not knowing Williamson's reason makes it hard not to interpret the labyrinth of tunnels as a metaphor for a mind searching for meaning, for a purpose, in the mysterious subterranean darkness of the unknowable.

The tunnels also spark our imaginations. How might they be used?

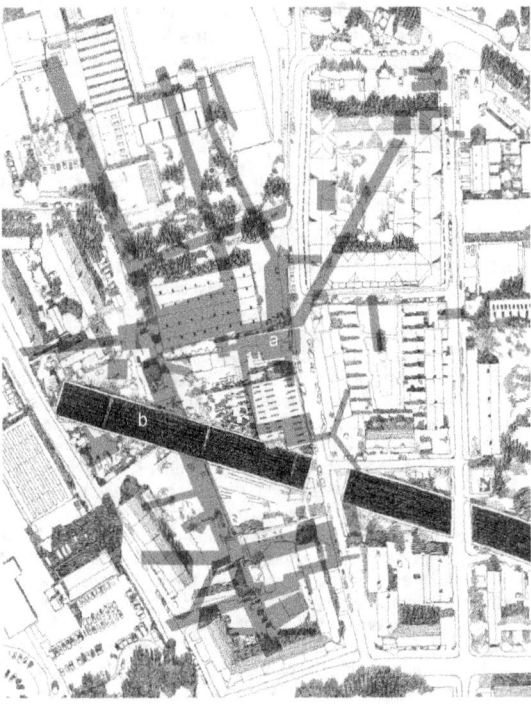

The Edge Hill area of Liverpool with Williamson's tunnels shaded. (The darker stripe, b, is the cutting for the later railway entering its own tunnel on its approach to Lime Street station.) Williamson's house stood near the epicentre of the tunnel complex, at a.

The tunnels would suit purposes that hide from the light of day: covert religious practice; interment of the dead; refuge from nuclear attack; sewage and waste disposal... or perhaps dancing to rock music. There is no indication Williamson had any of these in mind.

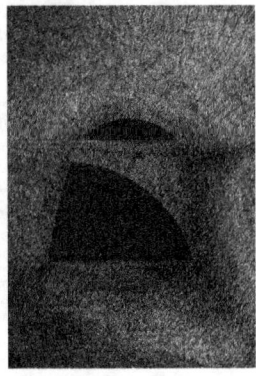

METAPHOR

PATINA
fabric infused with life

'We have long forgotten the ritual by which the house of our life was erected. But when it is under assault and enemy bombs are already taking their toll, what enervated, perverse antiquities do they not lay bare in the foundations. What things were interred and sacrificed amid magic incantations, what horrible cabinet of curiosities lies there below, where the deepest shafts are reserved for what is most commonplace.'

Walter Benjamin, trans. Jephcott and Shorter – 'One-Way Street' (1925–6), in *One-Way Street and Other Writings*, 1985.

Walter Benjamin uses an architectural metaphor for the scars life makes on our psyches. Buildings themselves record the wear and tear of life with their own scars. In the quotation below, Rainer Maria Rilke describes the exposed inside wall of a demolished house, complete with torn wallpaper, stains, broken toilet pipes, smells... The wall has absorbed, and become a metaphor for, the lost life of the house.

'Will anyone believe there are such houses? No, they will say I am misrepresenting. This time it is the truth, nothing omitted, and naturally nothing added. Where should I get it from? Everyone knows I am poor. Everyone knows it. Houses? But, to be precise, they were houses that were no longer there. Houses that had been pulled down from top to bottom. What was there were the other houses, those that had been standing next to them, tall neighbouring houses. Apparently these were in danger of falling down, since everything alongside had been taken away; for a whole scaffolding of long, tarred timbers had been rammed slantwise between the rubbish-strewn ground and the bared wall. I don't know whether I have already said that it is this wall I mean. But it was, so to speak, not the first wall of the existing houses (as one would have supposed), but the last of those that had been there. One saw its inner side. One saw at the different storeys the walls of rooms to which the paper still clung, and here and there the join of floor or ceiling. Beside these room-walls there still remained, along the whole length of the wall, a dirty-white area, and through this crept in unspeakably disgusting motions, worm-soft and as if digesting, the open, rust-spotted channel of the water-closet pipe. Grey, dusty traces of the paths the lighting-gas had taken remained at the ceiling edges, and here and there, quite unexpectedly, they bent sharp around and came running into the colored wall and into a hole that had been torn out black and ruthless. But most unforgettable of all were the walls themselves. The stubborn life of these rooms had not let itself be trampled out. It was still there; it clung to the nails that had been left, it stood on the remaining handsbreadth of flooring, it crouched under the corner joints where there was still a little bit of interior. One could see that it was in the paint, which, year by year, it had slowly altered: blue into moldy green, green into grey, and yellow into an old, stale rotting white. But it was also in the spots that had kept fresher, behind mirrors, pictures, and wardrobes; for it had drawn and redrawn their contours, and had been with spiders and dust even in these hidden places that now lay bared. It was in every flayed strip, it was in the damp blisters at the lower edges of the wallpapers; it wavered in the torn-off shreds, and sweated out of the foul patches that had come into being long ago. And from these walls once blue and green and yellow, which were framed by the fracture-tracks of the demolished partitions, the breadth of these lives stood out – the clammy, sluggish, musty breath, which no wind had yet scattered. There stood the middays and the sicknesses and the exhaled breath and the smoke of years, and the sweat that breaks out under the armpits and makes clothes heavy, and the stale breath of mouths, and the fusel odor of sweltering feet. There stood the tang of urine and the burn of soot and the grey reek of potatoes, and the heavy, smooth stench of ageing grease. The sweet, lingering smell of neglected infants was there, and the fear-smell of children who go to school, and the sultriness out of the bed of nubile youths. To these was added much that had come from below, from the abyss of the street, which reeked, and more that had oozed down from above with the rain, which over cities is not clean. And much the feeble, tamed domestic winds, that always stay in the same street, had brought along; and much more was there, the source of which one did not know. I said, did I not, that all the walls had been demolished except the last–? It is of this wall that I have been speaking all along. One would think I had stood a long time before it; but I'm willing to swear that I began to run as soon as I had recognized that wall. For that is the terrible thing, that I did not recognize it. I recognize everything here, and that is why it goes right into me: it is at home in me.'

Rainer Maria Rilke, trans. Herter Norton – *The Notebooks of Malte Laurids Brigge* (1910), 1992.

PSYCHO-ARCHITECTURE
movies

Plato's metaphor of the cave has remained a potent trope through more than two thousand years. It describes the situation when we go to the cinema, where we do not see the truth of the world but only the shadows others decide to project on the wall in front of our chained heads. The same applies to television and to the internet; the screen is our contemporary cave wall.

The metaphor of the cave is a device used by screenplay writers and movie directors too.

There is a scene in the movie *Paris, Texas* (Wim Wenders, 1984) in which Travis Henderson (Harry Dean Stanton) talks to Jane Henderson (Natassja Kinski) through the glass screen of a peep-show parlour booth (similar to a prison visiting booth). The faces of each and the other are filmed superimposed; each seeing themselves and the other as reflections (shadows) projected on the glass (cave wall) that divides them from each other.

The architecture of the scene does not merely accommodate the action. It contributes significantly to the psychological situation in which each of the characters finds themselves alone; separated, emotionally and physically, from the other. As in Plato's metaphor of the cave, the architectural situation is a metaphor for the psychological.

Modus *(Lisa Siwe and Mani Maserrat, 2015)* is a Swedish crime drama made for television (TV4) and based on a storyline by novelist Anne Holt. At one point the murderer, Richard Forrester (Marek Oravec), is in his caravan deep in a snowy forest (right). It is as if the caravan is a metaphor for his own skull. Inside, like one of the captives in Plato's cave, Forrester is kneeling, whilst images – presumably significant episodes from his past – flicker on the walls. These are the shadows that trouble his mind.

EVIDENT AND HIDDEN
my 'hotel' dreams

In *The Bible* Jacob had a dream that was architecturally metaphorical*. Maybe we all have dreams that involve architecture. Those dreams are, almost by definition, metaphorical. But often the metaphors are elusive. Dream analysis and therapy is about finding the right metaphorical interpretations of our dreams, or at least ones that seem to make sense.

One of my own recurrent dreams (only occasionally does it border on nightmare) is set in a hotel. The setting varies: sometimes it is a modern hotel with long carpeted corridors and a bewildering lift (elevator) system; sometimes it is the irregular, old world labyrinth of a country-house hotel; and sometimes the latter version has extensive gardens, maybe with guest cottages scattered amongst orchards and kitchen gardens. In these dreams I am rarely scared, but usually I am engaged in a search, trying to find my way to something; I never know exactly what. I do not ever feel that I am in the hotel alone; but neither do I remember seeing, or relating in meaningful ways to other guests or staff. No doubt a Freudian psychotherapist reading this will already have made a tentative diagnosis, but I have my own analysis.

* Jacob dreamt of a ladder stretching up to heaven (see page 87). The ladder, physically impossible though it is, is clearly a metaphor for a traversable link between earth and heaven.

      My analysis of these dreams is that they draw on the hotel – the generic rather than any specific hotel – as a metaphor for the common situation in which we all find ourselves. We are all aware of what we see around us – the evident – but we are also aware of the agency of forces, influences and provision that is concealed from us – the hidden. Hotels are prime architectural/metaphorical settings for the juxtaposition of evident and hidden. As guests we inhabit the evident – lobbies, lounges, bars, dining rooms.... But, behind the scenes, is the realm of the hidden operatives: the administration offices; the kitchens; concierges' rooms; cleaners' stores; porters' luggage stores and so on. Of course there are waiters, receptionists, cleaners, porters – sprites, Ariels, fairies... – that flit between the two realms making things happen and providing various services. But we guests do not, as a matter of course, penetrate into the hidden; we just know, if we bother to think about it, that it is there.

Cf. the quotation from Orwell on page 51.

      My psychotherapist (if I had one) might interpret my recurrent dream as a metaphor for a spiritual divide between the tangible world around and that of the gods that determine, influence and provide for our lives. But I do not think my dream is spiritual. I think it derives more from an awareness of the juxtaposition of the evident and the hidden even in the everyday, the mundane. That may be why I have spent so much time trying to access the hidden strategies architects use when designing buildings. It is appropriate that the dream my psyche uses to provide a metaphorical setting for this search is itself an architectural one – the often labyrinthine hotel.

LANDSCAPE METAPHORS

Frank Lloyd Wright conceived Fallingwater (1936) as formalised rock strata echoing the rock formations already on the site. Prehistorically, architecture cannot have originated anywhere other than in the landscape. Our first architecture (whether in prehistory or as children) was a matter of occupying places we recognised amongst the rocks and trees as appropriate to our needs and desires. Some architects have sought to mirror these origins by conceiving their works of architecture as built landscapes. Theatres might be designed to return performance to the slopes of hills overlooking a flat patch of ground. Houses might be conceived as rock terraces, caves or trees, or a camp on a beach. Thus the direction of conceptual flow between landscape (nature as found) and architecture (the contribution and interventions of the mind) is, if not reversed, made more complex.

HOUSE AS LANDSCAPE
Mohrmann House, Hans Scharoun

Hitler's Germany in the 1930s disapproved of Modernism, ordering that architecture be classical or vernacular. The Modernist Hans Scharoun, to avoid the authorities' attention, designed a number of family houses which outwardly appeared to be traditional but internally experimented with different ways of organising space.

As described in *Analysing Architecture* (fourth edition, 2014, pages 152–4) the geometry of making, with rectangular bricks and straight timbers, tends to produce rectangular spaces and buildings. In the Mohrmann House (1939, right) Scharoun wanted to resist this traditional tendency. The sides of the house visible from the road are arranged more or less rectangularly whereas the other sides have a more complex geometry – one that distorts the geometry of making to produce a freer arrangement of non-orthogonal spaces. It was as if Scharoun wanted to emulate the sort of non-orthogonal composition of places we might make settling a camp in the landscape. This desire might be traced back to nineteenth century concern about the dehumanising effect of industrialisation and a consequent wish to return to nature.

The non-rectangular interior of the Mohrmann House is conceived as a relaxed composition of places for living arranged as they might be in the landscape, below a cliff, amongst rocks and around a tree. There are places for all the principal activities of daily life: for sitting by the fire with friends and family, for cooking, for eating, for working, for playing the piano, for speaking on the telephone. Scharoun wanted these to relate to each other in 'natural ways' rather than being restricted by the tendency to the rectangular (orthogonal) of the geometry of making. In the lower drawing above you can see my interpretation of Scharoun's ground floor plan as a camp in a rocky landscape.

See also: Simon Unwin – *Twenty-Five Buildings Every Architect Should Understand*, 2015, pp. 243–54.

PERFORMANCE PLACE AS LANDSCAPE
Philharmonie, Hans Scharoun

After the end of the Second World War, Scharoun was freed from the Nazi diktat that architecture should be traditional (vernacular or classical) in style (see opposite). He remained interested in conceiving architecture as formalised landscape.

In the 1960s Scharoun designed the Philharmonie in Berlin (above) – the city's major concert hall – as a composition of terraces arranged as the slopes of a valley focussing on the performance area below. The hall's ceiling is conceived as a sky with lights as stars and acoustic reflectors as clouds. The organ pipes and light cables invoke the idea of rain falling from the sky.

Scharoun's design for the Philharmonie evokes the origins of performance (for example in ancient Greece) in natural landscape settings chosen because they had slopes and rocks looking down on a relatively flat area.

See also: Simon Unwin – *The Ten Most Influential Buildings in History: Architecture's Archetypes*, 2017, pp. 128–59.

LANDSCAPE SIMILES
Snøhetta, MVRDV, Gins

Various architects have alluded to landscape in their designs. In some cases the aim has been to evoke a country or region's landscape in built form, as in the Snøhetta and MVRDV designs below. Sometimes it has been a way of inducing effort in a building's inhabitants, so they might live forever.

Snøhetta's design for the Norwegian National Opera House in Oslo (2008, above), appropriately for a country that stretches deep into the Arctic, appears to float in the city's harbour as a gleaming white iceberg or fractured ice floe.

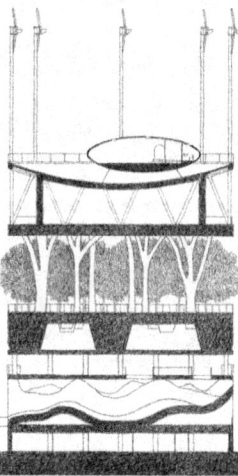

The Holland Pavilion at the Hanover Expo in 2000, designed by MVRDV, is a 'layer cake' of different kinds of landscape.

Madeline Gins and Arakawa designed the Bioscleave House as an internal landscape to keep its inhabitants fit.

See also: Simon Unwin – *Twenty-Five Buildings Every Architect Should Understand*, 2015, pp. 255–64.

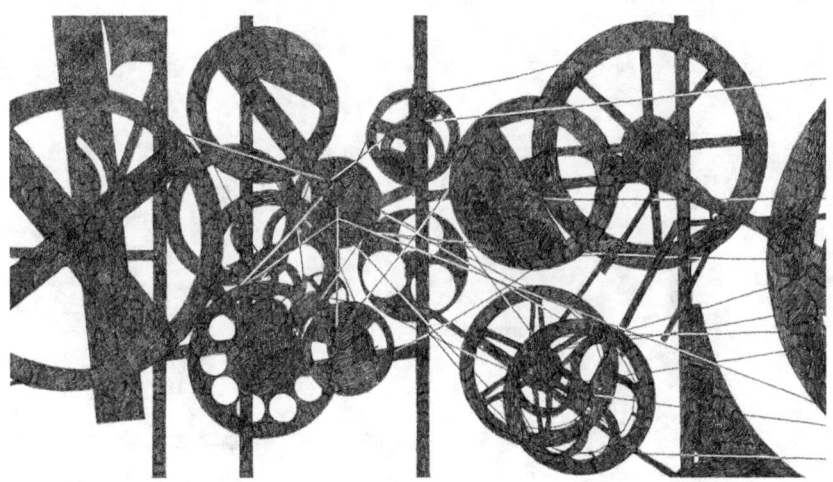

Jean Tinguely, 'Requiem pour une feuille morte' ('Requiem for a Dead Leaf'), 1967

MACHINE METAPHORS

One way in which architecture reciprocates the implicit compliments of psychologists and biologists who find it a useful quarry for metaphor is by trying to design buildings as if they were machines. Le Corbusier, for example, wanted architects to emulate the rationalism and the elegant puritan aesthetic of the work of engineers: bridges, motor vehicles, airplanes, ocean-going liners. It was not that he suggested that buildings should necessarily look like these things, but that architects should strive to achieve similarly evolved functional and aesthetic sophistication in their work, rather than be preoccupied with historical styles. His protagonism for this forward-looking aspiration was and continues to be seductive. But like many influential metaphors the precise implications are far from crystal clear.

BODY AS PALACE OF MACHINES
'Der Mensch als Industriepalast', Fritz Kahn

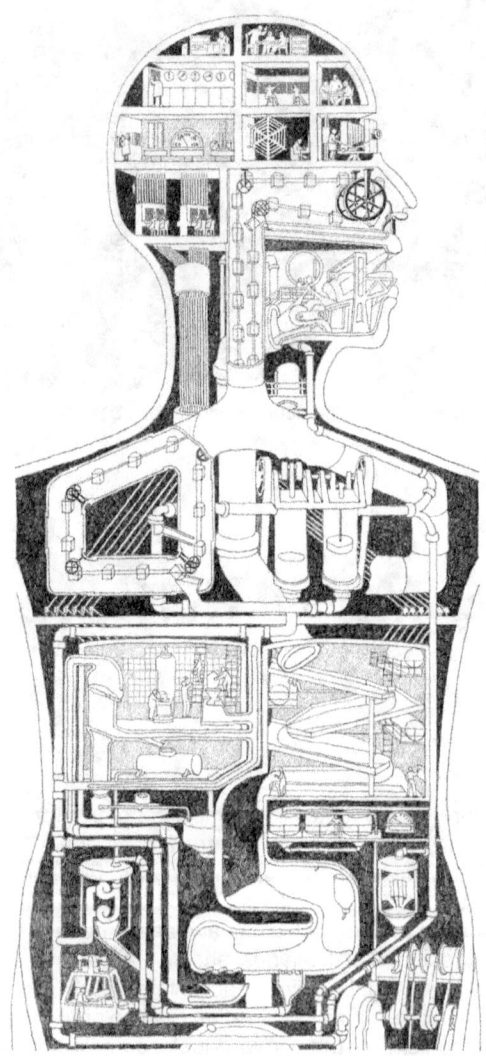

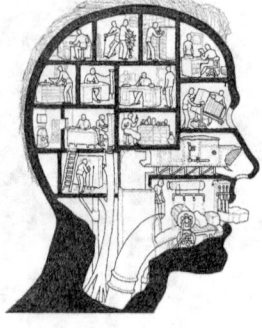

Architecture has been used in different ways as a metaphor for the workings of the human being. Jung and Freud used layouts of architectural space to describe the intangible layers of the psyche. Others have used architecture as part of a mechanical analogy to explain the workings of human organs and the controlling brain.

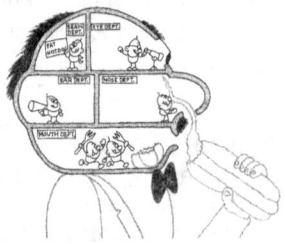

This drawing is based on one made for the German physician Fritz Kahn in the 1920s. It was titled 'Der Mensch als Industriepalast' ('Man as Industrial Palace', or 'The Human Factory'). Whereas psychologists used architecture as a metaphor to explain the workings of the human psyche, those interested in the interactive workings of the human organs found architecture and technology useful as a source of metaphor for their discipline too. Kahn's more detailed architecture of the head is illustrated top right.

The idea of the head as corporate HQ was taken up in cartoon strips such as 'The Numskulls' (see also page 117) in comics – e.g. The Beezer, The Dandy, and The Beano – published in the 1960s and 70s by Dundee-based publishers D.C. Thomson.

MACHINE AS MODEL FOR ARCHITECTURE
Le Corbusier – *Vers une architecture*

In the 1920s architects, especially Le Corbusier in his celebrated book *Vers une architecture* (1923), began thinking that buildings should be conceived as machines.

Le Corbusier argued that architects should strive to emulate the achievements, in the nineteenth and early twentieth century, of engineers. As well as great iron and steel bridges, he illustrated the motor car, airplane and ocean-going liner (left) as examples of the achievements of technology. Architecture, he argued, should kick itself out of its predilection for imitating styles from history and find a new architecture base on the idea of buildings as machines – 'the house is a machine for living in', 'the chair is a machine for sitting in' etc. Le Corbusier's polemic was aimed at stirring up architecture, making his colleagues think less about stylistic appearances and more about pragmatic performance and phenomenological experience. He wanted architecture without a mask (see page 58ff.).

HOUSE AS 'MACHINE FOR INHABITATION'
'Citrohan' House, Le Corbusier

' *"Citrohan" (not to say Citroën). That is to say, a house like a motor-car, conceived and carried out like an omnibus or a ship's cabin. The actual needs of the dwelling can be formulated and demand their solution. We must fight against the old-world house, which made a bad use of space. We must look upon the house as a machine for living in or as a tool... As to beauty, this is always present when you have proportion; and proportion costs the landlord nothing, it is at the charge of the architect! The emotions will not be aroused unless reason is first satisfied, and this comes when calculation is employed. There is no shame in living in a house without a pointed roof, with walls as smooth as sheet iron, with windows like those of factories. And one can be proud of having a house as serviceable as a typewriter.*'

'*Houses are built to live in, and not to look on.*'
Francis Bacon – 'Of Building', in *The Essayes or Counsels, Civill and Morall, of Franci Lo. Verulam, Viscount St. Alban,* 1625.

Le Corbusier, trans. Etchells – *Towards a New Architecture* (1923), 1927.

From before 1920, Le Corbusier was interested in designing what he called 'mass-production houses'. These, he argued, should be designed with the same attitude applied by engineers to cars, ships, airplanes, bridges... He did not suggest that aesthetics were irrelevant but that they could be trusted to look after themselves if designers combined common pragmatic sense and regulated proportion. Ornamentation and styles derived from past architecture were deemed decadent irrelevances.

One of Le Corbusier's mass-production houses was the Citrohan House (1922; model and section alongside, plans opposite). As you can see in the quotation above, Le Corbusier specifically applied the

model (different in some details from the published plans)

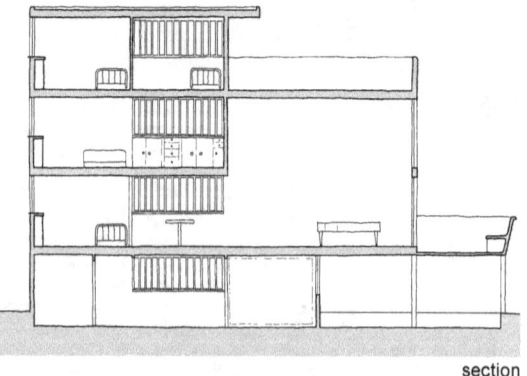

section

138 ANALYSING ARCHITECTURE NOTEBOOKS

machine metaphor to this house. Even so, you can also see from the drawings that this did not mean that he wanted the house to look like a machine. It was more that he thought that houses should be designed and made in straightforward, unornamented and elegant ways that satisfy their performance requirements with optimal efficiency using contemporary materials and technologies. It was the underlying pragmatic rigour of engineering that appealed to his moral sensibility, rather than the appearance of machines. He also felt that such rigour, allied with a sensibility attuned by geometry to proportion, could be relied upon to produce aesthetic quality – beauty in conception, appearance and use.

'The plan', Le Corbusier wrote, 'is the generator'. By 'plan' it seems he not only meant the floor layout of a building but also the idea, the intellectual life-force that gives vitality to a work of architecture, that (to use an apt metaphor) drives the machine.

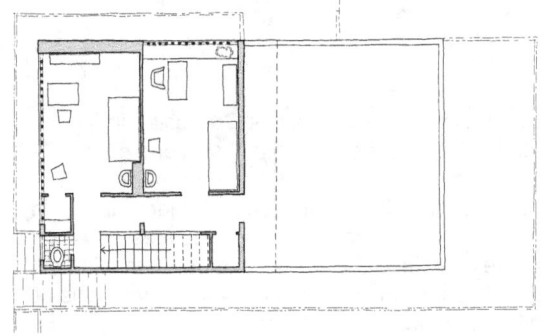

roof level

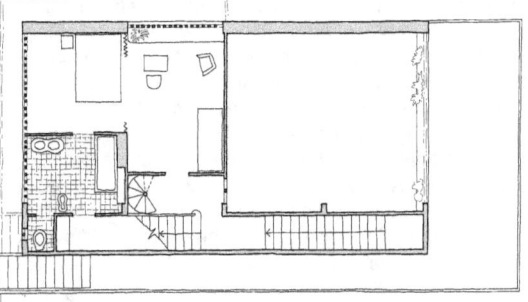

first floor

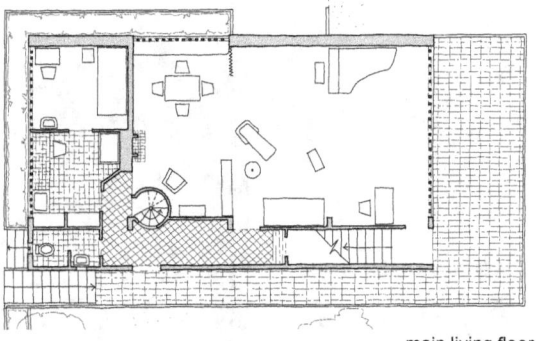

main living floor

The Citrohan House was conceived for mass-production. It is one of Le Corbusier's attempts to design a machine for living in.

The plans, section and a model photograph are in: Le Corbusier – Œuvre complète, Volume 1, 1910–29.

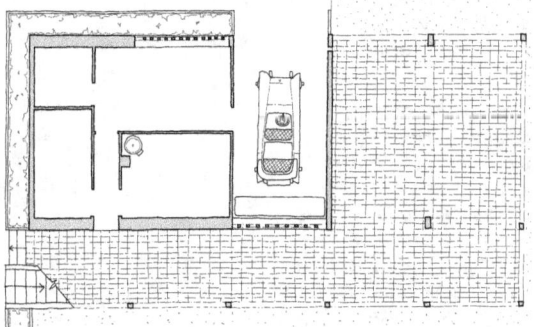

undercroft level

METAPHOR

139

MASS-PRODUCTON HOUSE
Dymaxion House, Buckminster Fuller

Around the same time as Le Corbusier, in the 1920s, the American architect and engineer Buckminster Fuller was begin to propose what he called the Dymaxion House, an idea he would develop over the following two decades. The name combined the words 'dynamic', 'maximum' and 'tension'. Fuller designed various versions at different times in his career.

The version illustrated below, the 4D, is from around 1930. Its structure is based on a single central mast from which floors and roof are suspended by tension wires. In this it is related to both yacht and suspension bridge technology. Services and vertical circulation were provided in the central core. The house was constructed from aluminium and could be assembled, from components light enough for one man to carry, in the same way we would assemble a flat-pack piece of furniture today. All versions of the Dymaxion House were designed for mass-production. They could even be disassembled for relocation.

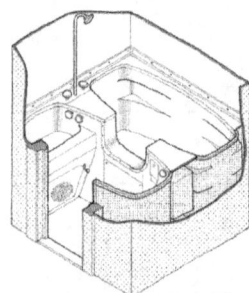

The Dymaxion Bathroom (1936, above) was constructed of pressed metal or moulded plastic panels and with a view to efficiency in the use of water and energy.

One version of the Dymaxion House (right), by Buckminster Fuller. As well as being conceived as a practical modern house it is also a clear example of architecture conceived as being detached from nature, rather like a space module.

HOUSES AS MACHINES
Charlotte Periand; Archigram

'A house is a machine for living in. Baths, sun, hot-water, cold-water, warmth at will, conservation of food, hygiene, beauty in the sense of good proportion. An armchair is a machine for sitting in and so on.'

Le Corbusier, trans. Etchells
– *Towards a New Architecture* (1923), 1927.

Le Corbusier was not the only architect to try to realise the metaphor that a house is a machine for living in. Some have even seen whole cities as machines, even one that, like a vehicle or some robotic animal, might be able to move. Although it is arguable that Le Corbusier was suggesting that houses should be designed with the same pragmatic efficiency as machines, rather than look like machines, some architects have sought to design houses and other living environments as if they were technologically equivalent to machines, built using the same manufacturing techniques used for cars, boats and airplanes.

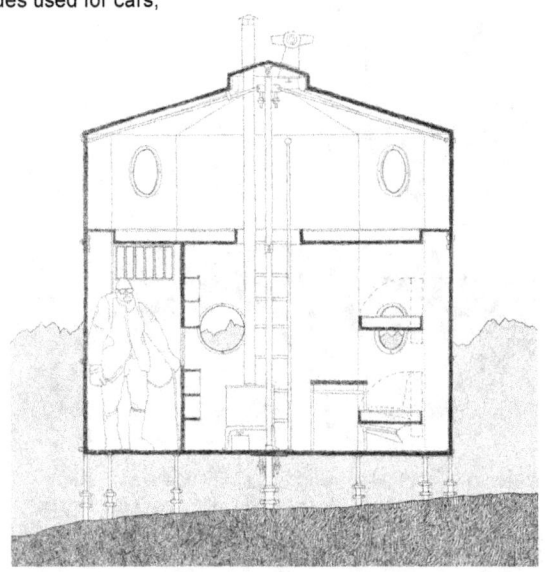

In 1938, a collaborator of Le Corbusier, Charlotte Perriand, designed 'le refuge tonneau' (right), a metal hut which could be transported to remote regions as a refuge for mountaineers and explorers. Every requirement – beds, cupboards, table, stove, energy generation… – was built-in to create a integrated whole, just as in a motor car or an airplane.

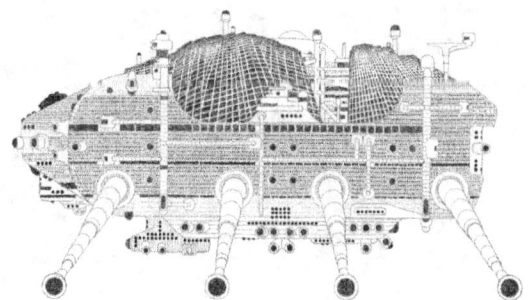

In 1964, Ron Herron of Archigram put forward the idea of a city that could move – The Walking City. It would walk around on legs like a huge mechanical animal (right).

SHIP METAPHOR
Villa E.1027, Eileen Gray (with Jean Badovici)

'The church may have been a ship, high-prowed, steering with all its company towards infinity.'

E.M. Forster – *Howards End*, 1910.

For centuries the ship metaphor has been applied to churches; with their 'naves' implying an etymological link with 'naval'; the church would be a ship to carry us through the storms of life. In the twentieth century the ship metaphor was seized by Le Corbusier for more secular and humanist purposes. For him the ship was evidence of humanity's technical genius, and a vessel that could carry us to distant lands.

Lewerentz's Church of S. Petri at Klippan alluded to the ship as well as the tree metaphor (see page 45), with a 'mast' 'below decks' and 'decks' that 'unbalance'.

This image (left) of the Aquitania appeared in Le Corbusier's Vers une architecture *(1923). The caption reads (translated by Etchells in 1927), 'a seaside villa, conceived as are these liners, would be more appropriate than those we see with their heavy tiled roofs'.*

One architect that took up this challenge was Eileen Gray. In 1926 she built a seaside villa near Cap Martin in the south of France (below). Evoking a machine serial number it was called Villa E.1027 – code intertwining her initials with those of her partner Jean Badovici.

Gray's villa evoked the idea of a decked liner, in which you could imagine travelling to distant lands.

See also: Simon Unwin – *Twenty-Five Buildings Every Architect Should Understand*, 2015, pp. 163–74 and 175–86.

MACHINE MASK
Pompidou Centre, Piano and Rogers

Despite the nineteenth-century critic, John Ruskin, urging that art, architecture and the crafts should not strive to achieve the perfection made possible by industrial production technology – the machine – architects in the 1920s found Le Corbusier's idea of the 'house-machine' seductive. Others found the growth of industrialisation and the dominance of machines unnerving.

Fritz Lang's 1927 movie Metropolis *imagined human beings as nothing more than cogs in an industrial machine. This was his view of the future sought by Le Corbusier and others; he saw it as dystopian.*

Le Corbusier may have wanted architecture without styles – without a mask – but the machine metaphor he espoused was destined to become a mask in its own right. In the hands of some architects the 'machine ideal' – the idea that architecture could emulate the pragmatic priorities of machines and engineering – was transformed into the 'machine aesthetic' – the idea that buildings might look like vast complicated machines.

'Architecture has nothing to do with the various styles.'
Le Corbusier, trans. Etchells
– *Towards a New Architecture*
(1923), 1927.

One eminent example of the machine aesthetic is the Pompidou Centre in Paris designed by Renzo Piano and Richard Rogers and completed in 1977. Painted in bright colours, the external architecture of this building combined the complex 'intestines' of an oil refinery with the ventilation systems of ocean-going liners, all framed in a steel 'exoskeleton'.

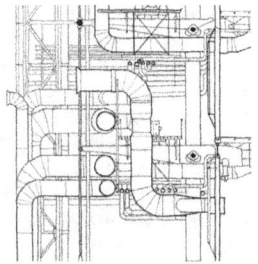

More for dramatic aesthetic effect than practical necessity, the architecture of the Pompidou Centre exposes the mechanical pipework of its ventilation and heating systems.

METAPHOR 143

INTEGRATING ARCHITECTURE AND PEOPLE
Fun Palace, Cedric Price

In the 1960s, the British architect Cedric Price extended the machine metaphor to present human beings and their contraptions – the rich multidimensional architecture (environment) that accommodates their lives – not as conceptually separate but as intertwined in mutual symbiotic relationships; i.e. as one big infinitely evolving machine, in which people were cast not merely as occupants but as participant beneficiary ingredients.

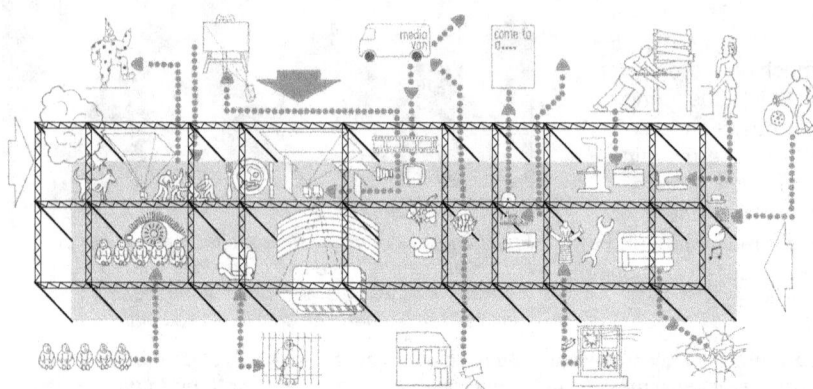

Although he drew images of his ideas for a Fun Palace (above), Price envisioned it would operate more as a system – even as an interactive organism involving (intermingling the agencies of) people and contraptions that could entertain, educate, feed them – rather than as a traditional building in which human activity is merely framed by stolid architectural fabric. The Fun Palace was presented as an interactive ever-mutating machine in which people, their activities (in particular recreational activities), and the physical infrastructures needed to frame and support those activities would interact in a dynamic, complex, ever-reactive and changing matrix of arrangements and relationships.

The Fun Palace concept was developed in collaboration with innovative British theatre director Joan Littlewood in the 1960s and is said to have influenced the design of The Pompidou Centre (page 143) in the following decade. Its architecture would be nebulous rather than concrete: conceived neither as a machine like a generator, that having been started could operate independently, nor one with people reduced to subordinate cogs slaving to achieve some supra-human purpose. Unlike the Pompidou, it would not necessarily look like a machine either. Rather, the Fun Palace concept sees human society and its contraptions as one complex interactive system, facilitated and kept vital by evolving cybernetic programmes. If the Fun Palace is metaphorically a machine, it is a political, social and economic one.

In hindsight the Fun Palace is less a design proposal than an architecturally imagined anticipation of our twenty-first-century relationship with the Internet, in which algorithms deliver to each of us personally tailored content. In place of the assumed intractable conceptual separation between machines (architecture as a machine for living) and people, Price posited a dynamic symbiotic fusion of the two.

THE MUSIC METAPHOR

Music has rhythm and melody; architecture has order and space. Music takes time; so does architecture. Music stirs emotion; architecture too. Though architecture involves pragmatic matters, it can be purely aesthetic. Though music is primarily aesthetic, it can tell stories too. We might think that words constitute the only language available to us. Both music and architecture are languages too: they have their structures (grammar and syntax) and their meanings (semantics). With nuances they may both express subtleties beyond verbal language. Both music and architecture, like language, can have regional 'dialects' and national identities. The music metaphor in architecture is where these shared differences from verbal language are established and celebrated.

HARMONY
music and proportion

Over two thousand years ago the Roman architect Vitruvius suggested architects should be conversant with the principles of music. Renaissance theorists interpreted this as a matter of proportion. Harmonies in music are achieved by geometric proportion in the relative rates of vibration causing different notes. Its seems plausible then that geometric proportion can result in visual and spatial harmony too.

'We shall therefore borrow all our Rules for the finishing our Proportions, from the Musicians, who are the greatest Masters of this Sort of Numbers.'

Leone Battista Alberti, trans. Bartoli – *Ten Books on Architecture* (1452), Book IX, Chapter V, 1955.

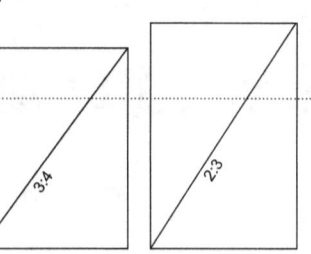

The proportions of musical intervals (above).

Harmonic proportions used in architecture (below).

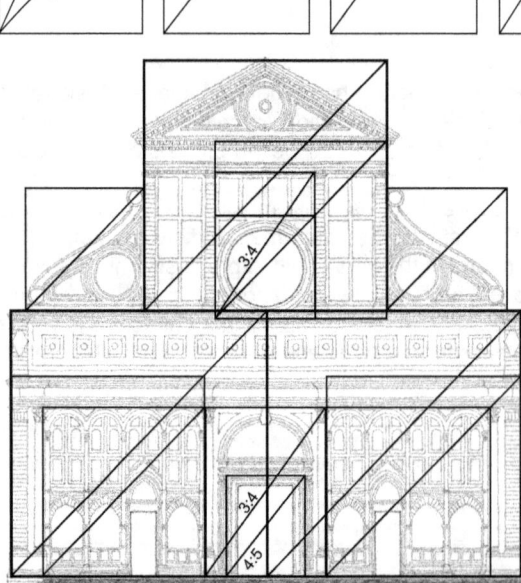

Architects also use:

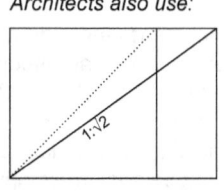

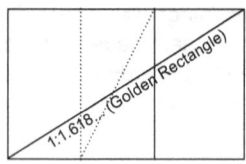

Alberti's S. Maria Novella in Florence (left) is a composition governed by squares and other simply proportioned rectangles. He sought the harmony of music in visual form.

ANALYSING ARCHITECTURE NOTEBOOKS

(NOT) FROZEN MUSIC
Goethe and Holl

' *"I have found among my papers," said Goethe, "a leaf, in which I call architecture frozen music. There is something in the remark; the influence that flows upon us from architecture is like that from music. Magnificent buildings and apartments are for princes and empires. When a man lives in such, he feels satisfied, and asks no more. This is contrary to my nature. In a splendid dwelling, such as I had at Carlsbad, I became slothful. A decent little room like this in which we are – somewhat disorderly-orderly – somewhat in the gypsy fashion – is what suits me; it leaves my inner nature free to act and create."* '

Johann Wolfgang von Goethe (1829), in Johann Peter Eckermann, trans. Fuller – *Conversations with Goethe in the Last Years of His Life*, 1839.

Goethe's use of music as a metaphor for architecture is vague but it is clear that it is very different from that of Alberti. Goethe creates a comparison between architecture and music not by means of geometry but more by emotion. The atmosphere of places framed by different kinds of architecture can influence feelings in a way similar to music. Goethe's reason for the adjective 'frozen' seems to relate to the apparent static nature of architecture compared with the movement of music. But if he had taken into account changes – in light, temperature and occupation through day, night and the seasons – that affect all places except those completely isolated from the outside world, then maybe he might have felt able to dispense with it.

A similar appreciation of the metaphorical relationship between architecture and music has been expressed more recently by the American architect Stephen Holl, who explains much of his own design work by comparison with various pieces of music.

> 'Music, like architecture, is an immersive experience – it surrounds you. One can turn away from a painting or a work of sculpture, while music and architecture engulf the body in space.'

Stephen Holl – 'Architectonics of Music', 2015: architectonicsofmusic.com.

Holl has also generated quasi-mathematical formulae in which sound and light are effectively seen as equivalent, with music the realm of sound in time and architecture the realm of light in space:

$$\text{MUSIC} = \frac{\text{material} \times \text{sound}}{\text{time}} \qquad \text{ARCHITECTURE} = \frac{\text{material} \times \text{light}}{\text{space}}$$

But the power of both Goethe's and Holl's appreciation of the metaphorical relationship between architecture and music lies in the realisation that both are phenomenological: both take and frame time; both move us, physically (in dance, or in moving around a space – building, city, garden...) and emotionally by influencing how we feel. In short, both include us not merely as spectators but as involved ingredients.

MELODY AND RHYTHM
music, movement and space

'And this is the other coding at St George's, the curvature & stony design of an unplayed musical score. Spiral form notation. Church as instrument. Unregistered pitch.'

Iain Sinclair – *Lud Heat*, 1975.

Iain Sinclair has not been the only one to compare the physical composition of architectural form – in this case one of Nicholas Hawksmoor's eighteenth-century London churches – with formal musical composition. He interprets St George's-in-the-East (right) as an architectural composition equivalent to a musical one. The church stands like a silent musical chord played on a grand organ.

Le Corbusier's mother was a musician; and it is arguable that music influenced his conception of architecture. For example, his promotion of a free plan within structural order is comparable with melody weaving through a rhythmic beat.

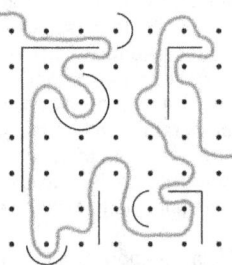

Hawksmoor's churches are like silent musical chords played on an organ.

In a 'Corbusian' free plan (right) walls and movement weave amongst columns like melodies within a beat.

Le Corbusier designed the monastery of La Tourette near Lyon in the 1960s. But the glass walls (visible in the first three floors above) were designed by another architect, one who was also a musical composer – Iannis Xenakis. These glass screens were designed according to musical form and proportions, and appear to undulate like a melody against the beat of the building's ordered structure.

NARRATIVE METAPHORS

The eccentric sanity of Jacques Tati's Monsieur Hulot is often illustrated with the help of architecture. On page 35 we saw Tati's humorous transformation of a modern house's windows into swivelling eyes. In the same film, *Mon Oncle* (1958), the hero of the film – M. Hulot – lives in the antithesis of a modern house (above). It is rambling and irregular, a confection of ad hoc additions. And Hulot reaches his own penthouse apartment (top left of the building) by the most circuitous route possible. Tati's device acts as an architectural metaphor; one that suggests that narratives derive charm not by direct rationality (as claimed by Descartes and modern architecture) but through meandering exploration.

PRESENCE
glass jar, picnic cloth...

Poets can be interested in the presence of things, their inferences and implications. Wallace Stevens, for example, reflected on the way an unpretentious glass jar could stand in the landscape – a work of architecture – representing human presence.

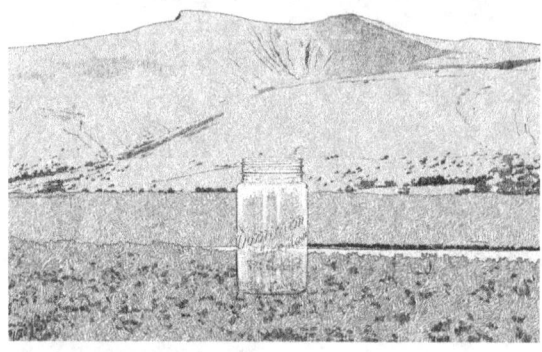

A glass jar, like a prehistoric standing stone, can gather the surrounding landscape into itself.

'I placed a jar in Tennessee,
And round it was, upon a hill.
It made the slovenly wilderness
Surround that hill.
The wilderness rose up to it,
And sprawled around, no longer wild.
The jar was round upon the ground
And tall and of a port in air.
It took dominion everywhere.'

Wallace Stevens – 'Anecdote of the Jar' (1919), in *Harmonium*, 1923.

And Seamus Heaney saw a white picnic cloth as a metaphor for a conversation; one that would be stained by the awkwardness of an ill-judged incident between a man (the poet), his partner, and 'another lady'.

'Our conversation...
... a white picnic tablecloth spread out
Like a book of manners in the wilderness.'

Seamus Heaney – 'A Dream of Jealousy', in *Fieldwork*, 1979.

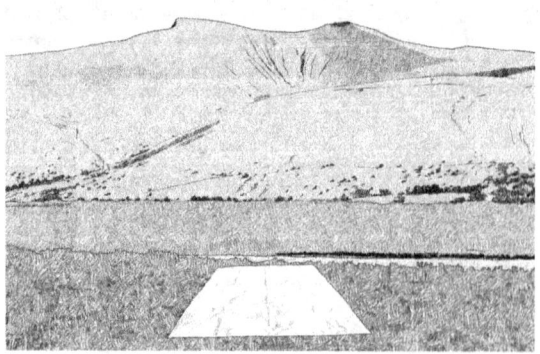

Even a simple cloth laid on the ground profoundly changes the world around. It, like a book, creates a world of its own, distinct in its boundaries. All architecture is like this.

GATHERING
Heidegger's bridge

'The bridge swings over the stream "with ease and power". It does not just connect banks that are already there. The banks only emerge as banks as the bridge crosses the stream... The bridge gathers the earth as landscape around the stream... Always and ever differently the bridge escorts the lingering and hastening ways of men to and fro, so that they may get to other banks and in the end, as mortals, to the other side... The bridge gathers to itself in its own way earth and sky, divinities and mortals.'

Martin Heidegger, trans. Hofstader – 'Building Dwelling Thinking' (1951), in *Poetry, Language, Thought* (1971), 1975.

Martin Heidegger alluded to the way in which a simple work of architecture – a bridge or a house for example – can gather the world into itself (like Wallace Stevens' jar, opposite). Its presence is not merely evidence of the presence of those that put it there but also a metaphorical representation of the order and sense their minds have projected into the landscape.

The world without mind has no sense or value. A work of architecture is necessarily a product of a conceiving mind. In however small a way, it changes the world. The mind's physical and psychological needs, its aesthetic sensibility, its social and religious beliefs... are projected into the world physically and organisationally by the architectural proposition. The work 'gathers' all these things into itself. It stands thereafter as a metaphor for the intellectual workings – the needs, sensibility, beliefs... – of the mind responsible for it.

Through the centuries a stream has cut for itself a channel as it descends to the sea. The landscape is as it is: mindless; without order or values.

But then we arrive and analyse the landscape around us. We project our sense on to it. We want our path to cross the stream. The erection of a bridge changes everything. Not only is the bridge an eye-catching feature of a picturesque scene. It stands as a metaphor for our presence and the sense we project into our world.

DIDACTIC METAPHOR
John Bunyan – A Pilgrim's Progress

*'Solidity, indeed, becomes the pen
Of him that writeth things divine to men;
But must I needs want solidness, because
By metaphors I speak? Were not God's laws,
His gospel laws, in olden times held forth
By types, shadows, and metaphors?'...
'The prophets used much by metaphors
To set forth truth; yea, who so considers Christ,
his apostles too, shall plainly see,
That truths to this day in such mantles be.'*

John Bunyan's *Pilgrim's Progress* is structured as a journey through a sequence of places, each with its own moral character and challenges. Bunyan, in his imagination and communicated to us through his writing, conjures up cities and a landscape through which his pilgrim progresses. That world, with its gates, pathways, sloughs, walls, castles, climbs, cities... is a metaphor for the psyche of a mind seeking moral certainty amidst doubt, evil and in the face of death. The landscape and its features, with their various meanings made clear by the labels Bunyan gives them, make sense of the world for the pilgrim; he gives his world an architecture that provides both narrative and moral structure.

John Bunyan – *Pilgrim's Progress*, 1678.

The world that Bunyan's pilgrim encounters, mapped below by Thomas Conder in 1778, is a narrative metaphor for his spiritual journey. Its components are landscape and architecture. The journey begins at the City of Destruction and culminates at the Gate of the Celestial City.

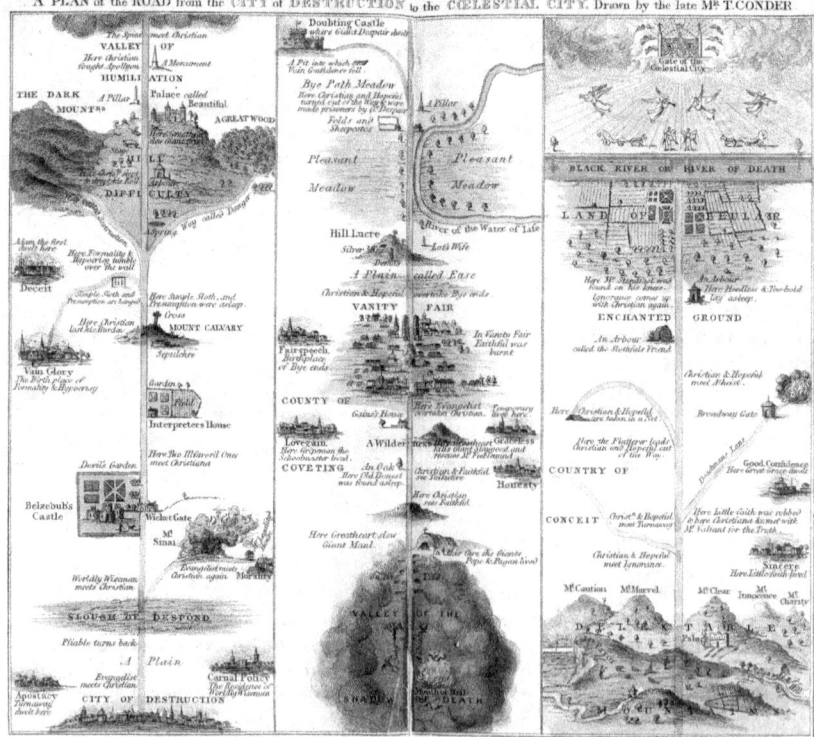

152   ANALYSING ARCHITECTURE NOTEBOOKS

SONGLINES
narratives we tell about our world

'One of the first images to reach the mind of an aboriginal child born at Ayer's Rock would be the sight of those great rocks and precipices, and one of the first stories told to him would be a simple myth explaining their creation. With a boy, this knowledge becomes richer as, with passing years, the tribal elders admit him deeper and deeper into the esoteric mysteries of the tribe until, by the time he is fully adult, Ayer's Rock and its myths are the central theme in his life. He belongs to a world completely dominated by the natural features surrounding him. It is a small world, but his knowledge of it is deep and strong. The young tribesman feels he is one of a continuous line of progenitors uniting him with the great tjukurapa creatures of the dim and ghostly past. They, his own forebears, brought into existence everything with which he is in daily contact; the monolith of Uluru, the cycle of the seasons, the pattern of his daily life, the ceremonial life, and the code of laws under which he lives.'

Charles P. Mountford – *Ayer's Rock*, 1965.

It might be thought that Australian aborigines have a culture without architecture; they do not build large and pretentious buildings. But like people everywhere, they do make places, and occasionally simple huts from bark or twigs. Their architecture is, however, much more sophisticated than that. Architecture is primarily the medium through which we make spatial sense of the world in which we live and, in such terms, it is clear that the stories aborigines tell about their landscape – sometimes called 'songlines' – constitute their architecture. In the way that all of us invest our surroundings with narrative, we are all aborigine architects. We hear and tell stories about the world in which we live; stories that condition how we act and relate to others. Below are some of the stories aborigines associate with particular places on and around Ayer's Rock.

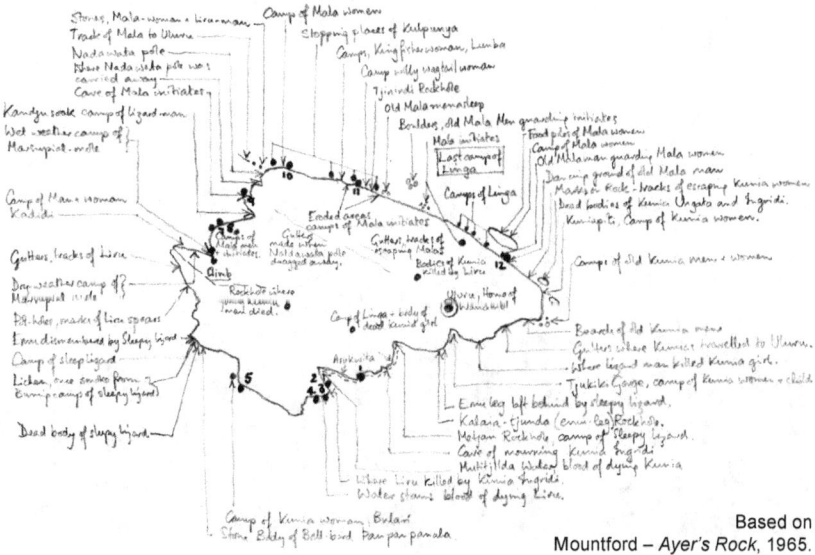

Based on Mountford – *Ayer's Rock*, 1965.

All works of architecture are elements in the stories we tell ourselves and others about the world in which we live.

Uluru (Ayer's Rock) is to Australian aborigines what the cathedral is to French Christians living in the city of Chartres. In both the ever-present mass, of rock or building, is the hub around which lives revolve. They are also invested with stories: personal memories and legends that are part of their communities' collective memory. Just as the crevices of Ayer's Rock are associated with Dreamtime events (from when the world was being created) involving emus and lizards, so too are the niches and windows of a great cathedral invested with stories of saints.

An important role of architecture, whether built or applied to natural features, is to be a metaphorical repository of narrative. Our personal stories are associated with our houses and neighbourhoods; our national and cultural stories are contained by our great historical works of architecture.

INTERPLAY
chessboard, courtroom, performance area

Towards the end of Shakespeare's *The Tempest*, Ferdinand and Miranda are discovered gently bickering, like an already married couple, over a game of chess – the game that involves intricate probes and parries; the interplay that culminates in mating, when a queen conquers her opposing king. Dramatically, the scene in *The Tempest* is a metaphor for the couple's incipient relationship. But it also suggests an architectural metaphor in that it centres on a place – sixty-four black and white squares arranged eight-by-eight. The chessboard's square matrix provides the architecture within which the battle is played – an architectural frame that accommodates interplay. Buildings too can be frames accommodating interplay – metaphorical chessboards – the settings for drama and narrative.

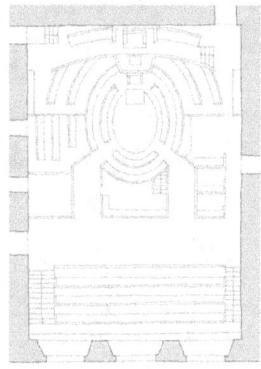

The courtroom is the chessboard on which games of justice are played.

A chessboard is a work of architecture; and any work of architecture is, to some extent, a chessboard. Rules governing movement in a building may be more variable but they are nevertheless there: exercised by walls, doorways, staircases, furniture… and the agency of people.

All works of architecture are to some extent performance places. They provide what Plato called 'the receptacle of becoming' – chora – time and space for change, interaction, unfolding narrative…

METAPHOR

The same applies to the places we live and work. Offices incorporate the mores, laws, rules of spatial behaviour of the organisations they accommodate as well as providing the landscape for the personal memories of those that work there. The New York Stock Exchange (above) is the Ayer's Rock of stockbrokers. In its heyday the trading floor of the Chicago Mercantile Exchange (below) 'sang' to the 'music' of traders shouting out and responding to orders for corn, soybeans, rice... Nowadays the 'songlines' that inform trading in financial institutions are the algorithms and connections of computer systems that facilitate global trading.

I worked for many years in the Welsh School of Architecture in Cardiff and I could tell many stories: about how the layout and the uses of rooms has changed; the offices inhabited by different friends and colleagues through the years; the idiosyncratic behaviour of eminent visiting architects (such as when I wheeled Berthold Lubetkin around the corridors with him tooting like a train at each corner); the ghosts of past professors, and the places where I argued with them; even the areas of wall that were the focus of particularly memorable student crits. For me and others, the School is a repository of countless memories.

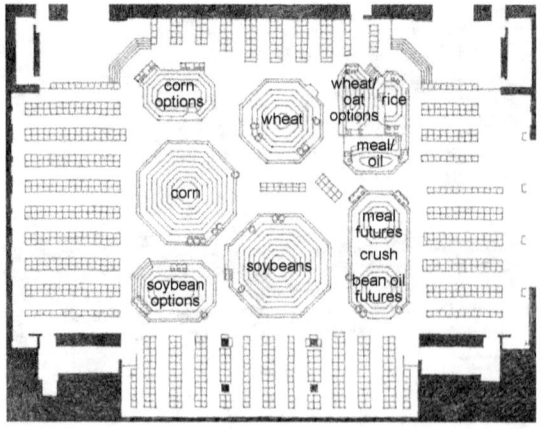

The Grain Room of the Chicago Mercantile Exchange was like a landscape with its own 'songlines'. Traders would sing out their orders in pits dedicated to different commodities. The architecture represented the narrative drama metaphorically as well as pragmatically. More recently the 'songlines' of such trading inhabit a cybernetic landscape inside computers.

METAPHOR FOR A MARRIAGE
Odysseus's bed

'Masons, when they start upon a building,
 Are careful to test out the scaffolding;
Make sure that planks won't slip at busy points,
 Secure all ladders, tighten bolted joints.
And yet all this comes down when the job's done
 Showing off walls of sure and solid stone.
So if, my dear, there sometimes seem to be
 Old bridges breaking between you and me
Never fear. We may let the scaffolds fall
 Confident that we have built our wall.'

Seamus Heaney – 'Scaffolding', in *Death of a Naturalist*, 1966.

In *Analysing Architecture* – the chapter entitled 'Primitive Place Types' – I used short descriptions from Homer's *Odyssey* (c. eighth century BCE) to illustrate some of the basic place types that have framed human life (and death) since prehistory: seat; tomb; cooking place; hearth; bed; altar; performance place; bath. In the *Odyssey* such descriptions are used to set the scene for a particular episode but there is an example, towards the end of the narrative, of a primitive place type used as a metaphor.

In Book 23 Odysseus has returned unrecognised to his estate in Ithaca, which he had left ten years previously to join Agamemnon's expeditionary forces on their mission to reclaim Helen (Agamemnon's brother's wife) from the Trojans. While away, Odysseus's own wife Penelope has been beset by 'suitors' who have pestered her to choose one of them as a replacement husband and squandered the resources of Odysseus's estate. The returning Odysseus has killed the suitors but Penelope is not sure that he actually is her husband. She comes up with a way to find out.

' "What a strange man you are", said the cautious Penelope. "I am not being haughty or contemptuous of you, though I'm not surprised that you think I am. But I have too clear a picture of you in my mind as you were when you sailed from Ithaca in your long-oared ship. Come, Eurycleia, move the great bed outside the bedroom that he himself built and make it up with fleeces and blankets and brightly coloured rugs. This was her way of putting her husband to the test. But Odysseus flared up at once and rounded on his loyal wife. "Lady", he cried, "your words are a knife in my heart! Who has moved my bed? That would be hard even for a skilled workman, though for a god who took it into his head to come and move it somewhere else it would be quite easy. No man alive, not even one in his prime, would find it easy to shift. A great secret went into the making of that complicated bed; and it was my work and mine alone. Inside the court there was a long-leaved olive-tree, which had grown to full height with a trunk as thick as a pillar. Round this I built my room of compact stonework, and when that was finished, I roofed it over carefully, and put in a solid, neatly fitted, double door. Next I lopped all the branches off the olive, trimmed the trunk from the root up, rounded it smoothly and carefully with my adze and trued it to the line, to be my bedpost. I drilled holes in it, and using it as the first bedpost I constructed the rest of the bed. Then I finished it off with an inlay of gold, silver and ivory, and fixed a set of gleaming purple straps across the frame. So I have shown you the secret. What I don't know, lady, is whether my bedstead stands where it did, or whether someone has cut the tree trunk through and moved it". At his words her knees began to tremble and her heart melted as she realized that he had given her infallible proof.' (trans. Rieu, 1946)

Odysseus's bed is a poetic example of how the identification of place (a work of architecture) blends, mingles, fuses... life, providence, emotion and form. It is easy to interpret as metaphor; not a verbal metaphor but an architectural metaphor described in words. Odysseus himself was the architect, and the bed a metaphor for his marriage with Penelope. The bed itself possesses its own metaphorical power independent of the words used to describe its creation.

These drawings show the stages in which Odysseus created his bed. It is a clear example of a rudimentary work of architecture in which elements that are there already are recognised and amended to identify a place. In this instance each element and stage of construction has its own metaphorical meaning:

1 First, Odysseus saw the olive tree – associated with Athena (Odysseus's guardian goddess) and with wisdom and peace – and recognised its potential as strong and immovable support for his and Penelope's marital bed.

2 Then he defined and protected the area around the tree with a wall (and roof), taking advantage of the presence of one wall of his palace courtyard that was already there.

3 Third, he amended (trimmed, carved and polished) the tree's trunk to fit his purpose.

4 And finally he added elements to the trunk to create the bed.

These are four stages in any work of architecture, even in more sophisticated examples: 1 recognition of the potential of existing elements; 2 definition and protection of the place; 3 exploitation and refinement of existing elements; and 4 design and construction of additional elements. The result is the identification of a place – a work of architecture.

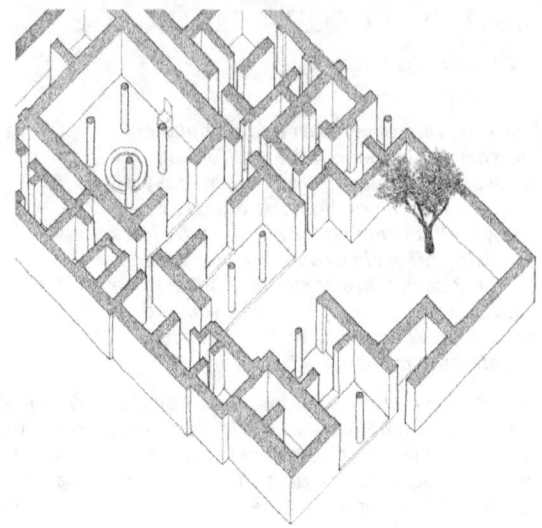

1   The olive tree is a metaphor for the feminine principle. It is Athena's tree and a symbol of wisdom and peace. It is rooted in the earth and promises fruit. It can be interpreted as a metaphor for Penelope herself.

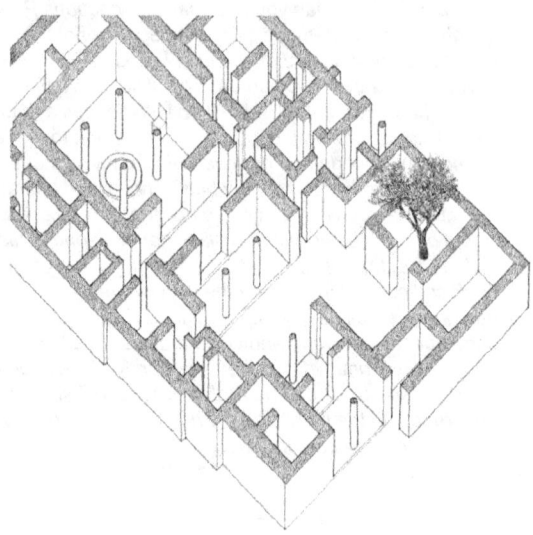

2   Odysseus sees the tree's potential and defines its place, embracing it with walls and sheltering it with a roof. The room becomes a shrine to the feminine principle, to Penelope, to wisdom, peace and the protectress Athena.

Odysseus's bed is replete with metaphorical connotations, making it a powerful device in the conclusion of Homer's narrative. The captions beneath each drawing give some metaphorical interpretations of each stage of the bed's creation.

The fundamental metaphorical power of Odysseus's bed is that it represents the strength and stability of his marriage with Penelope.

The metaphor Odysseus's bed is imbued with is not a merely narrative device, it lives in the architecture described. Architecture, as language, is a medium of metaphor too. Built form can accommodate metaphor just as well as can words; and one's appreciation (assimilation) of such metaphorical potential, though less verbally explicit, can be just as affecting channelled through our architectural as through our verbal imaginations.

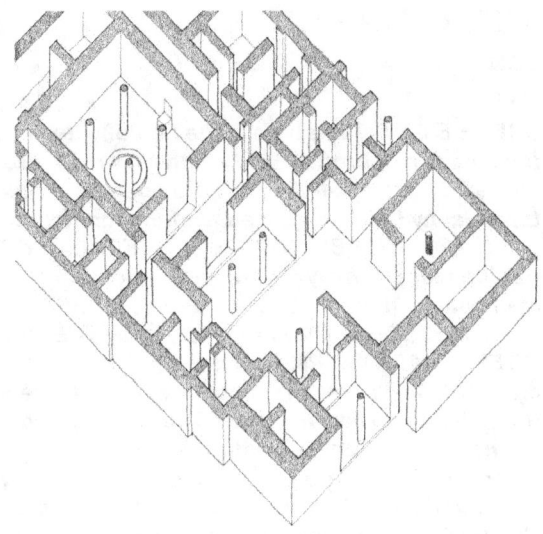

3 Odysseus trims and shapes the tree – as a pillar of the matrimonial bed. (Is this to be compared with Pygmalion's ivory statue, Petruchio's 'taming' of Kate in The Taming of the Shrew, or Henry Higgins' coaching of Eliza Doolittle in George Bernard Shaw's Pygmalion?)

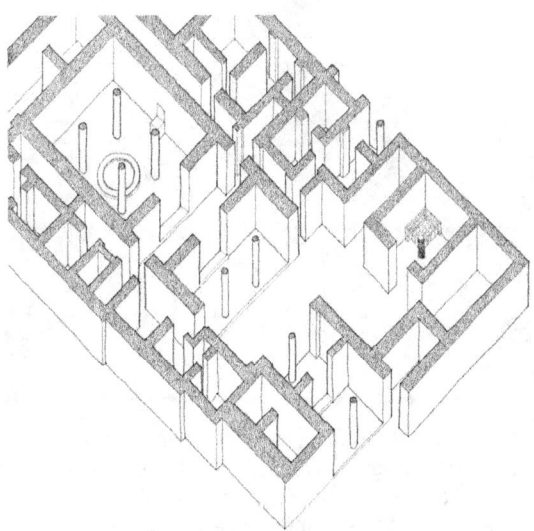

4 From the shaped trunk Odysseus fashions the bed – locus of procreation and the physical manifestation of his marriage to Penelope. Firmly rooted, both the bed and the marriage have withstood Odysseus's ten year absence and the challenges of Penelope's suitors.

Though some have claimed that archaeological remains of Odysseus's palace on Ithaca have been found, others insist Homer's hero was purely fictional. I have used Nestor's palace at Pylos – remains of which have been found – as the basis for these drawings because Odysseus's might be presumed to have been similar in layout. (See also page 74.) Nestor features in Homer's narrative; Telemachus – the 'fruit' of Odysseus and Penelope's bed – visits him near the beginning of the narrative to enquire after his father.

IMPERSONATION
Jean Genet – *The Balcony*

SCENE EIGHT '*The scene is the Balcony itself which projects beyond the façade of a brothel. The shutters, which face the audience, are closed. Suddenly all the shutters open by themselves. The edge of the balcony is at the very edge of the footlights. Through the windows can be seen THE BISHOP, THE GENERAL, and THE JUDGE, who are getting ready. Finally the french windows are flung wide open. The three men come out on the balcony. First THE BISHOP, then THE GENERAL, then THE JUDGE. They are followed by THE HERO. Then comes THE QUEEN, MADAME IRMA, wearing a diadem on her brow and an ermine cloak. All the characters step forward and take their positions with great timidity. They are silent. They simply show themselves. All are of huge proportions, gigantic – except THE HERO, that is, THE CHIEF OF POLICE – and are wearing their ceremonial garments, which are torn and dusty. Then, near them, but not on the balcony, appears THE BEGGAR. In a gentle voice, he cries out: "Long live the Queen!"*'

The Balcony, with characters from the 2014 performance at Teatro García Lorca de Fuente Vaqueros, in Granada, Spain.

The Balcony (1958) is a play by Jean Genet inspired by the 1930s Spanish Civil War. It begins in a brothel, with clients acting out roles of bishop, general and judge for sexual gratification. A civil war rages outside. When the equivalent real dignitaries are killed, the clients, robed in the exaggerated costumes provided by the brothel, are presented to the crowds in their place, with the Chief of Police dressed as 'The Hero'. Irma, the brothel's madam, becomes 'The Queen'. The eponymous balcony is the stage for the presentation of the replacement dignitaries to the crowds. And the instrument of their transformation (apotheosis) is the balcony's doorway. This happens in Scene Eight (above) which encapsulates the crux of the play: that identity (role, status, authority...) is often more a matter of assertion than actuality.

Genet's title *The Balcony* (*Le balcon*) is metaphorical. Architecture has always been an accomplice of power. It provides the platform that underpins the assertion of authority as it presents itself to 'the people'. It also provides the doorway that frames the drama of moments of appearance (right), and which is often an instrument of transformation from one state of being into another; in this case from brothel client to Hero, Judge, General, Bishop and from madam to Queen.

Doorways work both ways. And balconies can be frames for humiliation as well as adulation. On the 21 December 1989, Romania's head of state, Nicolae Ceaușescu, accompanied by his wife and other officials, tried to present a speech to a large crowd in Bucharest. A few days earlier he had ordered his security forces to open fire on demonstrators in Timișoara. During the speech dissent amongst the crowd grew in confidence and it became clear that Ceaușescu's rule was coming to an end. The people had decided that he was not a 'real dignitary' but a tyrant. The Romanian Revolution had begun. He and his wife were summarily executed four days later on Christmas Day.

On 18 July 2016, US Presidential candidate, Donald Trump, makes his entrance at the Republican National Convention in Cleveland, Ohio. His status is reinforced by the drama of his silhouetted appearance through a grand doorway (the size of the doorway being in metaphorical relation to the status and authority he wanted to project).

On 21 December 1989, Nicolae Ceaușescu (on the left) tried to present a speech from the balcony of Central Committee Building in Bucharest. It turned out to be his last public appearance. Four days later he and his wife were executed. Part of the television coverage of the speech is available on YouTube. You can see that while a balcony can provide a platform for power it can also be the locus of humiliation.

When Mr and Mrs Ceaușescu left the balcony of the Central Committee Building it was to meet their death. The balcony stands as a memorial to their humiliation as well as their earlier adulation. The doorway, as a memorial marking the end of their actual as well as their political lives, remains a metaphor for their consignment to history.

HEIGHTS
gods and angels watching (over) us

Architecture contributes to narrative. It does so in scripted drama, whether in plays, movies or television series. Architecture in the real world contributes to narrative too. There are many instances. Some exploit high precipitous places because of the sense of danger they evoke. Many thrillers, for example, involve characters teetering, clinging, being pushed over, falling from… the precipices of high buildings. In other examples the high parapets of buildings are the places from which saints, angels, superheroes, artists, spies and detectives… watch over us looking our for suspicious activity. These narrative situations are only made possible by the architecture that provides the buildings on top of which they stand, ready to swoop to our aid or retribution.

Standing high on pinnacles saints look over the city of Milan from its cathedral.

In the film Wings of Desire (Wim Wenders, 1987), angels watch benevolently over their charges.

The quintessential image of Batman is of him standing high on a parapet prepared to swoop down to save some victim of crime or disaster.

The artist Antony Gormley has placed steel casts of his own body on high buildings in various cities. He seems to be suggesting that artists survey the world like angels or superheroes.

The metaphorical allusions of settings and architecture are as important as music in generating the atmosphere and affecting our subliminal interpretation of movies, artwork and television dramas.

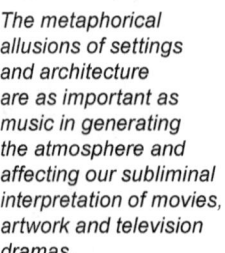

In thrillers and crime dramas directors often place detectives in high places where, like angels of justice, they can watch over suspicious events. This is Kate Fleming (Vicky McClure) in the BBC's Line of Duty, series 2, (Jed Mercurio, 2014).

PARADISE
metaphors for heaven

'Great Denis, open the door of Paradise
And protect Suger through thy pious guardianship.
Mayest thou, who hast built a new dwelling for thyself through us,
Cause us to be received in the dwelling of Heaven,
And to be sated at the heavenly table instead of at the present one.
That which is signified pleases more than that which signifies.'

Religion is one of the great employers of architectural metaphor. It does so both ways: it uses references to architecture metaphorically in its texts and scriptures; it uses architecture itself as metaphorical representation of beliefs and promises. Both Islam and Christianity find significance in the walled garden. It is a significance derived from the psychological peace and contentment we encounter in a well-ordered garden enclosed by walls but open to the heavens. Such seems to speak of humanity in harmony with God's creation. Nature and geometry come together to form a place of solace, a refuge from the rough world, a paradise.

Abbot Suger, trans. Panofsky – *On the Abbey Church of St.-Denis and its Art Treasures* (12thC), 1946.

The word paradise derives from the Old Persian word for a park or walled garden, پردیس , (pairidaeza). Used for heaven or a world of harmony and beauty, the word itself evokes an architectural metaphor by which the pleasure and psychological security you might feel in a walled, well-designed and well-tended garden is transferred to characterise a place of transcendence and peace; one that you might hope to encounter after death but may also enjoy whilst still living.

The wall divides the purity and harmony of the garden from the chaotic and troublesome world outside. It is also a metaphor for the intractable and inscrutable impenetrability of death. The doorway into the garden is cast as a metaphor for the moment of transition from life into death, the opening in the wall being the locus of that change that happens 'in raptu, in transitu, in ictu oculi' – 'in a vision, crossing a threshold, in the twinkling of an eye' (my translation from Donne's Latin).

In Domenico Veneziano's 'Annunciation' (1445) you get a glimpse of a paradise garden (a hortus conclusus) through the archway. Its pathways form a cross, with the one before us leading to a mysterious doorway in the distance.

John Donne – *Sermon XVII* (for Easter Day), 1624.

METAPHOR

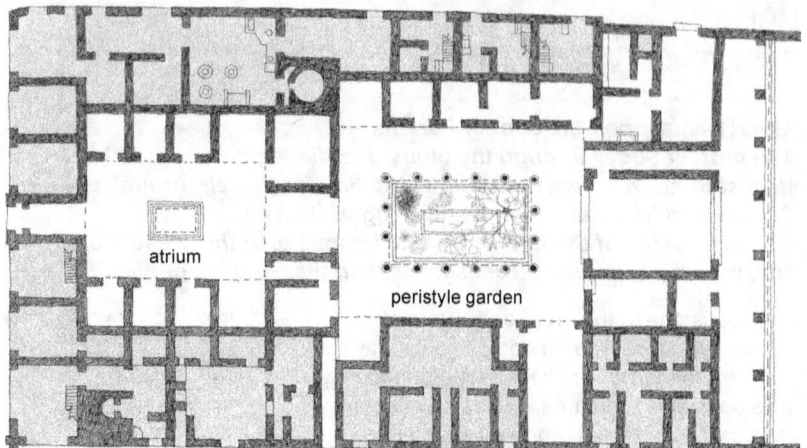

The metaphor of the paradise garden is more about pleasure and psychological comfort than about the daunting prospect of death. In this it offers solace in the real form of a place in this world. The characteristics of the paradise garden, though it was not then called such, originate in antiquity. They derive from the aesthetic, practical and psychological effects discovered when garden courtyards, separated from the everyday world outside, were formed to allow light and air into the centre of larger Greek and Roman houses.

Above is the plan of a wealthy house preserved in Pompeii – the House of Pansa. Like many Roman houses it has a peristyle garden at its heart which provides light, air, and the natural colours of vegetation – a peaceful place insulated from the bustle and dirt of the streets outside and cooled by a pond. As a refuge it may be seen from the entrance atrium as a promise (of escape from the world's tribulations) and as a demonstration of the superior domestic situation of the owner. It possessed key characteristics of paradise.

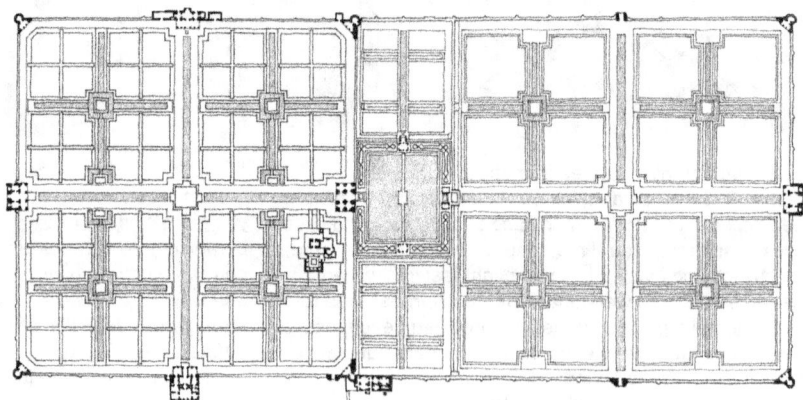

Islamic garden designers believe that geometric order is one of the defining characteristics of paradise. Their garden designs were ordered according to the Char Bagh, a quadrilateral arrangement of four canals and pathways representing the four rivers of paradise described in the Koran.

Above is the plan of the extensive Shalimar Garden near Lahore in Pakistan as laid out around 1640 CE where the Char Bagh is repeated at different scales. This Shalimar Garden was influence by another of the same name in Srinagar, Kashmir, laid out twenty years earlier for the Mughal Emperor Jahangir.

There are many versions of paradise in architecture.

Paradise might be conceived of as a place for personal contemplation, as in a Zen rock garden. Notice how, on the left, access to the deck, from which the rocks may be viewed, is extended, separating the paradise they occupy from the outside world.

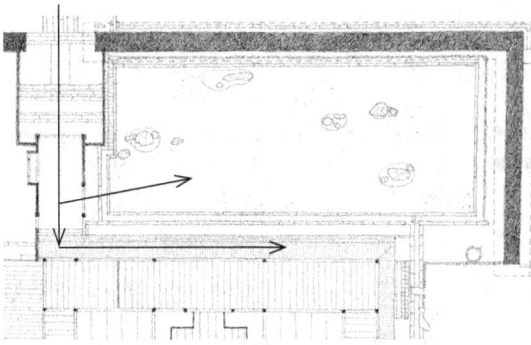

Ryoan-ji rock garden, Kyoto, Japan

Paradise might be thought to be best produced by a symbiotic interplay of providence and aesthetic decision (a collaboration between mind and nature). Sissinghurst has a number of small garden rooms based on the quadrilateral arrangement. But its overall arrangement is a more complex collage of existing features and aesthetic interventions.

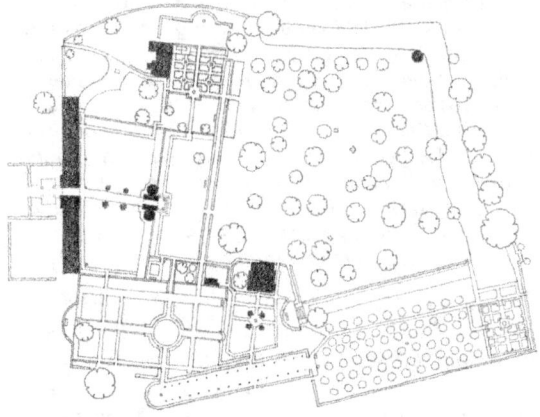

Sissinghurst garden, Kent, England

Or it might just be a personal refuge, away from the world. A carefully tended, sun-lit garden that caters for all the senses, emotional as well as physical.

One characteristic is certain: paradise is always a special world unto itself, separate from what we think of as the 'real world'.

Peter Aldington's Turn End, Haddenham, England

METAPHOR

GIANT PLAYPEN
Apple Headquarters, Foster + Partners

'We know by now that the internet is a giant playpen, a landscape of toys, distractions and instant gratification, of chirps and squeaks and bright, shiny things – plus, to be sure, ugly, horrid beasties lurking in all the softness – apparently without horizon… It is a world… "so responsive to our wishes as to be, effectively, a mere extension of the self" *. Until we chance on the bars of the playpen and find there are places we can't go and that it is in the gift of the grown-ups on the other side to set or move the limits to our freedom. We are talking here of virtual space. But those grown-ups, the tech giants, Apple, Facebook, Google and the rest, are also in the business of building physical billion dollar enclaves for their thousands of employees. Here too they create calibrated lands of fun, wherein staff offer their lives, body and soul, day and night, in return for gyms, Olympic-sized swimming pools, climbing walls, basketball courts, running tracks and hiking trails, indoor football pitches, massage rooms and hanging gardens, performance venues, amiable art and lovable graphics.'

* Jonathan Franzen

Rowan Moore – 'The Billion-Dollar Palaces of the Tech Emperors', in *The Observer* (*New Review* section), 23.07.2017.

Religions might offer the promise of paradise in the afterlife. Mughal emperors wanted it on this earth for themselves. 'Tech Emperors', as Moore calls them, know that providing paradise for their employees breeds esprit de corps and loyalty to the corporation. And that the best paradise will attract the best workers.

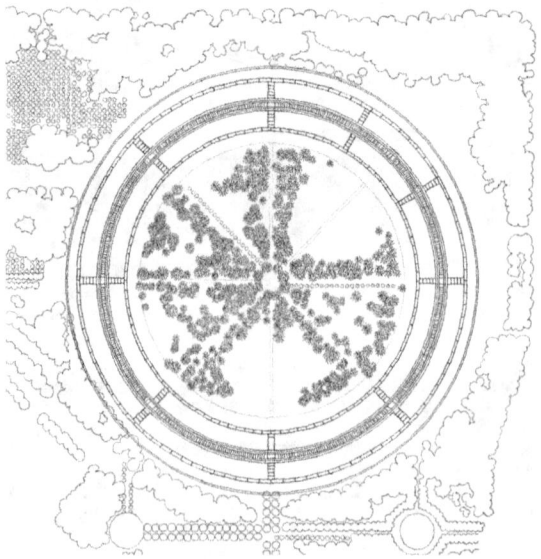

On the left is the plan of Apple's headquarters in Cupertino CA. Like the enclosure of a fortress or monastery, the circle – a mile in circumference – effects exclusion as well as reinforcing the idea of a cohesive community. It is presumably also a metaphor for the eternity the organisation intends to endure. Early versions of the landscaping (as shown), with the axial centralised quartered geometry of its courtyard (a hortus conclusus), are reminiscent of Mughal paradise gardens and the gardens of powerful elites through history.

PURGATORY IMAGINED
Samuel Beckett – *The Lost Ones*

The Lost Ones (1971) is a short novel by Samuel Beckett. It describes a strange and claustrophobic environment inhabited by two hundred souls. It reads like the account of a dream, and seems to want to be interpreted as a metaphor for human existence. The atmosphere of the story is dystopian, disturbing. As with all allegory (the narrative form of metaphor), we compare the narrative to our own lives. But in this story some correspondences seem to apply whilst others are elusive.

Beckett published The Lost Ones *first in French as* Le dépeupleur *(1970). He himself made the translation into English which was published the following year.*

Beckett's specifications for this claustrophobic world are precise. The two hundred souls occupy, or are confined in, a rubber-lined cylinder 18 metres high and with a circumference of 50 metres. There is an escape trapdoor exactly in the middle of the roof, which cannot be reached; and there is no indication where it might lead. There are twenty niches in the walls, all in the top half of the cylinder. They are arranged in 'irregular quincunxes' and some are linked by tunnels. There are fifteen ladders of varying length all with missing rungs. The shortest is 6 metres; the longest 16 metres, which means the ceiling can just be touched from its topmost rung. The souls, some of whom are related or married (though conditions make recognition difficult), either roam mindlessly and aimlessly across the floor, amble clockwise around the edge or queue to use the ladders, which they move within a peripheral zone. Some souls, having climbed a ladder, disappear for a while into one or other of the niche tunnels. The north is marked by an unmoving woman sitting in the foetal position with her back to the wall and her hair covering her face. The light in the cylinder is a dim and unchanging yellow. The temperature varies sometimes quite abruptly between 25°C and 4°. Skin is desiccated, sex random and infrequent. There is no space to lie down. The listless and moribund lean against the wall obstructing and annoying those who still care about climbing one of the ladders.

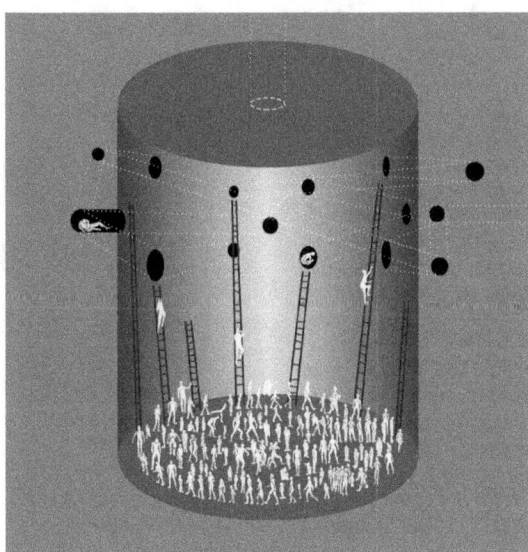

The Lost Ones has to be a metaphor for the human condition, one for which there is no precise interpretation. This cylindrical world contains elements of social dysfunction, of aspiration (the ladders), or refuge (the niches)… There even seem to be rules of behaviour as well as unavoidable squabbling. But the abiding atmosphere is one of hopelessness and futility. This circular world, of which the novelist was the architect, is no paradise. This architecture frames muffled despair.

DYSTOPIA
Yevgeny Zemyatin – *We*

Architecture is almost always an important ingredient in dystopian narratives, whether in films or novels. Whether in *Blade Runner* (Ridley Scott, 1982), *Brazil* (Terry Gilliam, 1985), *Mad Max* (George Miller, 1979)… *The Trial* (Franz Kafka, 1925), *1984* (George Orwell, 1948) or *We* (Yevgeny Zemyatin, 1921) the architecture not only provides the backdrop, it is also a metaphor for the ideology that governs the culture it accommodates.

Zemyatin's *We* is one of the earliest twentieth-century futurist novels. He wrote it not long after the Russian Revolution and at a time when architects were conceiving glass buildings.* The novel is set in a strictly Cartesian city in which all buildings are completely transparent (my image of the city is below). The use of curtains (to provide privacy for sex) is governed by application and the issuing of certificates. The city is bounded by a high wall that keeps nature out.

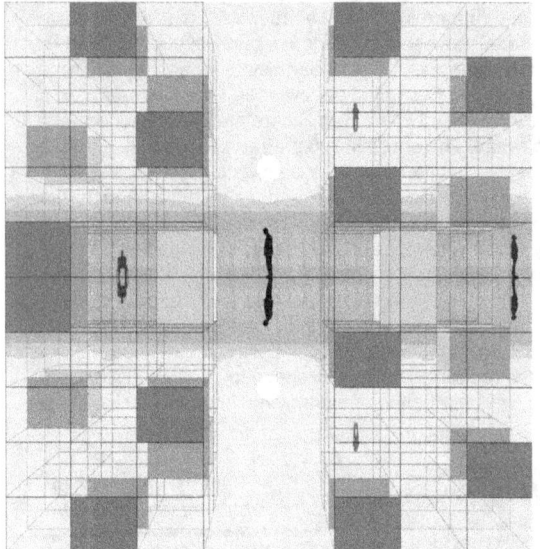

We *is set in a city where orthogonal geometry dictates everything and all buildings are glass; metaphors for the strictness of the ruling regime and for the exposure to scrutiny of all aspects of life (except sex, when permission to use curtains may be sought). Unpredictable and unruly nature is excluded from the sterile world of the city by a high perimeter wall.*

'*Dear O– was to come in an hour. I felt agitated, agreeably and usefully. Home at last! I rushed to the house office, handed over to the controller on duty my pink ticket, and received a certificate permitting the use of curtains. This right exists in our State only for the sexual days. Normally we live surrounded by transparent walls which seem to be knitted of sparkling air; we live beneath the eyes of everyone, always bathed in light. We have nothing to conceal from one another; besides, this mode of living makes the difficult task of the Guardians much easier. Without it many bad things might happen. It is possible that the strange opaque dwellings of the ancients were responsible for their pitiful cellish psychology… At twenty-two o'clock I lowered the curtain and at the same second O– came in smiling, slightly out of breath…*'

* Mies's Glass Skyscraper project for Berlin was published in the same year as *We*.

Yevgeny Zemyatin, trans. Brown – *We* (1921), 1993.

PRIVACY
NEO Bankside Apartments, Rogers Stirk Harbour

Zemyatin's 1921 depiction of glass architecture as dystopian did not alter the course of twentieth-century architecture. The positive metaphors associated with glass walls prevailed over the negative, especially in the minds of patrons, corporations and government clients, even though individuals might occasionally feel uncomfortable in the lack of privacy or environmental discomfort they can create.

In 2016 the architecture critic of *The Financial Times*, Edwin Heathcote, wrote a review of a new residential block – the NEO Bankside apartments. Residents were complaining their domestic lives were visible through the full-height glass walls of their apartments from the equally recent extension to Tate Modern (Herzog and de Meuron). In his review Heathcote included a précis of the fascination architects and their clients have developed with glass architecture during the twentieth century.

The metaphorical, aesthetic and phenomenological (experiential) connotations of the glass wall are quite difficult to tease apart; as is evident in the imagery used to advertise the NEO Bankside development (above), which clearly highlights the elevated view across the city and what we might call the 'master of the universe' identity ascribed to the occupant (reminiscent of the famous image of Pierre Koenig's Stahl House, see page 94), but does not mention any impairment of privacy.

'The idea of a glass architecture chimed with notions of transparency being a "good thing". In the corporate world, transparency is a metaphor for good governance. You cannot do shady or back room deals in a building with neither shade nor back rooms. In the world of government it is even more so – it's almost impossible to imagine a new parliament building being built in a democracy that does not express itself through the slightly dim witted metaphor of transparency. Both Foster's Reichstag and Rogers' Welsh National Assembly building have glazed chambers so that their workings are open to the electorate; visually, at least. And then there's the house. This metaphor of transparency got carried through to the psychopathology of the domestic. It was a built expression of the idea that light cleanses and that interior dark corners (ciphers for the recesses of the subconscious) should be purged. Ludwig Mies van der Rohe's Farnsworth House* was the high point. It was completely transparent, and its owner hated it, feeling vulnerable and overlooked – despite the house being in the middle of the Illinois countryside. There was always an ethical dimension to transparency, the opening up of everyday life to the world, the throwing open of the metaphorical curtains.'

* see page 70.

Edwin Heathcote – 'People in Glass Houses', in *The Financial Times* (Houses and Homes section), 30.10.2016.

WATER SURFACE
mirror, interface, instrument of detection...

'Ahistorical, pre-sexual, in suspension between the archaic and the modern, we were as susceptible and impressionable as the drinking water that stood in a bucket in our scullery: every time a passing train made the earth shake, the surface of that water used to ripple delicately, concentrically, and in utter silence.'

Seamus Heaney – 'Crediting Poetry' (The Nobel Lecture, 1995), in *Opened Ground: Poems 1966–1996*, 1998.

The surface of water is a potent metaphor in architecture. It has various dimensions. Heaney sees it in the above as something akin to a seismograph registering not only the vibrations of the passing train but also as a metaphor for the subtle nuances of history, reverberations from the past.

The surface of water is used in architecture too. First, in the horizontal dimensions it is a place we cannot stand or walk unless we have supernatural powers; we have to cross it on boats or across bridges. Thus the surface of water can be a metaphor for separation or denial of access.

Second, in the vertical dimension it is an interface between air and water; in one of these realms we can breath, in the other we cannot. Thus the surface of water can be a metaphor for the moment of death.

And third, the surface of water reflects light and images. It can be a metaphor for illusion, insubstantiality, impermanence and the flickering nature of events driven by fickle circumstances.

The surface of water is also the mirror of Narcissus, into which he peered, transfixed by the beauty of his own image.

In prehistoric times some bodies – perhaps sacrifices, perhaps criminals – were 'buried' in bog water, beneath the surface of the underworld.

In Jean Cocteau's film, the eponymous Orpheus *(1950) enters the underworld through a mirror, as through the surface of water.*

When Sigurd Lewerentz and Gunnar Asplund landscaped the Woodland Crematorium (left) they placed a pond by the main chapel. As a reminder of the interface between life and death it is one of many metaphors in the crematorium.

INFERNO
Grenfell Tower

As I approach completion of this Notebook the media is focussed on the disastrous and horrific fire that engulfed the Grenfell Tower in North Kensington on 14 June 2017, killing dozens of people. Politicians and commentators have been quick to interpret it – the building, the architectural ideology from which it originated, the limitations and mistakes of its recent refurbishment, the disaster… – as a metaphor for local and national government irresponsibility towards social housing and for the failings of Neoliberal ideology. But one suspects that another metaphor, one that has been applied to high-rise buildings since the Tower of Babel, comes into play too: that the erection of towers, and the divorce from the security of the earth they effect, represents an abiding hubristic tendency of humanity (and especially of their architect agents); and that the eternal mandate of Nemesis is retribution.

ENDNOTE

There are two significant metaphors relevant to architecture that I have not given sections of their own in this Notebook, but they require mention here. They are important because they underpin all the more specific metaphors architects use. They are the 'game' metaphor and the 'language' metaphor.

The first of these suggests – as was observed by Johan Huizinga in his book *Homo Ludens* (1949) – that we human beings are, at our psychological core, game players; we have a predilection for rule systems (which we also like to transgress), strategies (in which we like to display cunning) and competition (in which we like to establish our superiority over others). Even when we depended on it to live, we turned hunting into a game. If we hunt in the financial markets rather than the natural wilderness we turn profit-seeking into a game. We play games when we seek a mate; we play games, in more than one way, as we bring up our children, helping them to learn about the world. Education, religion, politics... all can be described as games. And nowadays 'game theory' has become an influential trend in many disciplines, from economics to psychology. Seen in this way, all the metaphors we apply to architecture can be classed as 'games', each with their own rule systems and strategies, by which we all – as architects – give order, purpose, identity... to our intellectual and creative endeavours. We can choose to play 'the cottage metaphor game', 'the machine metaphor game', 'the genetic metaphor game', or the 'game of masks'...

The second – that architecture is 'language' – may not be a metaphor at all. It may merely be a consequence of the fact that our English language does not have an umbrella term (which would cover itself) for the various intellectual framing structures by which we make sense of our world and project narratives of how we see it and how it might be. Framing structures such as: ceremony and ritual; dance; music; mapping; picture making; sculpture; coding; mathematics; science (physics, biology, cosmology...); verbal language (philosophy, fiction, drama, scripture, discourse, reportage, poetry...) as well as architecture. We apply the word 'language' to all of these because we do not have another term.

In previous books (*Analysing Architecture*, for example) I have referred to architecture as a 'metalanguage'; it makes place for (encompasses, accommodates) all those other 'languages' (and so claims to be 'the mother of all the arts'). It provides an intellectual framing structure, mutable and plural, through which we can make spatial sense of the world in which we live. But that does not mean architecture works in ways directly analogous to verbal language.

The evidence of the preceding pages shows that architecture is a rich and multidimensional medium for metaphor. It serves creative disciplines that use language (philosophy, psychology, fiction, drama...) by providing metaphors; in particular, metaphors for sense and intellectual structure. More significantly for architects, architecture itself is a medium for metaphors, metaphors we inhabit, literally. It is by metaphor expressed in architectural form that we might find ourselves living in a 'temple', 'machine' or a 'ship', or buried in a 'womb' or a 'skull'.

Metaphors, whether verbal or architectural, are prompted by correspondence. Apparent correspondence between disparate things make us feel the world around us has a subliminal integrity. In our own communications – and architecture is a form of communication – we like to draw attention to, draw on, evoke those correspondences to satisfy our desire for a world that holds together rather than confounds. Metaphors are tension wires linking disparate parts of our perceptions together. In architecture, as in verbal language, they inform poetic plurality. Metaphor not only seasons our language, making it more colourful and poetic, it conditions and informs our relationship with and understanding of the world, including how we shape it.

As a Notebook, the task of this book has been to open a gateway (door, window, bridge... or whatever other architectural metaphor you choose) into this rich multi-dimensional realm of imagination. Those who at the outset might have wondered whether metaphor had any role in architecture may now, having browsed the preceding pages, enjoy exploring the metaphorical dimensions of architecture with some hint of the many-faceted dream-world into which the open gateway leads.

This book is primarily, though not exclusively, aimed at those who face the challenges of architecture as a creative discipline – architects, who work with form and space to make sense of the world and give identity to place. Metaphors are often a path to getting started with a design in a way that transcends quotidian pragmatism. This applies even to so-called 'functionalist' metaphors, in which 'quotidian pragmatism' is promoted as an ideal.

Think of any metaphor and it will affect how and what you design. As an idle example... take 'flower' as a metaphor. How would you design a house following that? It might have 'petals' and 'sepals' encircling an 'ovule' (subsidiary rooms arranged around a central living room or courtyard). It might have a corridor like a stalk branching to different coloured rooms? Perhaps it would open up to the outside in summer and close back down in winter? Maybe it will grow over time. Metaphor is the intellectual device that prompts ideas in the designing mind. And for the inhabitant, the manifestation of metaphor makes a house engaging and intellectually stimulating.

In language, metaphors tend to occur in passing; in architecture they are more consequential. When Ali Smith, in an Introduction to *Super Cannes*, refers to its author J.G. Ballard as 'pulling up the floorboards of literary tradition' we just see it as a lively way of vitalising Ballard's talent for innovation with a metaphor that evokes the idea of disruption. But Le Corbusier's invocation of the machine as metaphor for domestic (and other) architecture has had substantial consequences for the settings in which many people have found themselves living... (and maybe without the pragmatic advantages the metaphor seemed to promise).

As I said in the Preface to this Notebook, metaphors are often cast as treacherous. They may offer insight, but they can be over-applied and mask polemic or induce prejudice. In science, where unadulterated truth is sought, metaphors can cause problems. (Scientists use them even so.) Some critics and commentators have applied such reservations to metaphors in architecture too. In the early twentieth century, Geoffrey Scott (in his book *The Architecture of Humanism*) condemned 'romantic', 'mechanical', 'ethical', 'biological' metaphors as 'fallacies'. In the mid-twentieth century John Summerson cited various metaphors associated with the emergence of Modern architecture as contributing to a general 'Mischievous Analogy' afflicting architects and architecture at the time.

Supported by the evidence in this Notebook, I would counter the arguments of both Scott and Summerson by suggesting that far from inducing fallacy and mischief, metaphors are the essential tissue of imagination and poetry in architecture as in other disciplines.

Writers usually criticise particular metaphors because they differ from their own favourite, the one they subscribe to as closest to the 'truth' as they see it. But no metaphor – just as no species of life on earth – deserves condemnation and extinction, even if it might turn out to be malign (as was the role of the 'machine' metaphor in the murderous activities of the Nazis). We cannot do architecture, any more than we can write or speak, without them. There is no truth in architecture, only proposition and a yearning for sense. Metaphors should of course be judged according to their effect and aptness; but, as a species, they should also be celebrated. Metaphor is the breath of imagination that gives vitality to things that might otherwise be dull. Do you, as a prehistoric undertaker, merely dig a hole in the ground into which to drop your client, or do you conjure up the built manifestation of a womb, the womb of mother earth to which we all return. Do you, in the face of the Industrial Revolution, continue to build houses as if they were classical temples or medieval churches, or do you suggest that they might be better conceived as machines offering modern efficiency in domestic life?

At its most fundamental level, architecture is about identification of place. This is the bedrock on which all my own explorations are based. It might be considered primarily a functional concern – to identify places to sit, to cook, to sleep, to be – but the preceding pages have shown that a significant factor in the identification of place is the role of metaphor; it has been so since before we lived in caves. Is metaphor the most powerful aspect of place identification? Sometimes it seems that it is. When one phenomenon seems to illuminate our understanding of another, when apparent correspondence resonates through the universe, we can persuade ourselves we are consolidating the sense we seek. When this happens metaphor is the essence of the poetics of architecture. And poetry – where 'truth' is no more nor less than 'beauty' – is powerful in the extreme.

ACKNOWLEDGEMENTS

To Jonathan Adams, Eugenia Baibazarova-Unwin, Alice Brownfield, Fran Ford, Professor Wayne Forster, Professor Peter Blundell Jones, Merve Kaptan-Unwin, Professor Stephen Kite, Ted Landrum, Jack McCulla, David McLees, Christina O'Brien, Alan Paddison, Richard Powell, Sue Ryrie, Jennifer Schmidt, Emily Stanley, David Unwin, Trudy Varcianna, and many others…
Thank you!

BIBLIOGRAPHY

Rob Abin and Saskia de Wit – *The Enclosed Garden: History and Development of the Hortus Conclusus and its Reintroduction into the Present-Day Urban Landscape*, 010 Publishers, Rotterdam, 1999.
Janne Ahlin – *Sigurd Lewerentz, Architect 1885–1975*, MIT Press, Cambridge MA., 1987.
Leone Battista Alberti, trans. Bartoli – *Ten Books on Architecture* (1452), Tiranti, London, 1955.
Christopher Alexander – 'A City is Not a Tree', *Architectural Forum*, Volume 122, 1 April 1965, pp. 58–62.
Christopher Alexander and others – *A Pattern Language: Towns, Buildings, Construction*, Oxford U.P., New York, 1977.
Jay Appleton – *The Experience of Landscape*, John Wiley & Sons, Chichester, 1975.
Antonin Artaud, trans. Corti – *The Theatre and its Double* (1964), Calder, London,1993.
Augustine, trans. Bettenson – *Concerning the City of God Against the Pagans* (5thC CE), Penguin, Harmondsworth, 1972.
Gaston Bachelard, trans. Jolas – *The Poetics of Space* (1958), Beacon Press, Boston, 1964.
J.G. Ballard, eds. Sellars and O'Hara – *Extreme Metaphors*, Harper Collins, London, 2012.
Walter Benjamin, trans. Jephcott and Shorter – 'Naples' (1924) and 'One-Way Street' (1925–6), in *One-Way Street and Other Writings*, Verso, London, 1985.
Peter Blake – *God's Own Junkyard*, Henry Holt, New York, 1964.
Suzanne Preston Blier – *The Anatomy of Architecture: Ontology and Metaphor in Batammaliba Architectural Expression*, University of Chicago Press, Chicago, 1987.
Kent Bloomer and Charles Moore – *Body, Memory and Architecture*, Yale University Press, New Haven, 1977.
Peter Blundell Jones – *Architecture and Ritual: How Buildings Shape Society*, Bloomsbury, London, 2016.
O.F. Bollnow, trans. Shuttleworth – *Human Space* (1963), Hyphen Press, London, 2011.
Jorge Luis Borges, trans. various – *Labyrinths*, Penguin, Harmondsworth, 1970.
Pierre Bourdieu – 'The Berber House', in Mary Douglas ed. – *Rules and Meanings*, Penguin, Harmondsworth, 1973.
Joanna Brück – 'Body Metaphors and Technologies of Transformation in the English Middle and Late Bronze Ages', in Brück, editor – *Bronze Age Landscapes: Tradition and Transformation*, Oxbow Books, Oxford, 2001.
John Bunyan, eds. Sharrock and Wharey – *Pilgrim's Progress* (1678), Oxford U.P., 1975.
Italo Calvino, trans. Weaver – *Invisible Cities* (1972), Harcourt Brace, San Diego, 1974.
Bruce Chatwin – *The Songlines*, Franklin Press, London, 1987.
Chuang-Tzu, trans. Giles – *Chuang-Tzu: Taoist Philosopher and Chinese Mystic* (4thC BCE), 1889, 1926.
Emma Clark – *The Art of the Islamic Garden*, Focus Press, Sevenoaks, 2004.
Peter Collins – *Changing Ideals in Modern Architecture 1750–1950*, Faber and Faber, London, 1965.
John Dee – *Mathematicall Praeface to the Elements of Geometrie of Euclid of Megara* (1750), facsimile, Kessinger Publishing, Whitefish MT., undated.
Gilles Deleuze and Félix Guattari, trans. Massumi – '1837: Of the Refrain', in *A Thousand Plateaus* (1987), Continuum, London, 2004.
René Descartes, trans. Haldane and Ross – *Discourse on the Method* (1637), Wordsworth, Ware, 1997.

Mircea Eliade, trans. Sheed – *Patterns in Comparative Religion*, Sheed and Ward, London, 1958.
Mircea Eliade, trans. Trask – *The Sacred and the Profane: the Nature of Religion*, Harcourt Brace and Co., San Diego, 1957.
Pierre Evreinoff, trans. Nazaroff – *The Theatre in Life*, Brentano's, New York, 1927.
Wooster Bard Field – *Architectural Drawing*, McGraw-Hill, New York, 1922; also available at: archive.org/details/architecturaldr00frengoog
Henri Focillon, trans. Beecher Hogan and Kubler – *The Life of Forms in Art* (1934), Zone Books, New York, 2013.
Jean Genet, trans. Frechtman – *The Balcony* (1957), Faber and Faber, London, 1958.
Arnold van Gennep – *The Rites of Passage*, Chicago University Press, Chicago, 1960.
Andri Gerber and Brent Patterson, eds. – *Metaphors in Architecture and Urbanism: An Introduction*, Transcript, Bielefeld, 2013.
Johann Wolfgang von Goethe (1829), in Eckermann, trans. Fuller – *Conversations with Goethe in the Last Years of His Life*, Munroe, Boston, 1839.
Erving Goffman – *The Presentation of Self in Everyday Life*, Doubleday, New York, 1959.
Stephen Grosz – *The Examined Life: How We Lose and Find Ourselves*, Chatto & Windus, London, 2013.
Seamus Heaney – 'Crediting Poetry' (The Nobel Lecture, 1995), in *Opened Ground: Poems 1966–1996*, Faber and Faber, London, 1998.
Seamus Heaney – 'A Dream of Jealousy', in *Fieldwork*, Faber and Faber, London, 1979.
Seamus Heaney – *The Redress of Poetry*, Faber and Faber, London 1995.
Seamus Heaney – 'Scaffolding', in *Death of a Naturalist*, Faber and Faber, London, 1966.
Edwin Heathcote – 'People in Glass Houses', in *The Financial Times* (*Houses and Homes* section), 30.10.2016.
Martin Heidegger, trans. Hofstader – 'Building Dwelling Thinking' (1951) and '...poetically man dwells...' (1951), in *Poetry, Language, Thought* (1971), Harper and Row, London, 1975.
Stephen Holl – 'Architectonics of Music', 2015, at: architectonicsofmusic,com.
Homer, trans. Rieu – *The Odyssey* (c. 700 BCE), Penguin, Harmondsworth, 1946.
Johan Huizinga – *Homo Ludens: a Study of the Play Element in Culture*, Routledge, London, 1949.
Carl Gustav Jung, trans. Winston and Winston – *Memories, Dreams, Reflections* (1963), Collins, Glasgow, 1977.
Robert Kerr – *The English Gentleman's House*, John Murray, London, 1864.
Ted Landrum – *Midway Radicals & Archi-Poems*, Signature Editions, Winnipeg, 2017.
Anthony Lawlor – *The Temple in the House*, G.P. Putnam's Sons, New York, 1994.
Le Corbusier, trans. de Francia and Bostock – *The Modulor: a Harmonious Measure to the Human Scale Universally Applicable to Architecture and Mechanics* (1948), and *Modulor 2 (Let the user speak next)* (1955), Birkhäuser, Basel, 2004.
Le Corbusier – *Œuvre complète, Volume 1, 1910–29*, Les Éditions d'Architecture, Zurich, 1964.
Le Corbusier, trans. Etchells – *Towards a New Architecture* (*Vers une architecture*, 1923), John Rodker, London, 1927.
W.R. Lethaby – *Architecture, Mysticism and Myth*, Macmillan, New York, 1892.
John Locke – *Essay Concerning Human Understanding*, Thomas Bassett, London, 1689.
James Malton – *An Essay on British Cottage Architecture: Being An Attempt to perpetuate on Principle, that peculiar mode of Building, which was originally the effect of Chance*, Hookham and Carpenter, London, 1798.
Thomas Mann, trans. Lowe-Porter – *Joseph and His Brothers* (1933), Vintage, London, 1999.
Elizabeth Martin – *Architecture as a Translation of Music* (Pamphlet Architecture 16), Princeton Architectural Press, New York, 1994.
Mies van der Rohe – Inaugural address as Director of Architecture at Armour Institute of Technology (1938), in Johnson – *Mies van der Rohe*, Secker & Warburg, London, 1978.
Charles W. Moore, William J. Mitchell and William Turnbull Jr. – *The Poetics of Gardens*, MIT Press, Cambridge MA., 1988.
Rowan Moore – 'The Billion-Dollar Palaces of the Tech Emperors', in *The Observer* (*New Review* section), 23.07.2017.
Charles P. Mountford – *Ayers Rock*, Angus & Robertson, Sydney, 1965.
Robert A. Nisbet – *Social Change and History*, Oxford U.P., New York, 1969.
Christian Norberg Schulz – *Meaning in Western Architecture*, Rizzoli, New York, 1980.
Michael Pawlyn – *Biomimicry in Architecture*, RIBA, London, 2011.
Plato, trans. Jowett – *The Republic* (c. 370 BCE), Oxford U.P., 1888.
Rainer Maria Rilke, trans. Herter Norton – *The Notebooks of Malte Laurids Brigge* (1910), Norton, New York, 1992.
John Ruskin – *The Poetry of Architecture* (1837), George Allen, London, 1893.
Joseph Rykwert – *On Adam's House in Paradise: the Idea of the Primitive Hut in Architectural History*, Museum of Modern Art, New York, 1972.

Cosimo Schinaia, trans. Lo Dico – *Psychoanalysis and Architecture: the Inside and the Outside*, Karnac Books, London 2016.
Thomas Schumacher – *The Danteum*, Triangle Bookshop, London, 1993.
Geoffrey Scott – *The Architecture of Humanism*, W.W. Norton, New York, 1914.
Vincent Scully – *The Earth, the Temple, and the Gods: Greek Sacred Architecture*, Yale U.P., New Haven, 1962.
Sinan, trans. Crane and Akin – 'Record of Construction' (1588?) and 'The Treatise Charmingly Named Record of Buildings' (1588?), in Gülru Necipoğlu ed. – *Sinan's Autobiographies: Five Sixteenth-Century Texts*, Brill, Boston, 2006.
Alison Smithson – *Team 10 Primer*, MIT Press, Cambridge MA., 1968.
Ettore Sottsass, ed. Barbara Radice – *Design Metaphors*, Rizzoli, New York, 1988.
Oswald Spengler, trans. Atkinson – *The Decline of the West* (1918), Allen and Unwin, London, 1934.
Philip Steadman – *The Evolution of Designs: Biological Analogy in Architecture and the Applied Arts* (1979), Routledge, Abingdon, 2008.
Wallace Stevens – 'Anecdote of the Jar' (1919), in *Harmonium*, Knopf, New York, 1923.
Abbot Suger, trans. Panofsky – *On the Abbey Church of St.-Denis and its Art Treasures* (12thC), Princeton U.P., 1946.
John Summerson – *The Classical Language of Architecture*, Methuen, London, 1964.
John Summerson – 'The Mischievous Analogy', in *Heavenly Mansions*. W.W. Norton, New York, 1963.
Oliver Taplin – *The Stagecraft of Aeschylus: the Dramatic Use of Exits and Entrances in Greek Tragedy*, Oxford U.P., 1977.
D'Arcy Wentworth Thompson – *On Growth and Form* (1917), Cambridge U.P., 1961.
Miranda Tufnell and Chris Crickmay – *Body Space Image: Notes Towards Improvisation and Performance*, Dance Books, Alton, 1990.
Victor Turner – *Dramas, Fields and Metaphors: Symbolic Action in Human Society*, Cornell U.P., Ithaca, NY., 1967.
Victor Turner – *From Ritual to Theatre: the Human Seriousness of Play*, John Hopkins U.P., Baltimore MD., 1982.
Simon Unwin – *Analysing Architecture*, Routledge, Abingdon, 2014.
Simon Unwin – *Doorway*, Routledge, Abingdon, 2007.
Simon Unwin – *The Ten Most Influential Buildings in History: Architecture's Archetypes*, Routledge, Abingdon, 2017.
Simon Unwin – *Twenty-Five Buildings Every Architect Should Understand*, Routledge, Abingdon, 2015.
Simon Unwin – *Villa Le Lac*, iBooks, 2014.
Robert Venturi – *Complexity and Contradiction in Architecture*, Museum of Modern Art, New York, 1966.
Robert Venturi, Denise Scott Brown, Steven Izenour – *Learning from Las Vegas*, MIT Press, Cambridge MA., 1977.
Vitruvius, trans. Hicky Morgan – *The Ten Books on Architecture* (1stC BCE), Dover, New York, 1914.
Rudolf Wittkower – *Architectural Principles in the Age of Humanism* (1949), W.W. Norton, New York, 1952.
Henry Wotton – *The Elements of Architecture* (1624), Gregg International, Farnborough, 1969.
Frank Lloyd Wright – 'In the Cause of Architecture', in *The Architectural Record*, Volume XXIII, March 1908.
Frank Lloyd Wright – Preface to *Ausgeführte Bauten und Entwürfe* (1910), in Kaufmann and Raeburn, eds. – *Frank Lloyd Wright: Writings and Buildings*, Meridian, New York, 1960.
Iannis Xenakis, trans. Kanach – *Music and Architecture*, Pendragon Press, 2008.
Frances A. Yates – *The Art of Memory*, Routledge & Kegan Paul, London, 1966.
Frances A. Yates – *Theatre of the World*, Routledge & Kegan Paul, London, 1969.
Yevgeny Zemyatin, trans. Brown – *We* (1921), Penguin, Harmondsworth, 1993.

INDEX

10 Downing Street, London 53
30 St Mary Axe (Foster) 23
1984 (Orwell) 168

Abbot Suger 11, 12, 85, 163
Acropolis, Athens 94
African hut 80
Alberti, Leone Battista 27, 34, 146
Aldington, Peter 165
Alexander, Christopher 48
all the world's a stage 89
Almodóvar, Pedro 50
'a monstrous carbuncle' (Prince Charles) 23
anarchy 115
Andalusia Mansion, Philadelphia (Walter) 65
Andre, Carl 110
'Anecdote of the Jar' (Stevens) 150
'Annunciation' (Veneziano) 163
anthropomorphic geometry 29
Apple Headquarters, Cupertino (Foster) 166
Aquitania 142
Archigram 141
architect as god 18
architect as metaphor 95
architects of the earth 16
architectural cloning 106
architecture and philosophy 117
architecture as inherently metaphorical 20
Aristotle 3
Art of Memory, The (Yates) 122
Asplund, E.G. 11, 170
'a tear-drop on the cheek of time' (Tagore) 96
Augustine 93
Australian aborigines 153
axis mundi 11
Ayer's Rock 153

Bacon, Francis 138
Bachelard, Gaston 124
Badovici, Jean 142
Balcony (Genet) 160
Ballard, J.G. 18, 33, 174
Batammaliba house 16, 26, 41
Bâtiment qui contiendroit les Académies (Peyre) 68
Beano, The 117, 136
Beckett, Samuel 167
Beezer, The 117, 136
Behrens, Peter 60
Benjamin, Walter 89, 128
Bennett, Alan 55
Bernini, Gian Lorenzo 34
Biddle, Nicholas 65
Bioscleave House (Gins and Arakawa) 134
Blade Runner (Scott) 168
Blake, Peter 22
Blake, William 93
Blier, Suzanne Preston 16, 26
Boathouse, Laugharne 61
body as house 37

body as temple 37
body metaphors 25
bog burial 170
Bollingen Tower, Lake Zurich (Jung) 124
Botta, Mario 99
Boullée, Étienne-Louis 126
Brazil (Gilliam) 168
Breuer, Marcel 82
bridge (Heidegger) 151
Brown, Denise Scott 22
Brück, Joanna 25
Bryn Celli Ddu, Anglesey 7
Bunyan, John 152
Burton Dassett Church, Warwickshire 87

Calatrava, Santiago 36
Callanish, Isle of Lewis 25
Calvino, Italo 19
camera obscura 119
Campo de' Fiori, Rome 90
Cartesian grid 110
Casa Del Ojo de Agua (Dewes and Puente) 88
Casa Malaparte, Capri (Libera) 62
Casino at Marino, Dublin (Chambers) 60
Ceaușescu, Nicolae 161
Cèfalu Cathedral, Sicily 4
Chamberlain Cottage (Breuer and Gropius) 82
Chambers, William 60
chaos 115
Char Bagh 164
Chartres 154
Chekov, Anton 91
chessboard 155
Chicago Mercantile Exchange 156
Chichen Itza, Mexico 87
children under a tree 20
chora 155
Chuang-Tzu (Zhuang Zhou) 120
church 113
Citrohan House (Le Corbusier) 138
city of God 93
civil unrest 89
cliché 21, 67
Clipsham, Mark 41
clown 89
Cocteau, Jean 170
Collins, Peter 97
Columbo (Falk) 116
Conder, Thomas 152
Congrès internationaux d'architecture moderne (CIAM) 48
contending metaphors 19
Coop Himmelb(l)au 116
cottage metaphor 71
courtroom 155
Crazy House 116

Dachau concentration camp 54
Dandy, The 117, 136
Dante Alighieri 54, 76

Danteum (Terragni) 46
death-related metaphors 11
Descartes, René 109, 117
'Design of a door to enter into darkness' (Sottsass) 53
Dewes, Ada and Puente, Sergio 88
disaster 115
divine proportions of the human body 28
dome as sky 15
Dome of the Rock, Jerusalem 38, 40
Donne, John 163
Donowell, John 50
doorway 50
doorway metaphors 49
doorway of appearance 53
doorway in pyramid temples 54
doorway of death 54
doorway of intercession 53
doorway of salvation 52
doorway of transformation 51
Doric column 38
'Dream of Jealousy' (Heaney) 150
dreams 50, 123, 130
Dreamtime 154
duck and decorated shed 64
Dulwich Picture Gallery (Soane) 54
Dymaxion House (Fuller) 140

École des Beaux-Arts, Paris 68
Emin, Tracey 57
empty room (Chuang-Tzu) 120
English Gentleman's House, The (Kerr) 112
Equivalents (Andre) 110
Eumaeus's hut 74

fake chimneys 60
Fallingwater (Wright) 131
Farnsworth House (Mies van der Rohe) 70, 102
Fehn, Sverre 88
female metaphor 38, 40
Fibonacci series 31, 33
Field, Wooster Bart 104
Focillon, Henri 16
forest metaphor 46
Foster, Norman 44, 166
free plan 148
Freud, Sigmund 7, 43, 117, 123
frozen music 147
Fuller, Buckminster 140
Fun Palace (Price) 144

Gaius Fabricius Luscinus 76
game metaphor 172
Garden Tree House, Kagawa (Hironaka Ogawa) 44
Gatiss, Mark 108
gendered space 41
gender metaphor 37, 40
Genesis 19, 87
genetic metaphor 97
Genet, Jean 160
geometry 31
Gilbert of Swineshead 53
Gimson, Ernest 71

Gins, Madeline and Arakawa 134
Glacier Museum, Norway (Fehn) 88
Glass House (Johnson) 102
Glass Skyscraper (Mies van der Rohe) 168
Globe, London 51
God as architect 14
Goddard, Jean-Luc 62
Goethe, Johann Wolfgang von 147
Golden Mean 98, 99
Golden Rectangle 29
Gormley, Antony 162
Gray, Eileen 142
Greek Cross plan (Wren) 114
Greek temple 65
Green Mosque, Bursa 52
Grenfell Tower, North Kensington 171
Gropius, Walter 82
Gut Garkau, Lübeck (Häring) 111

Hagia Sophia 14
Häring, Hugo 111
harmony 146
Hawksmoor, Nicholas 148
Heaney, Seamus 157, 170
Heathcote, Edwin 169
Heaven 122
Heidegger's bridge 151
Hell 122, 171
Hephaisteion (Athens) 65
Herron, Ron 141
Heydar Aliyev Cultural Centre, Baku (Zaha Hadid) 98
Hironaka Ogawa 44
Hoban, James 64
Holland Pavilion, Hanover Expo 2000 (MVRDV) 134
Holl, Stephen 147
Holy Grail 80
Homer 62, 74, 157
Homo Ludens (Huizinga) 172
Hopkins House, London (Hopkins) 36
Hopkins, Michael 36
Hosios Loukas, Greece 52
Hôtel aux Champs-Élysées (House of Bacchus) (Ledoux) 39
house as landscape 132
house as machine for living in (Le Corbusier) 137
house as psyche 123
House at Riva San Vitale (Botta) 99
house, body as 37
house for H.J. Ullman (Wright) 100
House of Pansa, Pompeii 164
House of Pleasure (Ledoux) 39
Hovis bread advertisement 79
Howard, Ebenezer 78
Huizinga, Johan 172

igloo 42
Il Postino (Michael Radford, 1994) 1
imago mundi 16
Imperial Hotel, Tokyo (Wright) 101
Indiana Jones and the Last Crusade (Spielberg) 80
inferno 171

Ionic column 38
Ionic Order 104
Ionic Order (Vignola) 105
Isola Bella, Lake Maggiore 90
Izenour, Steven 22

Jacob's dream 130
Jewish Museum, Berlin (Libeskind) 116
Johnson, Philip 102
Johnson Wax Administration Building (Wright) 46
Judge, Malcolm 117
Jung, Carl Gustav 117, 123

Kahn, Fritz 136
Kéré, Francis 44
Kerr, Robert 59, 112
King's Speech, The (Hooper) 125
Knowledge, The (London taxi drivers) 111
Koenig, Pierre 94
Korowai tree-houses, New Guinea 88

Lady in the Van (Hytner) 55
Laertes' farm 74
landscape metaphors 131
landscape simile 134
Lang, Fritz 143
language metaphor 172
Lao Tzu 41
Larkin, Philip 61
La Tourette, Lyon (Le Corbusier and Xenakis) 148
Le Corbusier 31, 32, 33, 34, 69, 98, 112, 135, 141, 143
Ledoux, Claude-Nicholas 39
Led Zeppelin 87
Le Mépris (Goddard) 62
Lemercier, Jacques 93
Lennon, John 61
Leonardo da Vinci 28, 98
le refuge tonneau (Perriand) 141
Lewerentz, Sigurd 45, 85, 93, 142, 170
Libeskind, Daniel 116
life's patina 128
light as metaphor 12
Line of Duty (Mercurio) 162
Liverpool Metropolitan Cathedral (Gibberd) 24, 114
Llainfadyn 41, 72
Locke, John 121
Loftus Garden Village, Newport (Pobl Housing Association) 78
London taxi-drivers 111
Long Island Duckling 22, 64
Lost Ones, The (Beckett) 167
Lubetkin, Berthold 156
Lyons Station (Calatrava) 36

machine mask 143
machine metaphors 135
Mad Max (Miller) 168
Maeshowe, Orkney 6
male metaphor 38, 40
Malton, James 77
'Man as Industrial Palace' (Kahn) 136

Manhattan 111
mask metaphor 58, 60
mater ecclesia 51
mathematics 31
maze 115
McCulla, Jack 108
megaron metaphor 69
Merz School Extension (Coop Himmelb(l)au) 116
metalanguage 173
metaphor for a marriage 157
metaphor for communality 10
metaphor for order 111
metaphor for structure of the universe, architecture as 17
metaphor of the cave (Plato) 118, 129
metaphors for landscape 131
metaphors for presence 9
metaphors of communality 12
metaphors of interplay 155
metaphors of personality 55
metaphors of presence 150
metaphors of sense and nonsense 107
Meteora, Greece 87
Metropolis (Lang) 143
Michelangelo 28
Mies van der Rohe 70, 80
Milan cathedral 162
mind as storeroom of knowledge (Locke) 121
mind metaphors 117
Modica, Sicily 51
Modulor (Le Corbusier) 31, 33
Modus (Siwe and Maserrat) 129
Mohrmann House, Berlin (Scharoun) 132
Mongolian ger 41
Mon Oncle (Tati) 149
Monsieur Hulot (Tati) 149
Montalbano 62
Moore, Charles 84
Morris, William 109
mosque 113
mosque, Cordoba 46
mountain metaphor 8
Mount Olympus 162
music and proportion 146
music metaphor 145
MVRDV 134
'My Bed' (Emin) 57

Narcissus 170
National Gallery, London (Ahrends, Burton, Koralek) 23
Nautilus shell 98
Nemesis 171
NEO Bankside Apartments (Rogers Stirk Harbour) 169
Neruda, Pablo 1, 11
Nestor's' palace, Pylos 159
Newton Mausoleum (Boullée) 126
New Ways, Northampton (Behrens) 60
New York Stock Exchange 156
New York taxi drivers 111
Nietzsche, Friedrich Wilhelm 18
Nisbet, Robert A. 2
Norwegian National Opera House, Oslo (Snøhetta) 134

Number One Poultry (Stirling) 23
'Numskulls' (Judge) 117, 136

Odysseus's bed 157
Odyssey (Homer) 62, 74, 157
organic integrity 100
organic metaphor 80
origin of architecture 5
Orpheus (Cocteau) 170
Orwell, George 51

Pacioli, Luca 28
Palladio, Andrea 30, 34
Pantheon, Rome 7
paradise 163
Paris, Texas (Wenders) 129
Parker, Barry and Unwin, Raymond 78
Parthenon, Athens 17, 29, 32, 94
path of destiny 47
Pentreath, Ben 58
perfect human being 30
performance place as landscape 133
Periand, Charlotte 141
Petra, Jordan 87
Peyre, Marie-Joseph 68
Philharmonie, Berlin (Scharoun) 133
philosopher as architect 109
Piano, Renzo 143
picnic tablecloth 150
Pigsty, Fyling Hall 68
Pilgrim's Progress (Bunyan) 152
Pink Floyd 85
place and identity 56
place as character metaphor 57
'plan is the generator' (Le Corbusier) 112
Plato 117, 118, 129
Pleat, Zachary 95
poetry of architecture (Ruskin) 75
poet's house 62
Pollença, Mallorca 87
Pompidou Centre, Paris (Piano and Rogers) 143
Portmeirion (Williams-Ellis) 79
Poundbury, Dorset 78
Prairie House (Wright) 81
Price, Cedric 144
Prince of Wales 58, 78
proportion 146
proportion as metaphor 29
Pygmalion (Shaw) 159
Pyramid of Khufu, Giza 8

Quintilian 122

receptacle of becoming 155
'Red Disk' (McCulla) 108
regulating lines 32
Renault Distribution Centre, Swindon (Foster) 44
repression 125
Rhiwbina Garden Village, Cardiff (Parker and Unwin) 78, 84
Rhodia (Egyptian grave stele) 57
Richelieu, Loire Valley (Lemercier) 93, 109
Rilke, Rainer Maria 128

Rivett, Geoffrey 95
Robie House (Wright) 81
Rogers, Richard 143
Roi Soleil (Louis XIV) 67
Rolls-Royce radiator 67
Roman Holiday (Wyler) 90
Romeo and Juliet (Shakespeare) 37
Rousseau, Jean-Jacques 76
Ruskin, John 75, 93, 109
Ryoan-ji rock garden, Kyoto 165

Safed, Israel 35
Sangallo the Younger, Antonio da 88
Scharoun, Hans 132, 133
Schulman, Julius 94
Scott, Geoffrey 97, 174
Seagull (Chekov) 91
Sea Ranch (Charles Moore and others) 84
Second Vatican Council 114
sense (and truth) 2
Serie Architects 44
Serpentine Pavilion 2017, London (Kéré) 44
Serralta, Justino and Maisonnier, André 31
sexual metaphor 39
Shalimar Garden, Lahore 164
Shaw, George Bernard 159
Sherlock Holmes 108
ship metaphor 142
simile 21, 66
Sinan 14, 35
Sissinghurst garden, Kent 165
Skara Brae, Orkney 7
skeleton metaphor 36
skin metaphor 36
S. Maria Novella, Florence (Alberti) 27, 146
Smith, Ali 174
Snøhetta 134
Soane, John 54
Socrates 118
songlines 153, 156
Sottsass, Ettore 53
S. Petri Church, Klippan (Lewerentz) 45, 93, 142
Stahl House, Los Angeles (Koenig) 94
stairway to heaven 87
St.-Denis Abbey 12
Stevens, Wallace 150
St Fagans National History Museum, Cardiff 73
St George's-in-the-East, London (Hawksmoor) 148
Stoneywell Cottage (Gimson) 71
St Patrick's Well, Orvieto (Sangallo the Younger) 88
St Paul's, London (Wren) 113
St Peter's, Rome (Bernini) 34
Süleymaniye Mosque 15
Summerson, John 97, 175
Swiss Re (Foster) 38
Sydney Opera House (Utzon) 23

Tagore, Rabindranath 96
Taj Mahal, India 96
Talk to Her (Almodóvar) 50
Taming of the Shrew (Shakespeare) 159

Tati, Jacques 35, 149
Team 10 (Team X) 48
Tempest, The (Shakespeare) 37, 155
temple 113
temple, body as 37
temple metaphor 63
Temple of Concord, Agrigento 64
Temple of Venus, West Wycombe Park (Donowell) 50
Temple on the Illissus, Athens 104
Terragni, Giuseppe 46
theatre metaphor 91
'There is always a doorway someone doesn't let you through' (Sottsass) 53
'There is sometimes a door through which you are meeting your love' (Sottsass) 53
things fall apart (Yeats) 115
Thomas, Dylan 61
Thompson, D'Arcy Wentworth 97
Thoor Ballylee, County Galway 61
tiger 1
Titanic 24
Titanic Museum, Belfast (Kuhne) 24
Tomb of Agamemnon (Treasury of Atreus), Mycenae 6
Tote Refurbishment, Mumbai (Serie Architects) 44
Tower of Babel 19, 171
tracés régulateurs 32
tree metaphor, city 48
tree metaphor, maternal 45
tree metaphors 43
tree metaphor, structure 44
Trial, The (Kafka) 168
Trump, Donald 161
truth (and sense) 2
tunnels under Liverpool (Williamson) 127
Turn End, Haddenham (Aldington) 165
Turner, Victor 2

Uluru (Ayer's Rock) 154
Unité d'habitation, Marseilles (Le Corbusier) 18, 33
Urbs Beata Jerusalem 13

van Eyck, Aldo 48
Veneziano, Domenico 163
Venturi, Robert 22

vernacular architecture 80
Versaille 67
Vers une architecture (Le Corbusier) 137
Vignola, Giacomo Barozzi da 105
Villa E.1027, Cap Martin (Gray) 142
Villa le lac, Vevey (Le Corbusier) 69
Villa Rotonda, Vicenza (Palladio) 17, 30
Villa Savoye, Poissy (Le Corbusier) 17
Villa Stein (Le Corbusier) 32
Vitruvius 27, 28, 30, 34, 38, 98

Walking City, The (Archigram) 141
Walter, Thomas Ustick 65
Warhol, Andy 90
water surface 170
Welsh house 81
Welsh School of Architecture, Cardiff 156
Wenders, Wim 129, 162
Westminster Abbey, Chapter House 45
We (Zemyatin) 168
White House, Washington D.C. (Hoban) 64
wigwam 24
Williams-Ellis, Clough 79
Williamson, Joseph 127
windows as eyes 35
'Window Wanderland' 35
Wings of Desire (Wenders) 162
Wolfowitz, Paul 95
womb metaphor 6
Woodhenge, Salisbury Plain 46
Woodland Chapel (Asplund) 11
Woodland Crematorium (Asplund and Lewerentz) 170
word metaphors related to architecture 85
Wotton, Henry 27, 36, 57, 59
Wren, Christopher 113, 114
Wright, Frank Lloyd 46, 80, 100, 131

Xenakis, Iannis 148

Yates, Francis 122
Yeats, W.B. 61
yin yang 41

Zaha Hadid 98
Zemyatin, Yevgeny 168
Zen rock garden 165
Zhuang Zhou (Chuang-Tzu) 120

'He who has once begun to open the fan of memory never comes to the end of its segments; no image satisfies him, for he has seen that it can be unfolded, and only in its folds does the truth reside; that image, that taste, that touch for whose sake all this has been unfurled and dissected; and now remembrance advances from small to smallest details, from the smallest to the infinitesimal, while that which it encounters in these microcosms grows ever mightier.'
Walter Benjamin, trans. Jephcott and Shorter – 'A Berlin Chronicle' (1932), in *One-Way Street and Other Writings*, 1985.

For Product Safety Concerns and Information please contact our EU representative GPSR@taylorandfrancis.com
Taylor & Francis Verlag GmbH, Kaufingerstraße 24, 80331 München, Germany

www.ingramcontent.com/pod-product-compliance
Lightning Source LLC
Chambersburg PA
CBHW070939240426
43667CB00036B/2383